Belonging in a House Divided

Belonging in a House Divided

THE VIOLENCE OF THE NORTH KOREAN RESETTLEMENT PROCESS

Joowon Park

UNIVERSITY OF CALIFORNIA PRESS

University of California Press
Oakland, California

© 2023 by Joowon Park

Library of Congress Cataloging-in-Publication Data

Names: Park, Joowon, 1986- author.
Title: Belonging in a house divided: the violence of the North Korean
    resettlement process / Joowon Park.
Description: Oakland, California : University of California Press, [2022] |
    Includes bibliographical references and index.
Identifiers: LCCN 2022011149 (print) | LCCN 2022011150 (ebook) | ISBN
    9780520384231 (cloth) | ISBN 9780520384248 (paperback) | ISBN
    9780520384255 (ebook)
Subjects: LCSH: Refugees—Korea (North)—Social conditions—21st
    century. | Refugees—Korea (South)—Social conditions—21st century.
Classification: LCC HV640.5.K67 P38 2022 (print) | LCC HV640.5.K67
    (ebook) | DDC 362.8709519—dc23/eng/20220803
LC record available at https://lccn.loc.gov/2022011149
LC ebook record available at https://lccn.loc.gov/2022011150

Manufactured in the United States of America

32   31   30   29   28   27   26   25   24   23
10   9   8   7   6   5   4   3   2   1

Contents

Illustrations

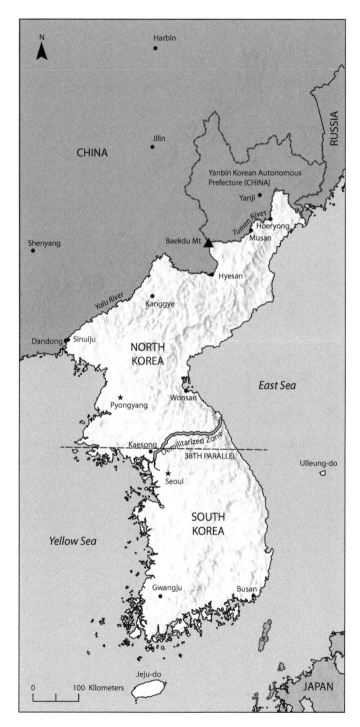

Map 1. Map of the Korean peninsula. Map: Joowon Park.

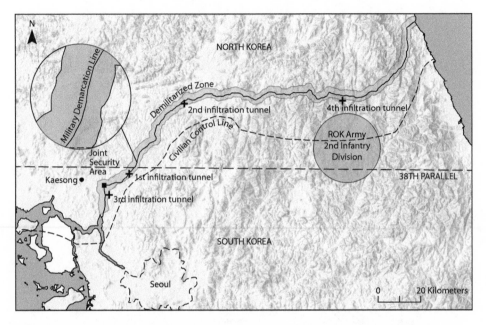

Map 2. Map of the Korean Demilitarized Zone. Note the location of North Korea's four infiltration tunnels and South Korea's 2nd Infantry Division, where the author was stationed. Map: Joowon Park.

Introduction

A HOUSE DIVIDED

A house divided against itself cannot stand.

BECOMING A SOLDIER

We stood on the dirt field, arms length apart. We formed imperfect rows and columns, which brought frantic scorn from the drill sergeants wearing red-capped black hats, uniforms in dark green digital camouflage, and shiny black boots. Our heads were all shaved, though we were still in our civilian clothes. At last, the national anthem played and we—the 1,200 newly conscripted men—saluted the South Korean flag. I felt a flurry of emotions, including nervous anxiety. I was anomalous, being in my thirties, and the drill sergeants failed to conceal their surprise upon seeing my mature face among mostly eighteen-year-olds. On this mid-September day in 2015, we had arrived at the 102nd Replacement Battalion in Gangwon Province in South Korea bordering the DMZ (Demilitarized Zone), a heavily fortified and militarized "no man's land" filled with landmines dividing the two Koreas. The 102nd Battalion was established in 1953 in the aftermath of the Korean War (1950–1953), and it served as a transit point where new conscripts received their uniforms and supplies before being transferred to the more remote units scattered along the DMZ to protect the nation from its northern neighbor.

1

Family, friends, and colleagues expressed shock, and sometimes horror, at the news of my conscription into the South Korean Army. My family had left South Korea for Kenya when I was eight. I have lived in the United States since I came to attend college, though my parents continue to live in East Africa. My military conscription was also received with disbelief because I was supposed to start my new job as a professor in upstate New York. Just a few months before my conscription, I had obtained my doctorate from American University in Washington, DC. However, my academic career would now be put on hold and I would be a soldier for the next two years.

Prior to national division and war, the Korean Empire (previously the Joseon Dynasty, 1392–1897) was annexed by Japan in 1910, putting the nation under imperial occupation until the end of World War II. The United States and the Soviet Union, competing for influence in Asia, agreed to "temporarily" divide the Korean peninsula into two trusteeships to oversee its decolonization. As agreed upon at the Yalta Conference, Soviet troops marched into the northern half of the Korean peninsula and US troops took control over the southern half, with the peninsula divided along the 38th parallel. During these high-level negotiations, Korean leaders were not present. Two US officers were called to the White House and used a *National Geographic* map to hastily divide the peninsula along the 38th parallel line of latitude, ensuring that Seoul, the capital city, fell under US control.[1] However, disputes over leadership, government, and the future of Korea ensued, and the US-backed South proclaimed statehood in 1948 with Rhee Syngman as president. The North established its own state shortly thereafter, supported by the Soviet Union and led by Kim Il-sung, a guerilla leader who had fought against the Japanese Imperial Army.

Desiring to forcibly reunify the peninsula, Kim sought approval from Joseph Stalin to invade South Korea. With the assurance of support from both the Soviet Union and China, North Korean tanks and soldiers launched a surprise attack across the 38th parallel on the morning of June 25, 1950. It sparked a devastating war that brought destruction to the peninsula, nearly five million casualties, and the involvement of military troops from all over the world. The United Nations forces, led by the United States, came to the South's defense and the sides battled back and forth. China eventually came to North Korea's aid, and the war ended in a stalemate after three long years. In 1953, an Armistice Agreement was signed to cease the fighting.

One consequence of the unresolved conflict—no peace treaty was ever signed, and the war continues to this day—was the establishment of compulsory military service in both Koreas.[2] In South Korea, the 1957 Military Service Act made military service mandatory for all able-bodied men, creating a gendered path towards full citizenship.[3] Evading conscription is a crime punishable by imprisonment and permanent banishment.[4] Since the 1950s, the Korean peninsula has become highly militarized, both sides fighting for the legitimacy of their statehood and employing large armies and amassing weapons in preparation for a future war. For example, North Korea has defied international norms and endured sanctions and condemnation to develop nuclear weapons. South Korea has built up its armed forces to become a top-ten military power, conducts annual war exercises with the US military, and has developed and deployed various missile defense systems.

The peninsula has been on the brink of reengaged war several times when North Korea attempted to assassinate two South Korean presidents (1968 and 1983), bombed a Korean Air flight from Baghdad to Seoul in 1987, and torpedoed the South Korean Cheonan naval vessel and fired artillery on Yeonpyeong Island in 2010, among countless other conflicts between the two countries. Furthermore, between 1974 and 1990, South Korea discovered four incursion tunnels beneath the DMZ. In preparation for a new war, North Korea had secretly dug tunnels deep underground (several kilometers in length from the north to the south) that would have allowed 30,000 of its soldiers to pass through each tunnel in a single hour.

When I was growing up in East Africa, my father used to tell me stories about the bitter cold nights in the DMZ and the intensive military training at his "White Skull" Division. Men were conscripted for three years at the time, and he half-jokingly advised me to find consolation in the fact that I would serve one year less than he had. My grandfather used to tell us stories about the Korean War at family gatherings. North Korean soldiers imprisoned and killed our great-grandfather (a civilian), and my grandfather would show us his father's shirt with the bullet holes as a vivid reminder. The question of division, therefore, interested me even from afar: what divisions would remain if the Koreas reunified? The two Koreas have both assumed reunification as a main objective, and have engaged in inter-Korean summits, family reunions, and economic collaborations. Recently, they sent a united ice-hockey team to the 2018 PyeongChang Winter Olympics. Though the Koreas are far from national reunification, it started to look more tangible as North Korean defectors, refugees, and migrants began to resettle in South Korea at the turn of the century, raising questions and hope about what a reunified Korea might look like.

RESETTLED NORTH KOREANS IN A DIVIDED KOREA

"None of you look like you're from North Korea!" a South Korean college student cheerfully exclaimed to her North Korean peers. The small room was dimly lit by fluorescent lights, warm and stuffy from the forty of us sitting behind the light brown rectangular tables arranged in a U-shape. Our bodies and clothes reeked of the smell of *samgyupsal* (grilled pork belly) we'd had for dinner. It was our evening coffee break after sitting through an hour-long lecture about pro-North Korean forces in South Korean society. The professor's first slide had read "Who is our enemy?" in big bold red characters, and he lectured us about the history of Korean communism, Kim Il-sung's efforts to bolster pro-North Korean groups within South Korea, the dangers of communist ideology, and the risks these forces posed to South Korea.

This Unification Workshop brought together two groups of college students: South Korean students and resettled North Korean students pursuing higher education in Seoul. Its purpose was for these students to get to know one another beyond cultural stereotypes and to discuss the challenges of reunification. It was 2013, two years before my military conscription, and a bus picked up the students in Gangnam on a Friday afternoon to escort them to a *pensyeon* (a rental house) in Gapyeong, a small city about an hour east of Seoul. The organizing NGO had received money from the South Korean government to host this two-day event, and the director of the fledgling NGO, Mr. Bak, had invited me to the workshop. A resettled North Korean living in South Korea, Mr. Bak regularly organized a variety of workshops addressing the themes of reunification and human rights. What made his workshops special, he emphasized to me, was that his participants always included both North and South Korean students.

The female South Korean student followed up her statement: "And you all have a great sense of humor too," which brought the participants to laughter.

"What did you expect?" asked Kichul, a North Korean student, showing no sign of amusement.

"I don't know, but you look no different from *hanguk* (South Korean) college students," she replied. She admitted that this was her first time meeting anyone from North Korea and that she was happy to have given up her precious weekend to come to the workshop.

Her seemingly innocent statement upset Kichul, though. The next morning, he told me it was something he had heard countless times while living in Seoul. "Do we only have one eye? No ears?" he asked me sarcastically. He was frustrated because South Koreans held a predetermined image of North Koreans, and it was always an image that depicted them as different and inferior.

North Koreans began arriving in South Korea in significant numbers following the heavy rainfall and floods of 1995, and the subsequent severe famines that led to mass starvation in North Korea. The natural disasters combined with North Korea's failed state plans and the dissolution of the Soviet Union and the Eastern Bloc—North Korea's main trading partners—contributed to the collapse of its Public Distribution System (PDS). The PDS, responsible for distributing food and resources to North Korea's citizens, proved much too inadequate. Approximately two to three million people died from hunger.[5] No longer able to rely on the state, ordinary North Koreans scavenged for food, engaged in black markets, and even fled the country. An estimated 200,000 to 300,000 North Koreans illegally crossed over to China between 1995 and 1999.[6] Some resettled in China permanently while others had more temporary plans, intending to return to North Korea when conditions improved. Although many humanitarian narratives frame this migration as a "search for freedom," it was predominantly hunger-driven and many became migrant laborers to "keep their families at home alive by taking on the role of breadwinner."[7]

Situated within a divided peninsula surrounded by oceans to the east and west, and with the highly militarized and securitized DMZ blocking direct entrance to South Korea, many North Koreans fled to China by crossing the Yalu and Tumen Rivers that serve as territorial boundaries between the two countries.[8] The majority of these border-crossers were from the poorer provinces with proximity to the Chinese border, while those in the core regions of North Korea near Pyongyang had less access to escape.[9] The familiarity of the cultural borderlands in the Yanbian Korean Autonomous Prefecture in China, with approximately two million ethnic Koreans residing and speaking the Korean language, provided a viable option. However, the borderland had always been a space of passage and it was the intensity in the number of crossings that marked this period as distinct from the past. Historically, migrants from both sides crossed over, formed families, conducted trades, and filled labor shortages despite the securitization of national borders.[10] The borderland was a place of fluidity, a space of constant crossings and maneuverings.

The Chinese policy in response to the influx of North Korean border-crossers has been to forcibly return these "economic migrants" to their home country. Pleas from human rights activists to protect North Korean refugees have had no success in preventing their forced repatriation. Kichul and his family secretly crossed the Tumen River to China in 2000, having little hope for survival in North Korea, but his parents were arrested by Chinese authorities and sent back to North Korea. Kichul was running errands in town when the Chinese police raided the apartment. He has since lost contact with his family and believes they are likely dead, as leaving North Korea without authorization is considered an act of defection and a political crime.[11] While many North Korean border-crossers have secretly and quietly settled in China, others, like Kichul, have eventually sought resettlement in South Korea due to the absence of legal status in China. The South Korean government grants citizenship to North Koreans and provides them with resettlement money, housing, job training, and education subsidies based on its 1997 Act on the Protection and Settlement Support for Residents Escaping from North Korea, in addition to claims about ethnic homogeneity of North and South Koreans sharing the "same" blood, history, and culture. Furthermore, Article 3 in its Constitution states that the "territory of the Republic of Korea shall consist of the Korean *peninsula* and its adjacent islands," allowing the country to assert itself as the sole and legitimate governing body of the

entire Korean peninsula.[12] Using this framing, North Koreans constitu-
tionally fall under the governing umbrella of South Korean territory, and
are thus considered deserving of citizenship.

The journey from China to South Korea, however, is not simple.
Without proper documentation, North Koreans in China have had to
enter foreign embassies in Beijing to claim asylum, or cross the Gobi
Desert into Mongolia. Others pay brokers or rely on NGOs and religious
organizations to help them traverse the Chinese mainland to reach a
country like Thailand in Southeast Asia.[13] In contrast to the Chinese, Thai
authorities do not forcibly repatriate North Koreans and instead transfer
custody to South Korean officials. North Koreans are then flown to South
Korea for resettlement.[14]

Over 33,000 North Koreans have resettled in South Korea, with
approximately 70 percent being women (see chapter 2 for a detailed discussion of this gendered migration). Following interrogation and security
clearance, newly arrived North Koreans receive mandatory cultural orientation at Hanawon, the government resettlement center, for three months.
Literally meaning "One Center" or "House of Unity" to symbolize the
reunification of the Koreas, North Koreans receive various trainings for
cultural adaptation to South Korea, assistance for their psychological
well-being, and career counseling sessions. Upon completion, the government provides them with apartment housing and resettlement money.[15]
There are over twenty-five regional adaptation centers in South Korea for
the purpose of assisting North Koreans to get settled into their new homes.
North Koreans also receive tuition waivers and vocational support.

Yet despite the shared history, culture, and language between the two
Koreas and despite this assistance, North Koreans continue to face many
obstacles during their resettlement in South Korea.[16] As the students at
the Unification Workshop highlight, resettled North Koreans are often
stigmatized, treated as outsiders, and perceived to be inherently different.
A South Korean professional who has worked for decades in the field of
North Korean human rights once told me that resettled North Koreans
are *gatjanhda* (not the same) as South Koreans, a phrase used pejoratively
in South Korea.[17] She claimed that North Koreans only know socialism,
and that their behaviors—stemming from the lack of a capitalistic mindset, responsibility, and self-sufficiency—are hard to change. These kinds of

stereotypes and prejudice have led many resettled North Koreans, like the college students at the workshop, to erase traces of their North Koreanness through grooming, fashion, and adopting a South Korean accent. While conducting ethnographic fieldwork, one of the things that stood out to me was that in public settings such as a restaurant, café, or on the subway many would lower their voices to speak about their identities, their origin, and their experiences in South Korea. They would speak at a near inaudible level and use semantic replacers such as "our people" or "our northern neighbors" to refer to North Korea.

Another obstacle for resettled North Koreans has been a sense of alienation. A community has been difficult to establish, as the South Korean government provides housing in random locations throughout the country (though many North Koreans desire to relocate to the Seoul metropolitan area after their first housing assignment). The availability of apartments is one reason for the dispersed settlement, but a concentration of resettled North Koreans and the potential for political dissent also weigh heavily on the government's resettlement plan.[18] And in areas with some concentration of resettled North Koreans, many choose to conceal their identities as Cold War politics and anti-communist rhetoric are still very much prevalent in South Korea.

An additional barrier to the formation of community has been the culture of fear and suspicion. Resettled North Koreans worry that there could be spies disguised as *talbukja* (a person who has fled North Korea, commonly translated as "defector"). This is one of the lessons that newly arrived North Koreans are taught at the Hanawon Resettlement Center. North Korean interlocutors have told me that they are cautioned to be wary—a North Korean spy could be your friend or your neighbor in the disguise of a *talbukja*. As a result, many North Koreans in South Korea live in social isolation, seldom communicating or networking with one another. One limited form of community for many North Koreans in South Korea has been through religious organizations, particularly Protestant churches—one of the sites of my participant observation, as I will explain later in this chapter.[19]

Recent findings show that North Koreans' suicide rate in South Korea is three times higher than that of South Korean citizens.[20] This is particularly alarming given that South Korea has the highest suicide rate among all countries in the Organisation for Economic Co-Operation and Development (OECD).[21] Furthermore, North Koreans drop out of school at twice the rate of their South Korean counterparts.[22] What forms of violence contribute to such disparities? How do past experiences of violence contribute to an ongoing experience of alienation, othering, and discrimination? What social and structural forces hinder successful resettlement? Do North Koreans feel a sense of belonging in South Korea? These are some of the questions at the heart of *Belonging in a House Divided.*

This book's main concern is how violence operates in and contributes to the experiences of citizenship and belonging for North Koreans resettled in South Korea. A central argument is that the North Korean embodiment of South Korean citizenship is often a violent process of belonging, becoming, and self-making, illuminating ongoing invisible forms of violence upon resettlement in South Korea. This ethnography reveals the structural obstacles complicating North Koreans' sense of belonging within South Korean society despite the seeming advantages of shared history, culture, ethnicity, and language. While most other cases of refugee resettlement around the world present the challenges of the host country's acceptance of refugees who are dissimilar to the larger citizen body (ethnically or culturally), I direct attention towards the various types of violence that occur even despite shared heritage, providing important insights into the interrelationship between violence and postwar citizenship.

CITIZENSHIP AND THE VIOLENCE CONTINUUM

The concept of citizenship has gone through many transformations—from the earliest Athenian model based on the Greek polis, to the expansion of the concept in the French Revolution, and to citizenship based on the nation-state system. With the emergence of modern citizenship based on the nation-state, citizenship meant belonging in one single polity, that status providing membership within the political community and the endowment of (theoretically equal) rights and entitlements coupled with that membership. This inclusion meant the exclusion of other individuals and groups, and the denial of their citizenship status and rights. However, during the 1990s scholars addressing issues of multiculturalism, transnational migration, and social exclusion expanded notions of citizenship beyond political-legal status.[23] During this "cultural turn" of citizenship studies, Will Kymlicka, for example, argued for a multicultural citizenship.[24] He emphasized the right to culture—an effort to include immigrants and people of color within the bounds of citizenship without requiring them to assimilate or erase their culture. Similarly, Renato Rosaldo defined cultural citizenship as the "right to be different and to belong in a participatory democratic sense."[25] Both Kymlicka and Rosaldo raised questions about how states should accommodate cultural diversity and how groups of different backgrounds could obtain equality within the polity. They viewed citizenship as a demand for full status and rights despite differences in culture, race and ethnicity, or socioeconomic status.

Further developing the notion of citizenship, social scientists have focused on the transnational, border-crossing, and boundary-transgressing phenomena that have characterized late modernity.[26] Studies emphasize the decoupling of citizenship from the state, detaching citizenship from classic territorial frameworks.[27] The global and the transnational are the new sites where citizenship is said to be embedded, and citizenship framed and conceptualized in universal notions. For example, Yasemin Soysal suggests the need to conceptualize citizenship based on "universal personhood," a post-national citizenship where membership is based on notions of universality instead of membership fixed in a state-based model.[28] Aihwa Ong frames "flexible" citizenship, with traditional elements normally associated with citizenship (such as rights and entitlements) disarticulated from each other and re-articulated with new practices and strategies of transnational mobility and flexible accumulation of capital.[29] However, while neoliberalism and the hegemony of capitalism are transforming citizenship, detaching it from the state, and exerting extra-territorial and extra-state configurations onto citizenship categories, nation-states will continue to exist and be significant in world politics in the foreseeable future. Most importantly, getting rid of nation-states and citizenship altogether is not what refugees and migrants in resettlement seek. On the contrary, the goal of asylum is the opposite—it is a pursuit of citizenship and belonging tethered to the host nation-state. *Belonging in a House Divided* contributes to these ongoing citizenship debates by examining the current and localized complexities of the still-relevant classic formulation of citizenship bound within national territories, the very form of citizenship and belonging for which North Koreans (and other refugees and migrants) are striving.

Citizenship is generally conceptualized in the dimensions of *status* within the state and the political, social, and civil *rights* coupled with membership. Based on this framework, many scholars suggest that citizenship is claim-making.[30] Ample ethnographic research documents practices, negotiations, and claims to citizenship status and rights in everyday life among people in various parts of the world such as Azerbaijani refugees in Armenia, Turkish Kurd refugees in Japan, or the urban poor in India.[31] However, conceiving citizenship as claim-making reduces it to a form of emancipation conferred by the state as compromise in response to the demands by marginalized subjects. While studies have revealed how citizenship is negotiated and claimed, citizenship is much more than status and rights bestowed by the state.[32] North Koreans in South Korea are already granted citizenship status and rights without explicit claim-making. Citizenship status for resettled North Koreans entitles them to the full political, social, and civil rights that South Korean citizens enjoy, in addition to other asylum benefits specifically for North Koreans. Their struggle is not about legal status and claims to certain rights, but rather their embeddedness within the overlapping layers of violence that constitute citizenship—despite the South Korean government's master narrative of ethnic homogeneity. Where both status and rights are granted to North Koreans in their resettlement processes without claim-making, citizenship confined to the juridical-political possessions of and claims to status and rights is inadequate.

This book decenters the notion of citizenship to further theorize it in relation to violence and debates on refugee resettlement around the globe. Refugees are central figures in the international system of nation-states,[33] and this book's main concern is how violence operates in and contributes to how citizenship is experienced. Citizenship also includes people's sense of belonging in the political entity and social body. In this ethnography, I examine the lived experiences of citizenship as belonging, which involves processes of embodiment, self-making, and becoming.[34] In other words, citizenship for resettled North Koreans is a complex process of becoming South Korean through self-making, which includes embodying, practicing, and performing a particular postwar Koreanness. For many North Koreans, embodying South Korean citizenship is a violent process in relation to power and inequality. Violence—visible and invisible, public and private, intentional and unintentional—permeates the experience of North Korean migration, shaping and defining every phase of their resettlement processes.

At the root of refugee policies is the fundamental presumption of the naturalness of the geographically partitioned nation-states from which refugees originate. In this contemporary "national order of things," refugees symbolize the failure of citizenship—the deterioration of the territory-state-subject relationship.[35] Refugees are approached as disquieting figures in the international nation-state system, problematic and displaced persons who disrupt the stability and security of that national order. Liisa Malkki writes that "our sedentarist assumptions about attachment to place lead us to define displacement not as a fact about sociopolitical context, but rather as an inner, pathological conditions of the displaced."[36] Refugees are further defined negatively by what they lack—without a political identity that is citizenship and belonging to a political community that is the nation-state, they are characterized by emptiness, incompleteness, and suffering having lost their identities by being uprooted from their homes.[37]

As a consequence of such bleak representations, methods to resolve refugee crises stem from problem-solving, short-term-fix point of views aimed at restoring order, maintaining peace and security, and reinstating persons "out of place."[38] These methods aim to resolve this "emergency" which challenges the concepts of nation-state and citizenship. The prevailing approaches instill the false notion that regaining citizenship through resettlement is emancipation from violence. For example, many ordinary North Koreans encounter various forms of violence living under their repressive regime. They face discrimination based on family history, preferential redistribution of resources to the elite class and the military, and a shortage of food and hunger for the ordinary populace.[39] In prisons, human rights organizations cite evidence of inhumane treatment, torture, and public executions.[40] When North Koreans cross the border to China, many are confronted with obstacles related to their vulnerable status such as labor exploitation, human trafficking, and living in hiding from the

Chinese police.[41] Therefore, granting new citizenship status and rights, according to the narratives of human rights activists, supposedly gives resettled North Koreans "freedom" and "liberation."

Belonging in a House Divided challenges the idea that violence is finished or over when North Koreans are provided asylum, or that they are newborn citizens, their lives restored to start afresh. This book provides a different perspective from the predominant narrative of North Korean migration, which tells a story of oppression, violence, and suffering in North Korea while freedom and liberation characterize South Korea. Complicating this narrative, I show that for resettled North Koreans violence is not just in the moment of brute force, or when personhood is assaulted by poverty, fear, repression, and state surveillance in North Korea. Violence is rather embedded in their everyday experiences of displacement and resettlement—it becomes routinized, unrecognized, and rendered invisible. I argue that a continuum of violence permeates North Koreans' migration experience and feeds into itself with multiple, overlapping layers to shape and define their experiences with citizenship and belonging. Following Nancy Scheper-Hughes and Philippe Bourgois, I use the concept of the violence continuum to close the distinctions and blur the boundaries between wartime and peacetime violence.[42] Violence is most commonly understood in discrete terms of physicality and visibility. We immediately think of wars and conflict, genocide, state repression, or revolutions because the assaults, inflictions of physical force, and brutalities we see are the most noticeable and easily traceable forms of violence many people experience. However, understanding violence as occurring along a continuum allows us to recognize invisible forms of violence including structural, symbolic, and everyday violence, and to see how they often produce, translate into, and reinforce other forms of violence.

Structural violence is the configuration of the large-scale forces, institutions, and social matrix—often historically driven—that produce inequalities, limit life chances, and lead to harm and suffering for the vulnerable.[43] It is a political-economic oppression manifested through poverty, health disparities, and exclusion, and experienced along the lines of class, race, ethnicity, nationality, or other social categories. This violence can stem from methods of institutional policies, responses, and practices of engagement. In the words of Paul Farmer, pathologies of power "crystalize into the sharp, hard surfaces of individual suffering" to damage bodies and moral experiences.[44] These include moments in everyday life where personhood is assaulted by insecurity, fear, and disease and illness. For example, prior to arriving in South Korea, both political and structural violence produce suffering and vulnerability for North Koreans. Many of my research participants faced hunger while the government redistributed resources to its elite and the military. Upon resettlement in South Korea, their stunted stature from malnutrition became an embodied mark of stigma, causing some to take growth hormones or contemplate limb-lengthening operations to increase their stature. Others turned to plastic surgery to erase traces of their "North Koreanness," or changed their accents, grooming, and fashion to meet gendered and classed expectations about the (South) Korean body. The internalization of such stigma, then, can lead to symbolic violence.

Symbolic violence, as theorized by Pierre Bourdieu, describes the inequalities of class and power in social relations and the normalization, naturalization, and internalization of that stratification.[45] Symbolic violence can be as simple as when a Korean man unconsciously hands a knife on the table to a woman to peel an apple, and the woman proceeds because she views it as the proper and right thing to do in Korean culture, thereby contributing to the reproduction of gender hierarchy. The key in this process is the subjects' complicity in the violence based on their habitus: "the structural and cultural environment internalized in the form of dispositions to act, think, and feel in certain ways."[46] Habitus—one's disposition and deportment, taste and desire—is acquired and embodied throughout one's lifetime of experiences and through family, education, and other social institutions.

The symbolic violence of postwar Koreanness in South Korea maintains social dominance and hierarchy through the legitimization of certain conditions that North Koreans misrecognize as natural or deserved. A common insult directed at resettled North Koreans is that they are selfish and cold-blooded for having escaped their country alone, leaving behind family members who are likely to be punished for their escape because, in North Korea, defection is considered a political crime. When resettled North Koreans begin to embody these Cold War ideologies as an accurate and deserved representation, and blame themselves—feeling guilt, shame, or grief—this insult becomes symbolically violent. Hoping to compensate for the guilt of having left behind family members in their home country, resettled North Koreans send remittances to family through an underground broker system. These transnational activities help sustain kinship and rebuild social ties, but in return create complex relationships of solidarity, demands and burdens, and obligations that are embodied violently. These types of sufferings become routinized into everyday violence, or the normalization of violence in everyday life and especially during times of seeming peace.[47] For the vulnerable, the everyday experience of violence, terror, or death often become routinized to the point of indifference.

Recovering from, overcoming, or undoing violence might be possible, but so is the opposite; despite resettlement, reconciliation, and peace, ongoing forms of violence blur the temporal boundaries between wartime and peacetime. Violence is not just in the very moment when it is enacted.[48] Experiences of violence and their legacies often extend into the present, and are reproductive and overlapping, challenging normative views of the temporality of violence. Past experiences in China, for example marriage to Chinese men or human rights activists' emphasis on human trafficking, lead to sexualizations of the female body in South Korea and become stereotypes that amount to a continuum of violence. Scheper-Hughes and Bourgois write that the "very idea that individuals and nations can heal and ultimately recover from violence falls prey to inappropriate and impoverished medical and psychological metaphors."[49] As in the case of the North Koreans in South Korea, and for many other refugee populations around the globe, the remembrance of violence in the places from where they have traveled remains vivid and manifests itself through embodied forms including but not limited to dreams, shame, grief, and insecurities. Fear and dread come to be felt inside the body. While not all North Koreans share all these experiences of violence along their journey, the pressures present at every juncture illustrate how violence impacts their resettlement.

Many studies on North Korean defectors, refugees, and migrants come from the frameworks of international security and human rights that document violations of human rights, the effects of famine, the trafficking of North Korean women, and the issue of statelessness in China.[50] Consequently, studies on resettled North Koreans in South Korea, particularly in scholarship published in the Korean language, focus overwhelmingly on their psychological health and the prevalence of posttraumatic stress disorders.[51] Because these people have reached a "safe haven" characterized as a land of freedom in direct opposition to oppressive North Korea, the central preoccupation in many of these studies is to make sense of the struggles of North Koreans to successfully integrate into South Korea despite hospitable conditions.[52]

In the Korean context, language operates to enforce the continuum of violence through its failure to communicate the violence. The words for violence in the Korean language are *pokryeok* and *pokhaeng*, both words describing the power (*ryeok*) and act (*haeng*) of brute force (*pok*). The language does not grasp invisible violence. Therefore, it is outside of what Koreans consider to be legitimate, normative categories and conceptions of violence. Linguistically, the types of invisible violence I describe in this book are not easy to grasp, but it is my hope that this ethnography provides a nuanced analysis of the ways that the continuum of violence operates on the Korean peninsula. But I want to be clear that my intention is not to reify North Koreans as tragic, suffering victims who only experience violence, but to use these stories and the theme of violence as a point of departure to explore and understand how they experience citizenship and belonging. These conditions, combined with South Korea's process of granting citizenship status and rights, the established government support system, and the discourse of shared ethnicity, make this an interesting case to explore the role of violence in the processes of belonging.

CATEGORIES OF IDENTITY

The official South Korean descriptor for North Koreans has undergone changes that have been political in nature.[53] In 1997, in response to the North Korean famine and increasing number of North Koreans seeking resettlement, South Korea passed the Act on the Protection and Settlement Support for Residents Escaping from North Korea, using the Korean word *bukhanitaljumin* (resident who escaped North Korea) to emphasize their escape. In 2005, the government changed the official label to *saeteomin* (new settlers), coinciding with South Korea's engagement policy towards

North Korea (that is, the Sunshine Policy). This new depoliticized label emphasized North Koreans' migration and settlement in a new country. North Koreans living in South Korea have had mixed reactions to the labels of *saeteomin* (new settlers) or *ijuja* (migrant) because they see the migrant label as putting them on the same footing as other, non-Korean, migrant workers in South Korea. In addition, they have argued that the migrant label only aids the Chinese policy of regarding North Korean border-crossers as economic migrants rather than providing them asylum as refugees.

The South Korean government has reversed course and now once again officially uses *bukhanitaljumin* (resident who escaped North Korea) even though the more informal word *talbukja* (North Korean escapee) continues to be widely used in the South Korean public sphere. However, because the syllable *ja* in the Korean language can often be used in negative ways—for example *nosukja* (homeless) or *dokjaeja* (dictator)—many have instead encouraged the use of the word *talbukmin*. The ending syllable *min* carries a more positive meaning and is used in many inclusive words such as *simin* (citizen) and *gukmin* (national).

"Defector," the most commonly used descriptor in English, is an imperfect translation of the words *bukhanitaljumin*, *talbukja*, or *talbukmin*, carrying problematic Cold War connotations of betrayal and political dissent. Labeling North Koreans as defectors grows increasingly inaccurate when the majority of them are fleeing their country due to conditions of poverty and material deprivation. On the other hand, though many North Koreans are indeed refugees in need of protection—some have been granted refugee status in various countries such as the United States and the United Kingdom—the South Korean government grants citizenship to North Koreans because its Constitution declares North Korea its sovereign territory. Thus, the Korean word for refugee—*nanmin*—is not publicly used to describe resettled North Koreans in South Korea.

As a result of this sensitive linguistic situation, throughout this book I am conscious of my use of labels such as defector, refugee, or migrant as a *sole* category of identity to describe North Koreans who leave their country. Identity, when used as a category of analysis, can have reifying consequences, flattening the multitude of people's experiences.[54] Others have warned that categories often have a sticky tendency, with the labels having a lasting impact on individuals.[55] Despite good intentions, labels can reorder experiences, disenfranchise the vulnerable, and reduce people to passive objects.[56] Accordingly, I refrain from using defector, refugee, or migrant as a singular identifying category to define the North Korean experience. For clarity, I often use "resettled North Koreans" or "North Koreans in South Korea" to refer to those that have gained South Korean citizenship and live in the country, as well as other descriptors to try to best describe the contextual circumstances.

ETHNOGRAPHY OF HOME

The film *Paris Is Burning* chronicles the members of the several Houses— likened to the fashion industry houses such as Chanel, Gucci, Prada, etc.— who "walked" and competed in the drag balls of New York City in the 1980s. The documentary explores the themes of gender, sexuality, class, and race by closely following the lives of the individuals involved and their desires, expressions of identities, struggles within their homes, material hardships, and future aspirations. These individuals were rejected from their familial homes for their gendered and sexual orientations, expelled from circles of kinship and the physical dwellings that make up the home, and the Houses of the ball circuit provided them with alternative forms of inclusion and belonging. However, these Houses did not replace the domestic, intimate sphere of the home, and Chandan Reddy writes that they were instead "the site from which to remember the constitutive violence of the home, and the location from which to perform the pleasures and demands of alternative living, while at the same time functioning as an 'interlocutionary device' between homes and queer subjects."[57] The Houses served as liminal entities, in Victor Turner's classic definition "neither here nor there; they are betwixt and between the positions assigned and arrayed by law, custom, convention, and ceremonial."[58]

I use this metaphor of the house to frame the political and national division of the Korean peninsula and the resettlement experiences of North Koreans. The Korean imagination contains a yearning for a whole home that is no longer divided. The divided Korea—believed to be in a temporary and liminal condition awaiting reunion—is a place from which we can reflect on the violence of citizenship and belonging. Whether one views the idea of the unity of the Korean ethnicity as "natural" or as a product of modernity, there is undeniably a strong belief in ethnic homogeneity that still pervades the Korean peninsula.[59] State and non-state actors in the two Koreas hold steadfast to the ideology of the "unity of Korean ethnicity" (*han minjok*), a people sharing the "same" blood as brothers and sisters, and a yearning for political reunion. Therefore, arguably the single most important issue for Koreans has been the question of reunification. When North Koreans resettle in South Korea, they are granted juridical citizenship status and rights. However, despite gaining paperwork and physical dwellings, they constantly search for home and a sense of belonging in South Korea.[60] They navigate the paradox of claims to ethnic homogeneity, all the while being treated as second-class citizens. Resettled North Koreans thus embody a liminal belonging in this divided peninsula.

As a Korean, I was conducting an ethnography of home. Yet, having spent the majority of my upbringing as a diasporic subject outside Korea, I found that my North Korean friends often knew South Korea better than I did, were more familiar with pop culture, and could navigate city life with far more ease than I could. At the same time, my particular experience growing up in East Africa provided me a connection to my North Korean interlocutors. Although we were all ethnically Korean, we felt like outsiders in South Korean society, and we shared similar longings for belonging, imaginations of home, and questions regarding our national identity— who we were and where we belonged (even though our background experiences differed greatly).

The site of this ethnography is in Seoul, the capital city of South Korea, and I travelled to various satellite cities in the neighboring Incheon and Gyeonggi Provinces to visit North Korean interlocutors and friends I came to know through my fieldwork. I conducted ethnographic fieldwork during the summer months of 2010 and 2011, long-term fieldwork from 2012–2014, and have continued sustained research over the years since. It is important to note, as a result, that this research should not be taken as a generalization of the experiences of *all* resettled North Koreans; my research participants left North Korea during a particular historical period following the 1990s famine and arrived in South Korea in the first decade of the twenty-first century.

The primary data come from participant observation in the day-to-day lives of resettled North Koreans and life-history interviews with them. I conducted participant observation in three main spaces in which the continuum of violence was made manifest, although I also spent a lot of time with my interlocutors outside of these sites and met other members within their social networks. First, language provided me privilege that granted me access to many spaces and relationships. I was an English teacher and tutor for North Korean students. I taught English to high school seniors in an after-school program at a North Korean alternative school in Seoul. Many of the students' education had been disrupted due to the North Korean famine and their migration to China. Thus, when I met them, they were many years older than the traditional high school student. I also became a tutor to these students and their friends once they entered college in subsequent years. I later came to realize that, by teaching English, I was participating in a larger violent system that requires resettled North Koreans to become South Korean by learning English—a form of cultural capital—to help them attend universities, obtain jobs, and achieve upward social mobility in South Korea.[61]

With some of the students I came to know, I also attended and participated in a church in Seoul. The members of the congregation included predominantly resettled North Koreans and a few South Koreans. Aside from the government, churches and religious organizations provide some of the most substantial resources and support to North Koreans resettling to South Korea. Churches are important spaces because they provide economic support, scholarships, and social services to North Koreans as incentives to attend their services and fellowships. Additionally, the evangelical mission of these churches is to bring Christianity to North Koreans.[62] There is no freedom of religion in North Korea and religious organizations are considered enemies of the state. It is often said that the official "religion" in North Korea is *Kimilsung-ism* (worshipping Kim Il-sung and allegiance to the Kim Dynasty). It is through religious conversion that South Korean evangelicals consider North Koreans saved, healed, and ultimately freed from the sins and evils of North Korea and communism.[63]

Thirdly, from 2012–2013, I was a researcher with the Seoul-based Database Center for North Korean Human Rights (NKDB) and participated in their various projects that included research on North Korean human rights, the economic status of resettled North Koreans in South Korea, and prisoners of war from North Korea. One of their ongoing perennial projects at the time was visiting the government's Hanawon Resettlement Center to survey newly arrived North Koreans on their experience with human rights violations in North Korea and China. Through my visits to Hanawon I was able to learn more about the education North Koreans receive in preparation for resettlement, including lessons on democracy and capitalism, and perhaps more urgent to the South Korean state, unlearning communism. Furthermore, resettled North Koreans are taught how to use an ATM machine and open a bank account, practice using public transportation, and learn South Korean accents, mannerisms, and culture. Clearly, both government and non-governmental organizations play important roles in assisting resettled North Koreans, and various ethnographic studies have captured the relations between these institutions and their North Korean subjects.[64] Therefore, my focus on violence and citizenship is framed by what I see as the limitations of the naturalized discourses and frameworks of South Korean NGOs and government institutions.

Participant observation in these spaces provided insight into the daily lives of North Koreans, their hopes and aspirations, the everyday challenges of resettlement, the navigation and negotiations of their identities, their self-presentation, and their complicated relationships with family members left behind in North Korea. The extensive, long-term personal relationships I developed through participant observation provided me the rapport crucial to conducting interviews and collecting oral histories. As I met new contacts and other members within my interlocutors' social networks at these various sites, my sample size diversified and increased through the snowball effect. Oral histories provided me a deeper glimpse into my interlocutors' entire trajectories: their lives in North Korea, their departure from the country, the experience of migration, and their resettlement experiences in South Korea. Interviews often took place in my interlocutors' homes, which were mostly located in working-class neighborhoods of Seoul. Most interviews were digitally recorded with permission, but in several cases when my interviewees preferred not to be recorded, I took notes. In this book, I only quote people directly when I am confident that I have captured their words precisely. To protect the privacy of my North Korean research participants, I use pseudonyms throughout. In addition to these ethnographic research methods, I collected government promotional materials, policy documents, media articles, and NGO reports, and carried out interviews with officials, human rights activists, and other experts on the issue of North Korean resettlement.

Moreover, where appropriate throughout this book, I draw on my military experience as a form of autoethnography to make connections between the enduring war on the Korean peninsula and the experiences of North Koreans resettled in South Korea. Research for this book was not the reason for my military conscription, but I spent two years as a soldier in the South Korean Army, from 2015–2017. As I began to explain earlier, my academic career was put on hold while I was stationed at a frontline infantry division along the DMZ. Through military service, I experienced firsthand some of the core themes of this book such as national division, militarization, nationalism, anti-communism, and citizenship. For example, I began to understand North Koreans' anxiety of being *gatjanhda*, a frequently used South Korean phrase which means, "not the same." In the event of war with North Korea, my division was responsible for counterinfiltration operations, meaning we would counterattack North Korean forces as the initial Guard Post troops retreated to safety. In preparation for a reescalation of war with North Korea, we constantly engaged in military exercises and trained for battle. In addition to physical exercises, part of our training included mental training, which involved indoctrination about North Korea as "the enemy," the very reason for our military conscription.

What did it mean for me to belong in this house divided? To me, despite having lived outside the Korean peninsula, citizenship and belonging meant military conscription. Military service was, as my drill sergeant insisted to me, a "special right" (*teukgwon*) to serve the nation. It was central to our citizenship, and we should proudly serve our time. Because of the history of the Korean division, the unresolved legacy of the Korean War, and the politics of anti-communism in South Korea, maintaining my citizenship meant that I had to serve in the military to protect the nation from the "North Korean enemy." However, as I had already been studying the experiences of North Koreans in South Korea, the military mindset was antithetical to how I viewed my North Korean friends and interlocutors.

ORGANIZATION OF THE BOOK

This ethnography follows the lives of the central interlocutors and friends I came to know during my fieldwork. The narrative is thus organized around their stories and life trajectories. Chapter 1, "Enduring Legacies of Division and War," provides a historical background to the contemporary migration of North Koreans by tracing the legacies of the Korean War and its enduring violence on the Korean peninsula. The chapter is driven by an enduring question: can reunion and the bond of kinship help overcome the political violence of national division and war? I address the conundrum of reunification through an ethnographic account of two siblings—a North Korean sister and her South Korean brother who later immigrated to the United States. Although they were both born in Seoul, they were separated in the aftermath of the Korean division. Over half a century later, she escaped North Korea in hopes of reuniting with her brother. Referencing my efforts to make their reunion possible, I explore Korean family reunions as a site of both violence and reconciliation. The nostalgic longing for a reunified Korea and the rhetoric of reconciliation and national healing symbolized by family reunions, as well as the increasing resettlement of North Koreans in South Korea, obscure the deeper impediments to overcoming war's legacies, its enduring violence, and the militarized landscape of the Korean peninsula.

Chapter 2, "The Chinese Dimension of the North Korean Migration," examines how the North Korean migration is intimately connected to China's one-child policy, history of son-preference, and gender imbalance. The majority of resettled North Koreans have been women. Although some do fall victim to human trafficking along the borderlands of North Korea and China and are sold into marriage, I complicate simplified notions of these women as trafficked or sold. Closely related to the gendered contours of North Korean migration is the stigma attached to North Korean women—that they are victims of trafficking, have had Chinese husbands, and have had children with these men. The notion of purity thus complicates their belonging in South Korean society.

Chapter 3, "The Body and the Violence of Phenotypical Normalization," analyzes the connection between structural violence, famine, and the processes of self-making. Poor nutrition and other forms of violence in North Korea have molded North Korean bodies; there are often physical disparities between North and South Koreans. Embodied experiences of hunger and malnutrition in North Korea—for example, stunted growth— contribute to the violence of phenotypical normalization in South Korea. North Korean bodies are marked as smaller, foreign, and strange in a surgically normalized society. Some choose to undergo cosmetic surgery to "correct" a variety of unwanted physical traits, and some men subject themselves to hormone intake and contemplate limb-lengthening operations in order to increase stature in a society where short height in men is viewed as undesirable.

Chapter 4, "Remittances and Transborder Kinship," explores the efforts of resettled North Koreans to maintain transnational kinship with their families back home through the practice of sending remittances. Despite the restricted nature of the North Korean state, brokers have developed complex networks throughout East Asia to enable remittances to North Korea, telecommunication, and even strategies to smuggle family members out. These transnational activities help sustain family relationships and rebuild social ties, but in return create complex relationships of solidarity, demands and burdens, and obligations that are embodied violently.

Chapter 5, "Constructing North Korean Deservingness," unravels the humanitarian discourse of violence used to draw compassion from the public sphere. This chapter analyzes the global contestations over granting refugee status to North Koreans, and the ways in which various humanitarian and governmental actors construct North Korean deservingness through representations of North Korean violence and suffering. Molded into a state of exception—inclusion into politics through their exceptional deservingness for protection—North Koreans are characterized as possessing only bare life, deprived of their political status and rights, and in need of asylum and emancipation to regain qualitative life.

Finally, in the conclusion I reflect on the question of belonging in a "house" that is divided. I grapple with the Korean concept of *gohyang* (home) to address the question of belonging that is at the heart of the experiences of resettled North Koreans in South Korea, and I argue that the violence continuum is enforced through the very incommunicability of violence in the Korean language. Relatedly, I examine the endlessness of the Korean War, the militarization of the landscape and the defensive architectural structures in South Korea, and the insidious ways that invisible forms of violence haunt the Korean peninsula.

1 Enduring Legacies of Division and War

Loss and vulnerability seem to follow from our being socially constituted bodies, attached to others, at risk of losing those attachments, exposed to others, at risk of violence by virtue of that exposure.

Judith Butler

Who will remember you if not your kin?

Ruth Behar

OPERATION CHROMITE

Boot camp was intensive and exhausting. In addition to the physically demanding training, we learned to fire the K2 assault rifle, throw grenades, and withstand the gas chamber. During my time in boot camp, and later as a soldier on the frontlines of the DMZ, I came to learn and embody military norms. Upon completion of training, a ceremony was held to commemorate our becoming soldiers, and I was assigned to the 2nd Infantry Division's 17th Regiment, a unit responsible for "counterinfiltration operations" (*daechimtujakjeon*) in the event of a North Korean invasion. The 2nd Infantry Division is stationed along the DMZ in the remote areas of Inje, Wontong, and Yanggu. The region has the lowest population density in South Korea, partly due to its proximity to North Korea but also because of its high mountains and deep valleys, blistering cold winters, and difficult terrain for travel.

When my mother came to the graduation ceremony and learned of my assignment in the Inje region, she said to me, with tears in her eyes and a warm embrace, *"Inje gamyeon eonje ona, wontonghaeseo mot salgessne"* ("When will you return once you go to Inje? It pains me to live"), quoting a well-known folk song. In the aftermath of the Korean War's ceasefire, as soldiers were stationed on this remote frontline, people sang this song to express their despair. The lyrics play with the region names of Inje (which also carries the meaning "now") and Wontong (which also means "pain" and "sorrow"), and have their origins in a funeral song: "When will he return once he leaves? It pains me to live." The transformed lyrics, likening the singer's feeling to the sorrow people felt when their loved ones died, express the anguish of sending one's family members to this very inaccessible and hostile region for military conscription.[1] When the military bus transported me from boot camp to the regiment's base, I was not only physically disconnected from the rest of society, but also socially isolated, as conscripted soldiers were not permitted the use of cell phones to communicate with loved ones, and our mobility was confined within the army barracks.

In 1950, early in the Korean War, the 17th Regiment played an important role in recapturing Seoul as one of the few South Korean units that participated in the US-led Operation Chromite. The city had fallen to the North Korean forces that invaded South Korea on June 25 to ignite the war. They crossed the 38th parallel with over 75,000 soldiers, heavy artillery, and tanks, and captured the capital city within days. In the next month, North Korean forces took control of nearly the entire peninsula as the fledgling South Korean troops retreated to the southeastern port city of Busan. Responding to this invasion, a United Nations force came to South Korea's defense with US General Douglas MacArthur as its commander. Judging that fighting North Korean troops head-on would lead to heavy casualties (the North Koreans were well-equipped and armed with aid from the Soviet Union and China), MacArthur ordered the UN forces to swing around the southern peninsula towards the western sea and make an amphibious landing in Incheon—the midpoint or the "waist" of the peninsula. Incheon is located near Seoul, and the UN forces would be able to attack the North Korean troops from behind, recapture the capital city, and cut off the supply lines to the southern half of the peninsula.

It was a highly risky operation with a very small chance of success. The narrow water channels into Incheon would make the warships susceptible to attacks by naval mines, and it would be difficult for many ships to enter quickly at once. Additionally, the extreme tides posed a great challenge, giving them less than two hours to make a swift landing. If the UN forces were unable to land before the water moved out, they would be stuck on the mudflats. For these reasons, the plan was opposed by the US Joint Chiefs of Staff.

"The only alternative," MacArthur responded to the top US commanders, "will be the continuation of the savage sacrifice we are making at Pusan, with no hope of relief in sight. Are you content to let our troops stay in that bloody perimeter like beef cattle in the slaughterhouse?"[2] He argued that the very handicaps posed by the unfavorable conditions would actually help the UN forces because the operation would be unexpected and the North Korean forces would be caught off-guard.

The date of the planned attack was finally set for September 15, 1950, when the tide would be at its highest. It was codenamed Operation Chromite after the mineral chromium, the chemical element used in stainless steel. Despite the odds, the Allied troops successfully landed in Incheon, taking the North Koreans by surprise as MacArthur had hoped, and the UN forces (along with South Korean military units like the 17th Regiment) recaptured Seoul. It was the first turning point in the course of a war that would last for another three years. Disregarding the warnings of a Chinese intervention if the Allied forces crossed the 38th parallel, the UN forces advanced into North Korea, captured Pyongyang, and pushed the North Korean troops north toward the Chinese border.

THE WOMAN FROM PYONGYANG

"There is a North Korean grandmother who recently arrived in South Korea," Kang said to me over the phone with excitement and a sense of urgency in his voice in 2012. I was with Dahae and Sunmi at the IFC Mall in Seoul. After finishing our English tutoring session, we had decided to visit the brand-new mall and have dinner at the food court. Kang, Dahae, and Sunmi were some of the students I had taught at an alternative school for resettled North Koreans in Seoul.

"She is a *talbukja* (North Korean escapee) from Pyongyang, but she was originally born in Seoul," Kang explained. To her misfortune, he continued, she happened to be in Pyongyang during the Korean War and thus became North Korean, while her family members remained South Korean. Five decades later, she fled North Korea hoping to reunite with her brother and uncle who, based on what she told Kang, had emigrated from South Korea to the United States. Her desire for this familial reconnection, rather than a desire to create a new life in South Korea, had led her to migrate.

Although I met many resettled North Koreans through the course of fieldwork, the news about this North Korean grandmother was surprising information to digest because there are not many resettled North Koreans who come from Pyongyang, the capital city of North Korea. Its residents have a higher quality of life in comparison to the majority of other North Koreans who live in the regional provinces and they normally do not have either political or economic reasons to leave their country.

"Her uncle is a famous aerospace engineer in America," Kang exclaimed, "she said he built the space shuttle that went to the moon!"

"You mean ... NASA? How does she know that?" I asked, bewildered by everything he was saying. Her claims sounded like some Hollywood script.

"They wrote her letters from America [to North Korea]," he answered. In addition to the uncle, Kang continued, she also had a brother who was a scientist in the United States. "Can you help find them? I told her that you could help since you live in Washington [DC]."

Unraveling Grandmother Ku's[3] story and her search for her family, this chapter explores the legacies of war and the human costs of separation from the lingering conflict between the two Koreas. One of those issues has been that of separated families (*isan gajok*). Following the Korean War, millions of Koreans found themselves on opposites of the 38th parallel. The South Korean expression for this catastrophe is *cheonman isan gajok*, or "ten million separated families." Nam Kim writes that "rather than denoting a calculated estimate," this expression instead "connotes a quantity of such great magnitude as to be virtually countless."[4] Since

1985, there have been over twenty-one rounds of state-sponsored, inter-Korean temporary family reunions—allowing family members to see one another for less than 24 hours before each side returns to their respective countries. However, Grandmother Ku's case differs in that she personally fled North Korea to seek reunion.

Family reunions do not necessarily lead to happy endings.[5] But they continue to serve as a stepping-stone to undo the historical violence on the Korean peninsula and as a micro-level template for national reconciliation, reunification, and the recovery of the "whole" Korean nation. At the 2018 Inter-Korean Summit between North Korean leader Kim Jong-un and South Korean President Moon Jae-in, the two pledged that "South and North Korea will reconnect the blood relations of the people and bring forward the future of co-prosperity and unification." Importantly, the summit outlined family reunions as one of the key ways to approach reconciliation: "South and North Korea agreed to endeavor to swiftly resolve the humanitarian issues that resulted from the division of the nation, and to [. . .] solve various issues including the reunion of separated families."[6]

Can family reunion—a symbol of past political violence but simultaneously of future hope and healing—and the affective bonds of kinship help overcome the political violence of national division? In examining family reunion as a site of violence, I illustrate how kinship can cloak relations of power in the glow of affect. The temporalities of the violence continuum complicate the desires and possibilities of family reunion. The violence of the division is enduring and without perceived crisis or rupture, but it is nevertheless pervasive, persistent, and reproductive, with new forms arising to fray interpersonal relationships and impose more suffering.

Kang and I met on a Saturday afternoon at the Junggye subway station, located on the northern outskirts of Seoul. In contrast to the affluent neighborhoods of Gangnam in southern Seoul, Junggye and its surrounding neighborhoods are home to many lower-class residents and, in recent years, North Koreans who are given government-subsidized apartments. Kang himself lived only two subway stops away. In his late twenties at the time, he had long curly hair with bangs that partially covered his face and were carefully styled with hairspray. There were big metal chains dangling from his pants and he wore jewelry on his fingers and ears. Each year he experimented with different fashion trends, but no matter the style, he was always dressed a little more extravagantly than his peers.

We first searched for a local store. We did not want to visit the elderly woman's home empty-handed. After buying a box of apples and pears, we located the apartment and entered the building. The apartment was handicap-accessible. The elevator's bottom half was covered on all sides with wooden panels while its top half had mirrors all around. It creaked as we stepped in. Kang pressed "5" and we headed up together in silence. We fixed our eyes on the yellow-lit numbers above the door as the elevator took us up to the fifth floor. I was nervous. Although I was hopeful, I did not feel very optimistic about the prospects of finding this woman's uncle and brother. But I was eager to hear her extraordinary story.

Grandmother Ku's apartment door was propped open and we knocked. In unison, we said "*Annyeonghaseyo halmeoni*" ("hello grandmother") as we removed our shoes before entering the one-bedroom apartment. The cold autumn breeze flowed from the entrance toward the balcony in the back, carrying a strong smell of fresh paint from the front door, just painted a few hours prior. The woman rose from the living room where she had been resting and lowered the volume on the television with a remote control. I noticed a figure of the Virgin Mary beside the TV as she did so.

Smiling, she quickly approached us and shook Kang's hands first. The old woman then greeted me with a slight bow. "Thank you for coming all this way," she said firmly, in a strong North Korean accent that she had acquired over the decades she spent living in Pyongyang. She looked younger, healthier, and stronger than someone I would have imagined in her seventies. Her black permed hair had gray roots and touched the top of her shoulders. Her tan face had many wrinkles and she wore thin, silver-colored wire-framed glasses. She was taller than most other North Koreans I had met, and taller than Kang. Kang had lived a less privileged life than this woman, including years of famine in North Korea. His stature embodied the structural and physical violence of malnutrition. This woman was stocky and stood straight.

Her apartment, in my estimation, was less than 500 square feet (or 14 *pyong* in Korean measurements), and the layout was similar to other resettled North Koreans' apartment homes I have visited—a tiny bedroom adjacent to the entryway and a small kitchen that led into the living room.

She did not have many personal belongings and the living room was sparsely furnished. There was no bed. She slept on a mat on her living room floor, not uncommon in Korea, where apartments are designed with an underfloor heating system called *ondol* instead of air vents. Her bedroom had only an old computer on top of a desk; she later told me she was taking a computer class with other newly resettled North Koreans at the local welfare center.

As soon as we sat, Grandmother Ku wanted me to understand that she was not originally from Pyongyang. Her encounter with me seemed to carry a deep sense of urgency, excitement, and nervousness, as I was her hope for reunion with her brother and uncle. She wanted this to be very clear: she was born in Seoul and she had escaped North Korea to return home—though her "home" was irrevocably changed by the violence of national division and war.

SEPARATED FAMILIES

Through a series of meetings with Grandmother Ku, I learned that her family had fallen victim to the national division and subsequent war. During the short five years between the 1945 division and the start of the Korean War in 1950, people frequently crossed the border between the two Koreas by foot, a stark contrast to the militarized reality today. Koreans viewed the division as ephemeral and expected an eventual and inevitable reunification of their country. They imagined (and the two Koreas still proclaim) the Korean people as a homogenous ethnic group with over five thousand years of history, culture, and language. In 1948, Grandmother Ku explained, she and her parents temporarily went to Pyongyang to visit her paternal grandmother, who was sick in the hospital. Her brother, however, remained in South Korea with extended family members.

"I still remember the tall grass touching my cheeks that night," she said, recalling the night when she left Seoul.

Grandmother Ku and her parents remained in Pyongyang longer than originally planned. But they could not have foreseen the devastating war that would soon be waged between the two Koreas. Her parents died during the war in the US bombing campaign that turned the city to rubble;

their bodies were never found. Grandmother Ku and her grandmother, taking shelter in the hospital, survived. But following the 1953 armistice, the DMZ became extremely militarized. Without a peace treaty, military troops from both sides patrol this zone against potential attack to this day, making cross-border movements by ordinary people nearly impossible. Grandmother Ku, unable to return to Seoul and with her parents deceased, had no choice but to stay in Pyongyang and live with relatives. She became North Korean, while her brother remained South Korean. Their identities developed on either side of the border that posed barriers for future communication and reunion. She asked me, "The family separated. Siblings separated. . . . What kind of a miserable misfortune is that?"

Like Grandmother Ku, millions of people were torn apart from family members on opposite sides of the DMZ. Although the two countries had officially entered a time of "peace," suffering would continue, especially north of the 38th parallel. Over half a century later she was back in Seoul but her South Korean extended relatives did not welcome her and wished no connection with her. She struggled to express how she felt about this experience, to articulate the shame of kin rejecting her. Language is often unable to express such experiences of pain and loss, and it is often through the burial of the unspeakable that one can overcome pain.[7] However, it was clear as she talked to me that she still held on to the hope of reuniting with her uncle and brother in the United States.

She handed me a paper on which she had written down the names of her immediate and extended family members, including their birth dates and education. I could see that she was from a highly educated and wealthy family. Her father, uncle, and brother all graduated from Seoul National University—the most prestigious university in South Korea, which only the most privileged Koreans could attend at that time. However, many South Koreans with kinship ties to North Korea, like Grandmother Ku's brother, faced ostracism and discrimination in South Korea, and he had emigrated to the United States in the 1970s.[8] The US Immigration and Nationality Act of 1965 opened the door to an influx of immigrants from countries like South Korea, China, and Japan.

In 1990, serendipity started to bring Grandmother Ku and her brother, Dr. Ku, back into contact. North Korea held the Pan-National Reunification Concert (*Beomminjok Tongir Eumakhoe*) in Pyongyang from October

18–23 and musicians from the Korean diaspora living in the United States, Canada, the Soviet Union, and China visited North Korea to attend. One of the participants was Dr. Ku's wife, Sarah, a former professional singer and Korean American member of a US choir group participating in the event. The North Korean authorities allowed these foreign guests to connect with any extended family members living in North Korea, and Sarah searched for her parents-in-law. Though she learned that they had passed away, the North Korean authorities introduced Sarah to Grandmother Ku. Sarah returned to the United States and shared with her husband the joyous news about the discovery of his long-lost sister. Shortly thereafter, in April 1991, Dr. Ku visited Pyongyang to reunite with Grandmother Ku. It was their first meeting in over four decades.

Upon his return to the United States, Dr. Ku began to send her letters, a practice which the North Korean government permitted for Korean Americans, Koreans from Japan, and other Korean diaspora with family in North Korea.[9] In addition to the letters, her brother also sent her remittances. She told me his monetary support helped her husband and children live through the extreme famine in the 1990s that was preceded by heavy rainfall and floods. The ecological disasters, combined with the dissolution of the Soviet Bloc and the North Korean regime's incompetence, contributed to the death of nearly three million North Korean citizens.

She recalled one of the earliest letters her brother had sent her. He boasted in the letter—not foreseeing its consequences—that their uncle was part of the team that had engineered the American space shuttle that went to the moon. During their initial reunion in North Korea, Dr. Ku had explained to her that their uncle (who also had emigrated to the United States from South Korea) was an aerospace engineer at NASA. In the letter, he sent her a picture of the space shuttle as proof.

"That letter and picture circulated around so much [among the North Korean authorities] that all the edges were worn and brown. It must have circulated for over a month before I received it!" she said. The North Korean State Security Agency opened all the incoming and outgoing letters to make sure there was nothing in writing that slandered North Korea. They only delivered letters with "non-threatening" information, and privacy in the correspondence was impossible.

"*Oppa* (older brother) doesn't know the sufferings I went through," she said, frustrated that she had not been able to share her experiences with him. For example, the bodies of her parents never having been found, they were recorded as "missing." North Korean officials assumed that they ran away to South Korea, and her *todae* (family background) thus became stained. Despite her South Korean origin and her tainted background, she said the authorities let her live in Pyongyang among other privileged North Korean citizens for propaganda purposes (as opposed to relocating her to a rural, poorer region of North Korea).

However, she was discriminated against, and her *todae* was passed down to her children: "My children could not get good occupations because of my South Korean origin, even though they excelled in their majors." Grandmother Ku snickered. "You want me to tell you a funny story? When my brother visited Pyongyang, the officials told him that our father was a national hero and patriot. But after he left, they said to me, 'Your father's betrayal is still a fact. Don't forget that.' I couldn't tell my brother the truth." After Dr. Ku left Pyongyang following that face-to-face reunion, the authorities interrogated her. They had eavesdropped on the conversation and they questioned everything she had said.

Grandmother Ku chuckled at the memories of it all. "Let's laugh. It's the past so let's just laugh. I must laugh. . . ." But her laughter was brief. "I have lived with such sufferings but my uncle and brother have no idea." They exchanged letters over the years, but in 2002, she told me, her government stopped delivering the letters—the last she had heard from her American brother.

Grandmother Ku left North Korea in 2009, but I learned during additional visits that she did not initially intend to come to South Korea. Unlike others who secretly escape North Korea, Grandmother Ku went legally to China with a government-issued passport for the purpose of visiting relatives. She crossed over from the North Korean city of Sinuiju to the Chinese city of Dandong—two border cities connected by a well-secured bridge.

"My brother will think I am a *dokaebi* when he hears this," she said, explaining how she obtained a passport. (A *dokaebi* is a goblin-like monster in Korean folklore known to have special powers, with which it bewitches and plays malicious jokes on people.) Grandmother Ku's daughter worked as an intermediary broker between Chinese and North Koreans engaged in cross-border trades. One of her daughter's clients was a Chinese woman of Korean descent with the same surname as Grandmother Ku's mother. Her daughter bribed the client in order to register this client's father as Grandmother Ku's maternal uncle. In the past, the existence of this fake uncle in China had provided Grandmother Ku the opportunity to visit China on multiple occasions.

Thus, when Grandmother Ku applied for a passport to visit her "family" in China, the North Korean officials issued it to her without much trouble. It did, however, come at a price and Grandmother Ku bribed the officials with approximately $1,000 USD. Her travel permit allowed her to visit her Chinese relative for two months at a time. Grandmother Ku had also requested a passport for her daughter, but despite the bribes she offered, the authorities denied her request. They considered the daughter "young," which meant that her chances of defecting to South Korea from China were high. Grandmother Ku told me that the officials, however, did not question her intentions because she was too old and would have no reason to betray the country, given that her children lived in North Korea and would be subject to punishment if she fled.[10]

In China, Grandmother Ku stayed at an acquaintance's house and wrote letters to her brother in the United States, hoping they could reconnect. But the letters were returned undelivered, and she ended up overstaying her permitted two-month period while she resent the letters and waited for his response. As punishment, her eldest son served three months in prison and he sent her a letter upon his release. In coded language, he advised her to go to South Korea instead of returning to Pyongyang. She faced punishment for not returning and her children worried she would not survive the demands of physical labor due to her age—the prisons are known for their long hours of labor, little food, and harsh treatment.

Grandmother Ku felt she had no choice but to embark on her journey to South Korea. She could not return to North Korea, and she could not stay in China since she was now unauthorized. Therefore, with the help of migration brokers, Grandmother Ku travelled by bus through the Chinese mainland toward southwest China, traversed the mountainous border area between China, Myanmar and Laos on foot, and got on a motorboat to secretly cruise through the Mekong River to reach Thailand. She was not alone, but with a group of other North Koreans desiring to reach South Korea. The boat was long and narrow, and they could sit only in a single column. As soon as they reached the Thai border, the brokers turned the boat around and hurriedly sped off. From there, they were on their own.

The North Koreans were given one instruction: find the nearest police station to turn themselves in. Unlike the Chinese government, the Thai authorities do not forcibly return North Korean refugees to their home country. Instead, they processed Grandmother Ku and the other North Koreans as unauthorized border-crossers and eventually transferred custody to South Korean authorities. After months of waiting in an overcrowded Thai detention center for refugee determination processing, Grandmother Ku finally made it to the South Korean embassy, where she would have to wait many more months before she could get on an airplane to South Korea.

BOUNDARIES REDRAWN

The prospect of finding Grandmother Ku's family was very slim given the dearth of information I had about them. Months passed with no success in locating Grandmother Ku's uncle or brother. One day, as I sat working at my regular coffee shop in Yeongdeungpo, a western neighborhood of Seoul where many immigrants reside, I searched for Dr. Ku on Facebook. There were numerous people with the same name. I scrolled down the list looking and clicking on each profile picture one at a time. One particular profile near the bottom immediately caught my attention. The profile picture was that of a space shuttle.

Chills and adrenaline rushed through my body. Goosebumps. Grandmother Ku had told me her brother had sent her a picture of a space shuttle, boasting that their uncle was an aerospace engineer. And here, I had stumbled upon someone with the same name as Grandmother Ku's brother and whose profile picture was a space shuttle. Many thoughts went through my head in that moment. I imagined the siblings reuniting and embracing one another with tears of joy. This would be a powerful reunion, one that could lead to important national and international conversations about the painfully lived realities of divided families and the ways to overcome historical violence and the division of the peninsula.

In hindsight, imagining anything other than a romanticized reunion would have been difficult. The catastrophe of national division and the hope for reunification are taught to North and South Koreans at an early age both institutionally and within the home, though with varying narratives, for example, about who started the Korean War. I had heard since childhood that "our wish is reunification." This affective view is something I learned even as I lived outside the Korean peninsula. Koreans know very well the following lyrics from a national folk song:

> Our wish is reunification
> Our wish is reunification even in our dreams
> Reunification carried out with all heart and soul
> Let us achieve reunification.
> Reunification will revive our nation
> Reunification will revive our people
> Reunification, come quickly
> Reunification, come.[11]

In reality, not all South Korean citizens long for reunification. Recent polls have shown that the younger generation of South Koreans express resistance to the idea of reunification, largely because of the threat of economic destabilization and higher taxes that would result from the absorption of North Korea into South Korea. However, the *concept* of reunification is still instilled in the Korean habitus. There is still the DMZ and there still exists a North and a South Korea. On the South Korean side, there is the Ministry of Unification and the President's National Unification Advisory Council. Numerous reunification-themed drawing, poetry, or writing competitions are held each year. People disagreeing with the idea of reunification signify that they are engaging with the idea, illustrating the very pervasiveness of national division and question of reunification, whether they are for or against it.

The desire and imaginary for Korean reunification reinforce the ideology of a divided nation that can rediscover itself through reunification that will repair the harm of past war. Furthermore, the reunification of East and West Germany provided tangible hope in the possibility for Korean reunification. Reunification is therefore deeply embedded in national politics on both sides of the DMZ, and the narrative of Korean family reunion—and to

Figure 1. This ribbon, with the word "reunification," is attached to a fence in the DMZ. Photo: Joowon Park.

an extent the relatively recent integration of North Koreans to South Korea—serves as a micro-level model for national reunion, as illustrated in the inter-Korean summit held between Kim Jong-un and Moon Jae-in.

Media footage also helps to romanticize reunification. One of the most highly anticipated and publicized reunions took place in 2000. This meeting showed images of tearful embraces between separated family members, reuniting briefly for less than a day. Nan Kim sees these temporary family reunions as political rituals that are part of ongoing state strategies "to foster new forms of national intimacy" and "facilitat[e] inter-Korean reconciliation and economic cooperation."[12] Both cinematic and real-life videos of divided families reuniting provide an ideal vision of family, an emotional glimpse of what national reunification might look like, hope for political reconciliation and the recovery of the Korean nation. These romanticized visions had been deeply engrained in me, making Grandmother Ku's story so compelling that I wanted to get involved in the search for her brother.

I nervously clicked on the Facebook profile. It showed that this man worked at a US national laboratory focusing on high-energy physics research. I searched this laboratory on the Internet and typed Dr. Ku's name into the search box. An office phone number was listed. It was a Tuesday evening in Seoul. Without internet service at my residence, I waited in the café nervously for several hours until 23:00 to dial this office phone number via Skype. In the United States, it was 10:00 on a Monday.

"Hello?" a man answered.

"*Annyeonghaseyo. Ku seonsaengnimgwa tonghwahago sipseupnida,*" I said in Korean—"Hello, I would like to speak with Dr. Ku."

"Who is this?," the man asked in English.

Answering him in Korean, I informed him that I was a friend of Grandmother Ku's. "Does this name sound familiar to you? I'm searching for her brother."

There was a long pause, and I wondered if he no longer understood or spoke Korean. He finally broke the uncomfortable silence and asked me again in English, "Who is this? How did you get this number?" His voice became increasingly tense and unsteady. "What is your relationship with her?" His English had a trace of Korean accent.

This time, in English, I reintroduced myself and explained to him Grandmother Ku's story, how I came to know her, and her desire to reconnect with him.

"This is a very personal issue and I do not want to discuss such matters over this phone," he said to me, again in English. My excitement had blinded me to the fact that I was calling a Korean American at his place of work, a national physics lab no less, about his North Korean sister. He provided me his home phone number and said, "Call me at six in the evening." There was a click and the connection went dead.

I was confused because I had expected a joyous response. Instead, he was suspicious of me. I sensed during this short exchange that he did not seem excited to hear his sister's news. Six in the evening was seven in the morning for me in Seoul. But it was difficult to fall asleep that night because I was anxious and his cold reaction to the news of his sister's whereabouts worried me.

I returned to the same café the next morning and called Dr. Ku. I was the only person in the café at this hour. He immediately picked up the phone. His voice was much more relaxed and I sensed that he was more accepting of me this time. We spoke entirely in Korean.

"Thank you for helping my sister, but I don't want to reconnect with her at this time," he said immediately. His straightforwardness caught me off guard. She must be nearing seventy years of age, he continued, and questioned how she was allowed to move around so freely in North Korea. I told him about the North Korean passport that had allowed her to travel to China.

"Did she leave alone? What about her children?" he asked. I explained to him that they were still in North Korea. "Her children are still in North Korea? How could she have fled alone knowing that her children will be punished?" He was bewildered, and could not comprehend how she could have done such a "selfish" thing. He then questioned her motives for leaving North Korea and why she desired to get in touch with him. He emphasized that he did not believe that she would intend him any harm, but he was suspicious of "others" in her vicinity. He hinted that there might be a scheme related to her escape, that someone in North Korea might be using her as an asset to get to him.

The conversation was moving in a direction I had not foreseen. I tried to ease his suspicion by telling him that the South Korean National Intelligence Service had already interrogated her and thoroughly checked her background. I also told him of her struggles in Pyongyang due to her origins in Seoul.

Dr. Ku began to share with me his family's story as he remembered it. His parents and sister *permanently moved* to Pyongyang willingly, he emphasized, while he stayed behind in Seoul with his uncle. This was a different narration of his family's separation; Grandmother Ku had told me her parents temporarily went to North Korea to take care of her ailing grandmother. After the war, Dr. Ku and his relatives in South Korea began to experience discrimination under the anti-Communist, authoritarian regime of Park Chung-hee, a former military general who overthrew the previous administration in a coup and ruled South Korea with an iron fist for eighteen years (1961–1979). Dr. Ku said his family members were persecuted due to their kinship ties to North Korea—because his parents and sister had defected to the communist north. Neighbors accused his family of being *ppalgaengi* (North Korean commies), a derogatory term regularly used to reference North Koreans. Others accused them of being spies living in disguise as South Koreans. He resented his parents for moving to North Korea, for had they stayed in Seoul, he would not have received such treatment. Due to the ongoing abuse, persecution, and constant surveillance in South Korea, Dr. Ku emigrated to the United States in 1973.

I asked him about his visit to Pyongyang in 1991. He told me he did not think the US government knew that he had visited North Korea. He had traveled to China first, and the organization that arranged his trip temporarily confiscated his US passport before he entered North Korea. His US passport therefore only marked his visit to China.

Dr. Ku's story differed from that of his sister's in another significant way. While Grandmother Ku told me that her government stopped delivering the letters in 2002, he said that he had stopped sending them.

Following their initial reunion in 1991, he claimed that North Korean spies in the United States began to torment him. The harassment began with phone calls from mysterious Koreans instructing him to buy Mercedes-Benz luxury vehicles for them. These individuals secretly visited him, barked orders at him (including orders to provide blueprints from his national laboratory), and even threatened to kidnap him. This is certainly not beyond the realm of possibility. North Korea has had a notorious history, and both the imports of luxury goods under murky circumstances and the kidnapping of people from various countries are part of that history.[13] Kim Jong-il often gave German cars as presents to his elite leaders in exchange for their loyalty.[14] What surprised me, however, was that these presents were given at the expense and suffering of diasporic Koreans like Dr. Ku.

He told me that the North Korean agents were interested in him because of his occupation as a US scientist. His relationship with his North Korean sister made him a potential asset to their spy network. The timing of Dr. Ku's reunion with Grandmother Ku and the eventual harassment occurred at a critical moment in North Korea's long-term geopolitical interests. In 1994, the Agreed Framework between the United States and North Korea specified that North Korea would not develop its nuclear program in exchange for US provision of light water reactors. Nevertheless, North Korea did secretly resume its nuclear programs throughout the 1990s.[15]

"She is my sister, and I'm happy to hear of her news. But I'm not capable of supporting her mentally or materially," he said. Unable to bear the ongoing harassment and fear, his Korean American wife—the same who had sought out Grandmother Ku during her visit to Pyongyang in 1990— divorced him. His family fell apart. Though he thought he had escaped the suffering in South Korea caused by his association with North Korea, his re-established ties with his sister had led to continued torment, this time haunting his new life in the United States. He said these were traumatizing experiences. These experiences likely constituted a form of violent subjectivation through the lingering legacies of war. While Grandmother Ku lived and experienced the violence of division, Dr. Ku lived with the violence of having a North Korean sister.

He had resolved to sever all ties to North Korea, and believed he had done so—until that day when I contacted him. I had naively assumed that their intimate bonds could overcome the past, bring these siblings together, and heal their sufferings. I had underestimated the damage done over the years, the political context, and the power of the violence continuum.

Feeling defeated, after Dr. Ku refused contact with his sister, I asked him if there was a way for me to contact their uncle, hoping he might be more receptive of her news. "He died three years ago, in 2009," he responded. That was the year Grandmother Ku left North Korea hoping to reconnect with her brother and uncle. Dr. Ku added that their uncle "was not that famous, just an ordinary engineer." Documents I later uncovered from the NASA archives confirmed that a man with their uncle's name indeed worked for NASA. A 1974 declassified document disclosed the kind of work this man did at NASA, particularly his involvement with the "Skylab" and "Apollo" programs.

Dr. Ku asked for my telephone number. I also provided him Grandmother Ku's number in case he had a change of heart. He said he would need time to think things over but that I should not tell Grandmother Ku about our conversation. If he wanted to talk to her, he would call her directly. I agreed to respect his request.

"Be careful," he warned. "Keep away from the North Korean radar." His parting words disturbed me and left me unsettled as I hung up the phone.

SPIES AND SPY DISCOURSE

After hearing Dr. Ku's experience, I began to have doubts about the truth of Grandmother Ku's narrative and I questioned whether she might be entwined in some kind of North Korean espionage. It could have been possible that Grandmother Ku was a political plant. My, and Dr. Ku's, suspicion of Grandmother Ku is not unique. Many North Koreans resettled in South Korea receive similar treatment. They are met with doubt and accusation—a major obstacle that my North Korean interlocutors recounted to me during my research.

People also often demonize North Koreans and, like Dr. Ku, call them selfish for having escaped alone from their country, leaving behind family members who will likely be punished by the North Korean authorities as a consequence of their escape. The guilt can be overwhelming, and some internalize the insults directed at them and punish themselves. One North Korean woman I came to know refused to turn on the heat in her apartment during the winter months. Heat was a luxury her family did not have access to in North Korea, and she could not sleep comfortably knowing that her family had no electricity and were sleeping in the cold.

When North Koreans arrive in South Korea, they undergo scrutiny and interrogation by the South Korean NIS (National Intelligence Service). NIS officers interrogate North Koreans desiring resettlement about all aspects of their life in North Korea. North Koreans are instructed to write testimonies explaining the details of their birthplace, residence, family, occupation, reasons for their flight, what they did in China, and for how long. It is only after months of interrogation and a determination that they are not spies that North Koreans are allowed resettlement in South Korea.

In South Korea, when someone is unfamiliar with some way of life—a pop culture reference, music, television show, celebrity, fashion, and the like—people often tease each other by asking, "Are you a North Korean spy?" North Koreans become the subject of jokes. These jokes and ongoing suspicion of North Koreans illustrate the ongoing legacies of Cold War politics, the troubled history of North-South relations, and the espionage activities in South Korea by real North Korean spies. There are everyday fears that North Korean spies are in South Korea living in disguise.

Real cases of spies among resettled North Koreans have emerged. Between 2003 and 2013, there were forty-nine recorded cases of North Korean spies in South Korea, and nearly half of these involved a person charged with espionage activities while disguised as a North Korean defector.[16] On the other hand, the NIS has also been found guilty of falsely framing resettled North Koreans as spies in the past.[17] Furthermore, some conservative factions of South Koreans have gone as far as calling the South Korean president Moon Jae-in a "commie" for his efforts at peace and friendly relations with North Korea. All this makes the stakes high for resettled North Koreans, becoming one major reason many try to erase any traces of their origin and hide their identities upon resettlement in South Korea.

As my conversation with Dr. Ku planted a seed of doubt in my mind about Grandmother Ku, making me question whether I was foolish to believe everything she had told me, I fell prey to the same everyday spy discourse that stigmatizes North Koreans. The tinted lens through which North Koreans are viewed in South Korean society is probably the reason Grandmother Ku had emphasized to me that she was born in South Korea, that she was different than the other North Koreans in South Korea, and that she had simply returned home.

I had believed Grandmother Ku's version of events, and the narrative in this chapter revolves around her version of events because of the personal interactions and friendship I had developed with her, while I never met Dr. Ku. However, what is important here is what they illustrate about everyday spy discourse. Instead of trying to decipher the truth of their stories, it is more imperative to see how these larger structural complexities and violence fracture relationships and strip resettled North Koreans of their sense of belonging. Whether a North Korean in South Korea is a spy is hard to determine, and this is one of the reasons why resettled North Koreans are placed under the care (or surveillance) of local policemen upon resettlement.

Grandmother Ku frequently asked me if there was any news regarding her brother. I told her I needed to return to the United States to find him. It was painful to have to withhold her brother's news, especially since she hoped her brother would help her children get out of North Korea. I considered telling Grandmother Ku that I had found her brother but that he was unwilling to reconnect with her. I wanted to tell her because I knew she was anxious to get word of him. I wished she could move on with her life and not expect anything from her brother. It pained me to withhold this secret. I had been pulled into a "gray zone" of heightened moral ambiguity. [18] I became complicit in Grandmother Ku's suffering. As much as I wanted to tell her the news of her brother, I could not for ethical reasons. He had specifically requested that I keep this a secret from her, and I had just as much responsibility to protect him as I did her. And as her story remained unresolved, I struggled with this dilemma and felt unsettled. I wished her no harm, but I withheld the news for which she desperately waited.

In early 2013, several months after I contacted her brother, I made my way to Grandmother Ku's house because she insisted on cooking me dinner. She prepared kimchi stew, seafood pancakes, and fried fish along with other side dishes. Scooping the steamed rice into my bowl, she mentioned that every time she ate, she thought about her children and the shortage of food in North Korea. She offered me too much food, but I did not decline her generosity.

During our conversation that evening, Grandmother Ku cursed a man named Ryu Kyung, a public figure and former Deputy Director of North Korea's State Security Agency. "Ryu Kyung, that bastard. . . . He should have issued my daughter a passport before he died. That's why I'm here alone." According to her, it was also Ryu Kyung who ultimately granted her the passport she needed to cross into China. She knew him personally, and this surprised me. Ryu Kyung was a powerful man in North Korea and a close associate of Kim Jong-il until 2011, when he fell out of favor and was secretly executed.[19] North Korea experts cite this execution as a strategic decision to remove Ryu Kyung from the political sphere, and to consolidate power around Kim Jong-il's son and successor, Kim Jong-un.[20]

Grandmother Ku and Ryu Kyung's relationship apparently went back several decades, to when he was a child. She told me her eldest son was friends with him and that Ryu Kyung often came to play in her home. Moreover, she revealed to me, Ryu Kyung and those under him had been the ones responsible for contacting her brother. Some agents even visited her brother in the United States, she said.

"You mean like spies? Spies in the US?" I asked.

"There are spies everywhere. Don't underestimate North Koreans," she replied. Grandmother Ku explained that she had constantly worried that North Korean spies were excessively bothering her brother. She was aware that they had contacted him on many occasions and made bizarre requests. She was appalled when Ryu Kyung complained to her that her brother did not treat his agents well when they visited him. She said she was furious and scowled at Ryu Kyung, demanding "Why are you contacting him without my permission? Why are you making visits to him? You have all lost your minds!" She asked me, "Would you like it if someone you didn't know kept visiting you?"

One day, she said, agents from the North Korean Worker's Party (*Jungangdang*) brought her a fake South Korean passport so she could accompany them to the United States. They showed her her brother's bank statement and said, "Look how much money he has. Let's get money for you and your family." She told me she did not know if the bank statement were real, but she assumed it was fake because that was the largest amount of money she had ever seen in her life. The real objective was for her to persuade Dr. Ku to come to North Korea. As a US scientist with North Korean ties, her brother was valuable to the North Korean regime.

"I'm originally a good person. But after these things happened to me, only wickedness remained. My suspicions increased and my mouth became more reticent. Sometimes, however, wickedness became handy and helped me," she said, referring to her verbal fights with the North Korean officials. Her words suggested she now considered herself a "bad person," having embodied and internalized this notion of "wickedness." Grandmother Ku refused to cooperate with the authorities. She told the officials, "Kill me instead. Or maybe I'll kill myself. If I die, they [her brother and uncle] have no reason to come to North Korea."

Grandmother Ku worried the spies had harassed his brother so much that her brother might harbor ill feelings toward her. If I was to ever find her brother, she begged, I should explain to him her story. She began to cry, saying that the years of built-up misunderstandings would require he understand her side of the story in order to resolve the past. She was a strong, fiery woman, and this was the first time I had seen her get so emotional.

"I'm distressed that I left my children, and I'm distressed I came all the way here but have yet to find my brother. I constantly ponder how I will bring my children to South Korea."

KINSHIP AND REUNION

Several months later, I tried to reach Dr. Ku again. It was possible that my phone call, even with my best intentions, could cause more suffering. I promised myself that if he did not pick up I would never call again.

Dr. Ku answered the phone.

I greeted him, and immediately recognizing me, he responded in English, "I'm so busy. . . . I don't want to talk."

In English, I began to say, "Yes . . . uh . . . is there any way we can talk. . . ."

But he interrupted angrily before I could finish. "*Ani, jeonhwahajima-seyo*" ("No, do not call me"), he said in Korean. Switching back to English he added, "I don't need!" and abruptly hung up.

Whatever the reason that Grandmother Ku's parents had decided to go to North Korea prior to the Korean War, their actions would have severe consequences on their children's lives. Grandmother Ku lived under the violence of the North Korean regime for the next half century. Dr. Ku lived with the violence of having a North Korean sister, as he and his extended family members were persecuted in South Korea due to their kinship ties to North Korea and ultimately decided to emigrate to the United States. And although Dr. Ku initially sought reunion with his sister in the 1990s, this connection led to further torment and violence.

I was motivated to help reunite Grandmother Ku and Dr. Ku because many other Korean families have been torn apart by the division of the peninsula and the Korean War. Many of these separated families still long to reunite with lost family members, and some desire to return to the place of their ancestors. As divided families age, approach death, and die, time is of the essence. The living testimonies fade away. I hoped that Grandmother Ku's reunion with her brother would be a timely illustration of the violence of division and war on the lives of Koreans. Her story carries significance, but not in the way I initially hoped.

In this chapter, I have illustrated how kinship can cloak relations of power and violence in the glow of affect. For the Ku siblings, kinship could not reconcile violence—families are driven apart and families take sides. And yet, as Jane Collier, Michelle Rosaldo, and Sylvia Yanagisako note, the family is "sacralized in our minds as the last stronghold against The State, as the symbolic refuge from the intrusions of a public domain that constantly threatens our sense of privacy and self-determination."[21] Because kinship plays a fundamental role in the lives of many people across various societies, I assumed that Grandmother Ku and her brother—linked by their intimate bond of kinship—would be happy to see each other. Trapped in my own habitus, structured by a normative understanding of sibling bonds and cloaked by the affective glow of reunion, I had hoped and expected Dr. Ku would also seek reunion with his sister.

Grandmother Ku's hope to reunite with her family complicates the ideology of reunion, and her story illustrates that not all family reunions lead to healing or closure. I had imagined their embracing one another, tears washing away the past experiences that haunted them. No matter what had happened in their past, their blood relations as siblings would bring them together, reconcile their pasts, and restore their relationship. Their wounds would heal and their scars would disappear over time. However, I could only stand by helpless, to discover that I had fallen victim to the illusion that such enduring political and interpersonal violence could be overcome through the "natural" bonds of kinship and reunion.

Ruth Behar writes in *Vulnerable Observer*, "Call it sentimental [. . .] but I say that anthropology that doesn't break your heart just isn't worth doing anymore."[22] The hope I had for Grandmother Ku's reunion with her brother was heartbreaking. But I wonder, was it worth doing? I am devastated knowing that my hope for their reunion likely inflicted more harm on Dr. Ku, shoveling up a past he wished to remain buried and re-opening his scars. My hope—my vision of a joyous reunion—had become another source of violence.

This story has an equally complex epilogue. In the summer of 2019, Dr. Ku phoned Grandmother Ku, and the two siblings communicated with one another for the first time in nearly three decades. And at last, I was able to tell Grandmother Ku of my earlier encounter with Dr. Ku and my reasons for withholding the event from her for many years. Sitting on the same living room floor where we initially met in 2012, she graciously accepted my apology and began to tell me more about her conversation with him. Though they spoke briefly on the phone, she told me he had reservations about the possibility of reuniting in person. He continued to have fear and distrust. She had aged considerably since the last time I saw her. Seemingly hearing my thoughts, she said, "I will soon be in 8th grade," using the South Korean idiom of expressing age by grades. She was approaching eighty years old, and time was running out. Though she had tried on several occasions to locate her children in North Korea through brokers, the searches had been unsuccessful. Six decades ago she had been separated from her brother across the DMZ, and now, by another twist of fate, the situation was reversed and she was in South Korea longing for her children and grandchildren in North Korea.

Grandmother Ku's story illustrates the legacies of national division, war, and the temporalities of violence that still haunt the Korean peninsula. The nostalgic longing for a reunified Korean nation and the sentimental rhetoric of reconciliation and healing symbolized by family reunions obscure the much deeper impediments to overcoming the war's legacies and the state of militarization. Koreans feel this separation with their bodies—the violence lingers and haunts them like a phantom limb. There is no violence in the form of crisis or rupture, but it is nevertheless pervasive. The two Koreas may be many years removed from the political violence of division and the historical event of the Korean War, but it is clear that invisible forms of violence endure to extend far and wide across time and geography. Yet, it is difficult to pinpoint and name the perpetrators of the interpersonal violence experienced by the Ku siblings; the violence they have suffered is intimately embedded in broader structures of power and closely linked to the history of suffering on the Korean peninsula. They are at once participants in and victims of social forces and events beyond their control.

2 The Chinese Dimension of the North Korean Migration

Why did I have to be born in North Korea? We are the same people, but why did I have to be born there and now receive these types of stigma and discrimination in South Korea? I think we North Koreans all have thought this at least once.

A North Korean woman, in conversation with author

CHINESE INTERVENTION IN THE KOREAN WAR

I was several months into military service when North Korea conducted its fourth nuclear test on January 6, 2016 at 10:30 in the morning. The detonation of a miniaturized hydrogen bomb put the entire South Korean military on high alert. Soldiers on holidays returned to base as soon as possible. All visitations were cancelled. We were ordered to get combat-ready, pick up our assault rifles from the command center (they are always locked up when not in use), and be on standby. For the next week, our rifles did not leave our sides. We ate with the guns on our backs strung over our shoulders, carried them with us while using the restroom, and slept with them in our arms. We dwelt in a hyper-militarized state, feeling uneasy and wondering when things would return to "normal," that is, to a condition of war- and defense-readiness that had been normalized in our minds as "peaceful."

In the evening the soldiers chattered with one another about the potential for conflict, and some joked about which of them, in the event of war with North Korea, would drop their rifles and desert their duties. "I will shoot you in the back if you run, coward," a cocky private said, poking fun at his peer. A few corporals told a story about a soldier on guard-post duty who had a psychological breakdown and shot his partner in the chest during their night duty. Our conversations turned to the battles of the Korean War and the Chinese intervention in the Korean conflict. One legend that had been passed down was about the long winter battles fighting the Chinese forces that had entered the Korean peninsula. No matter how many soldiers were killed, more Chinese soldiers kept coming, running over the dead bodies of their comrades like a human wave.[1] The Chinese outnumbered the UN forces by ten times, and the barrel of the guns turned so red hot that the UN soldiers peed on their guns to help cool them off. Some urinated into the water-jacket of machine guns to get them to work. The water-cooling systems had failed, despite the freezing weather, causing the guns to overheat and malfunction.

Following the success of Operation Chromite (the Incheon Landing and the recapture of Seoul discussed in the previous chapter), the UN forces had advanced into North Korean territory in September 1950. They eventually pushed the North Korean People's Army as far back as the border with China along the Yalu and Tumen Rivers. Reunification via conquest, and the end to the war, seemed within reach. Although there were warnings that China would enter the war if the UN forces crossed the 38th parallel, the UN Commander General Douglas MacArthur shrugged them off because the Chinese military lacked aerial forces. The UN's superior airpower, MacArthur believed, would wipe out the Chinese in the event of their intervention.[2]

However, the UN forces failed to gather intelligence on the Chinese People's Volunteer Army troops that secretly crossed the Yalu River into the Korean peninsula. The Chinese "volunteer" soldiers marched at night and their camouflage helped avoid aerial detection. Mao Zedong had feared that the if the UN forces were successful in the war, the United States would pose a major threat to China.[3] The North Korean leader Kim Il-sung, prior to launching his surprise attack on South Korea, shrewdly lobbied for support from both the Soviet Union and China, often using Joseph Stalin's words to gain support from Mao, and vice versa. When China intervened in the war, Stalin sent aerial aid to support the Chinese attack on the UN forces.

With the Chinese and Soviet intervention, the Allied forces found themselves in retreat. There were heavy casualties on all sides and the UN forces lost ground in North Korea. Years of fighting did not yield results and the two Koreas found themselves in a stalemate. North and South Korea ended up occupying roughly the same territories along the 38th parallel as they did prior to the war, and in July 1953, an armistice was signed. The DMZ—and the Military Demarcation Line within it—was established to divide the two Koreas yet again. The Chinese intervention in the war changed the fate of the Korean peninsula, and its alliance with North Korea continues to the present day. The North Korean migration to South Korea cannot be explained without discussing the consequences of Chinese policies. As we will see in this chapter, Chinese politics, and China's steadfast alliance with North Korea, complicate the transnational mobility of North Koreans in violent ways.

GENDERED MIGRATION AND THE ONE-CHILD POLICY

"My name is Dahae. Nice to meet you," she said to the others sitting at the table. It was her first time at church, and Soyang, who had brought her that day, had promised she would not leave Dahae's side. But at that moment, as the youngest of the group, Soyang was shuttling instant coffee to her *eonnis* and *oppas* (older "sisters" and "brothers"). After the morning service and lunch in the church cafeteria, the group had an hour break before Bible study commenced in the afternoon. Many of them attended both Sunday service and Bible study because the church—mostly comprised of resettled North Koreans but also a few South Koreans—gave them monthly allowances in exchange for their attendance. Dahae and Soyang wished they were elsewhere on a Sunday afternoon, but they had come for the scholarship money.

"When did you arrive in South Korea?" asked Jinsung. Although he was South Korean, he had attended the church the longest and was the de facto leader of the young adult group. "And how long were you in China?" he asked unabashedly. Jinsung was not shy and always asked questions that others posed with more care. But Dahae hated to publicly talk about the several years she had lived in China. She had left North Korea at the age of sixteen, and Soyang, Sun (another North Korean), and I all knew that Jinsung's questions had made her uncomfortable. She had anticipated she might receive these questions and it was the reason she had refused for so long to come to church.

"Did you know Dahae went to school with us?" Sun interjected, changing the subject. "Dahae, Soyang, and I were in the same class, and *ssaem* (teacher) taught us English," he said, waving his hand in my direction. Sun was several years older than both Dahae and Soyang, but he had dropped out of school and became a *kkotjebi* (wandering, homeless child) during the North Korean famine. But we all knew Sun as one of the brightest among his classmates. He was an avid reader, always carrying a book with him wherever he went, the topics ranging from Chinese politics to Western philosophy. The most recent book in his backpack was the Korean translation of *Justice* by Michael Sandel.

A few weeks later, I rode the escalators to the ground level of Sadang subway station, and I immediately saw the Hyundai sedan with its hazard lights blinking. On other Friday mornings I would have taken the subway to the opposite side of Seoul, from my residence in Yeongdeungpo to Gyeongbokgung station—the location of the Database Center for North Korean Human Rights (NKDB) where I was an affiliate researcher at the time. It was two degrees Celsius on this foggy November morning, and the four of us researchers from NKDB were on our way to Anseong, a city approximately 80 kilometers from Seoul, to spend the day conducting interviews at the government resettlement center called Hanawon, which literally means "House of Unity." The center sits on a slight hill and the spiked walls and security cameras give the place an intimidating look, though the brown-brick buildings and facilities resembled a small college campus. When we arrived, the security guards took our photo IDs and in exchange handed us visitor passes. On the pass was the phrase *igoseun kkumi saneun jip* (a house where dreams live).

We had a full day ahead of us. We each had three two-hour interviews with North Korean women from the 171st cohort. North Koreans are given cohort numbers as they arrive each month at Hanawon, and North Koreans resettled in South Korea often greet each other by asking "*hanawon myeot ginya?*" ("which cohort are you?") The women that day had experienced forced repatriation from China, human trafficking along the Chinese-North Korean border, forced abortion in a North Korean detention facility, and physical labor as punishment. One woman was a witness to a public execution. At the end of the day, we would survey the next cohort about human rights violations in North Korea, from which the NKDB team singled out interview subjects for the next month. With the findings from these surveys and interviews, NKDB published their annual series, *White Paper on North Korean Human Rights*.

Hanawon was established in 1999 in response to the increasing number of North Koreans seeking resettlement in South Korea. Prior to 1998, there were less than one thousand North Koreans resettled in South Korea, and nearly nine out of ten (88 percent) were men. These North Koreans were mostly high-profile individuals: soldiers, diplomats, and government officials who had the ability and opportunity to leave their country. Their defection was "proof" of the superiority and legitimacy of South Korea, and they were welcomed by the South Korean government because they provided valuable intelligence during the Cold War era. They were granted big monetary rewards—*uisa byeonhosa wie gwisunjaga issda*, "on top of doctors and lawyers are defectors," was a well-known phrase in the 1980s. However, in the aftermath of the collapse of the Soviet Bloc and the North Korean famine in the 1990s, ordinary citizens began to leave their country on a scale incomparable to the previous five decades. By the turn of the century, thousands of North Koreans sought resettlement in South Korea every year, and the majority were women. Today, women make up 72 percent of the North Korean population in South Korea, and there are now two Hanawons: the main facility that houses entirely women and children, and a secondary facility in Hwacheon, Gangwon Province.[4]

Many factors likely contribute to this gendered migration. First, North Korean women gained more mobility than men as a result of the traditional public vs. private division of labor in North Korea. Men work in the public, government-monitored sphere while women are traditionally assigned to domestic roles. The result has been that it has been easier for women to escape North Korea because their absence will not be noticed until much later than it would take for the authorities to notice men's absence from the organizational structure of the workplace. Men's absence from work would immediately raise alarm and lead to swift investigation. As one North Korean man stated, "When men don't show up at work the office starts searching for them. [...] Men are scared to move around."[5] Relatedly, North Korean men are bound up in military service for ten

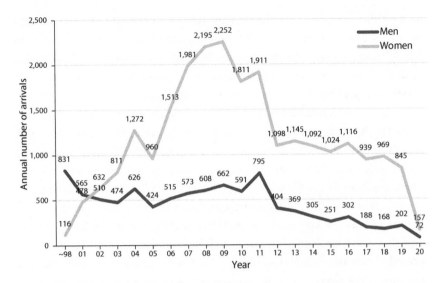

Figure 2. This graph shows the annual number of North Koreans resettling to South Korea by gender. Source: Ministry of Unification.

years. The mandatory conscription and the length of service inhibit their mobility, decreasing the chances of their defection and migration.

When one of my North Korean interlocutors, Hosung, was discharged from his army duties, he returned to an empty house, to his surprise. His family had left to escape the famine in North Korea. He too found a way to cross over the Chinese borderland to the Yanbian Korean Autonomous Prefecture in Jilin Province, where many ethnic Koreans reside. He reconnected with his family, and they eventually sought resettlement in South Korea because living without legal documents in China had become unbearable. When I asked Hosung how he felt coming to an empty home after ten years of military service he replied, "Of course I was very confused and angry. But they did what they had to do to survive, so I hold no grudges." His younger brother Jacob (who had taken on a biblical name upon converting to Christianity in South Korea), who at the time of the family's escape was too young for military conscription, laughed while he sat next to us and acknowledged that what they did was a bit harsh.

Another element contributing to the gendered migration has been the growth in economic activities of North Korean women. With the disintegration of the Eastern Bloc in the 1990s, the series of natural disasters and extreme famine in North Korea, and the state's own mismanaged policies, its Public Distribution System began to fail, and ordinary citizens could no longer rely on the state to provide them with food and other basic resources. Women, by participating in the growing *Jangmadang* or black markets in North Korea, became increasingly responsible for their family livelihoods. As breadwinners, women crossed into China to seek temporary jobs and earn money, or with plans to smuggle in goods to North Korea. Many found work in the gendered spaces of service industries such as restaurants and karaoke bars, textile factories, and some in online chat rooms.

In addition to the availability of work, there was a strong demand for North Korean women in China. In the last few decades, China has experienced gender disparity as a result of its one-child policy and its cultural history of son-preference. The Chinese state began to advocate for family planning at the regional level in the 1960s in response to its rapidly growing population, and it implemented birth control policies at the state level in the 1970s. A popular slogan at the time illustrates these biopolitics: "One is too little; two is just right; three is too much." In 1982, the Family Planning Policy (commonly known as the one-child policy) was written into the Chinese Constitution in an effort to decrease the nation's fertility rate and stem population growth. A new slogan was propagated: "It is good to only have one."[6] Although there were some special exceptions in rural areas or for people of marginalized ethnicities, the one-child policy was generally strictly enforced. If people could only have one child, they desired sons, and many engaged in sex-selected abortions.[7]

The policy officially ended in 2015 with an amendment that allowed couples to have two children. However, there are 34 million more men than women in China today as a consequence of this policy.[8] Particularly in rural China, there has been a shortage of marriage-aged women due to both demographic changes and increasing rural-to-urban migration. In addition to migration to seek work in urban areas, because of the gender disparity women have had opportunities to marry up, to find partners in higher socioeconomic classes. These larger forces have left rural Chinese bachelors searching for brides, creating what many in migration studies would frame as a "pull" for North Korean women "pushed" by famine and poverty in North Korea.[9] Though the "push and pull" framing centralizes the agency of individuals, women's choices to cross the border—and others' decisions to not leave North Korea—are influenced and constrained by larger structural forces such as the biopolitical regulation of citizens, regional inequalities, global warming and ecological degradation, and the situatedness of North Korea and China within the global economy.[10]

Many narratives point to the 1990s as the beginning of the cross-border migrations, but the Chinese-North Korean borderland was historically a space of fluidity, cultural familiarity, and kinship.[11] From 1950–1970, during the periods of China's Great Leap Forward and Cultural Revolution, many ethnic Koreans from China migrated to North Korea to escape the economic hardship and discrimination they experienced as ethnic minorities.[12] Furthermore, cross-border marriages were a common practice and labor migrations were frequent. In 1958, the Chinese Ministry of the Interior passed along an official document from the Chinese Consular Affairs Department of the Ministry of Foreign Affairs to all its provincial bureaus titled, "Internal Opinions on Marriages between Chinese [Men] and [North] Korean Women."[13] Cross-border migration in the borderlands of North Korea and China occurred regularly, which explains why North Koreans in turn saw China as a viable option when they faced famine. And as an act of reciprocity, Chinese citizens in the borderlands were generally accepting and accommodating of North Korean border-crossers. Borderland mobility was understood by local people as a strategy for survival.

Exactly how many North Korean women have migrated to China is unknown. In 1999, the North Korean government acknowledged that about 200,000 of its citizens had crossed over to China.[14] My colleagues at NKDB estimate that closer to 300,000 North Korean border-crossers lived in China at the peak of the famine. It is difficult to discern an exact figure because North Korean border-crossers live in hiding in China, where official policy is to arrest and return the "illegal economic migrants" to North Korea. Many border-crossers were also temporary laborers or engaged in cross-border trades. Others have sought resettlement in South Korea to obtain legal status and resettlement benefits, although they must first navigate the Chinese mainland with the help of brokers (and missionaries and humanitarian organizations) to intermediate countries like

Mongolia and Thailand. The women that stayed in China assimilated into local communities through marriage, becoming care-givers and home laborers, learning Chinese, and creating families of their own.

CROSS-BORDER MARRIAGES AND SILENCE AS RESISTANCE

The significant number of female North Korean border-crossers to China and the rise in intermediary marriage brokers have led to human rights narratives centered on the trafficking of North Korean women. Such narratives have appeared alongside mass-circulated images of starving North Korean children and the country's notorious political prison camps. In regular visits to Hanawon to research human rights violations in North Korea, NKDB researchers asked North Korean women questions about their experiences with cross-border trafficking, forced repatriation, and sexual violence. In countless reports from other NGOs, human rights activists have produced a singular narrative of North Korean women as victims of sex trafficking, even though most cross-border trafficking occurs for marriage, and not for the sex industry.[15] Undoubtedly, some women are duped into false promises of job opportunities or the security of a good marriage. However, prevailing human rights discourse fails to consider a more nuanced understanding of women's mobility. North Korean women complicate the sweeping discourse of the victim-narrative by expressing multiple motivations, desires, and experiences with cross-border marriages.

Soonbok, a woman in her late twenties, sought out brokers to secure a better future in China and negotiated with them about whom she would marry. Soonbok left North Korea twice. The first time she left, a female merchant offered Soonbok ¥200 CNY (roughly $25 USD) to help carry her bags over the river. Soonbok accepted the offer in order to make some money, but she was unaware that the "river" the merchant referred to was the actual border between North Korea and China. Upon crossing the border, the two were arrested by Chinese authorities and deported. The punishment for crossing the border was physical labor in a detention center for three months, but this did not prevent Soonbok from desiring to leave North Korea again.

"I disliked life in North Korea. I came to hate it. I had tasted freedom during my few days in China," she told me, referring to her first experience crossing the border. After her forced repatriation and imprisonment, Soonbok and her mother sold goods on the black market to make a living, an activity that she found to be embarrassing. Therefore, Soonbok sought out the same female merchant hoping to leave North Korea again and the merchant introduced her to a North Korean soldier stationed at the border. At night, the soldier put Soonbok on his back and crossed the river with care, making sure he did not slip on the rocks.

"He got paid," Soonbok said referring to the soldier. "A broker met us on the Chinese side and gave him money. It seemed they knew each other. The broker told me, 'Since you do not know Chinese, you have to get married and learn to speak. And you can send money to your family.' I did not think of it as being sold. I thought of it as getting married."

Marriage offers security to North Korean women without legal status, decreasing the chance of arrest and deportation. Soonbok and the broker travelled further north. She stayed with the broker for several weeks, and he sheltered and fed her until she chose her partner. During their time together, the broker introduced her to several men. However, she found them displeasing to her taste and rejected the transactions. "I met four people in total," she told me. "The broker was so mad he almost hit me! I knew I had to get married, but I did not like the men."

She eventually accepted the fifth man the broker introduced to her. Although he was "ugly," she said, he was a "good, smart man." Her husband paid the broker ¥14,000 CNY (approximately $1,700 USD in 2003). She proudly stated to me that her transaction price was twice more than the average selling price of North Korean women at the time. Soonbok was not a passive victim; she asserted her agency throughout. She was able to reject the candidates for marriage the broker introduced to her, and she was able to negotiate and choose whom to marry. Soonbok viewed the border-crossing and marriage as opportunities to secure a better future and improve her life circumstances, and she became an active participant in her own trafficking. Later, after negotiating with her husband, she resettled in South Korea alone, and though he refuses to send their child to her, they continue to communicate regularly.

As I further developed relationships with many North Korean women during their resettlement, I learned that many of the women maintained good relationships with their Chinese husbands. Though she was not sold into marriage, thirty-nine-year-old Kyungok had also viewed cross-border marriage as a chance to start a new life. In 1994, her father passed away and her family struggled to make ends meet and to put food on the table. If they were lucky, they had soup every other day, and the everyday hunger and poverty became key factors in her decision to migrate to China.

"My mother insisted I go and marry into a good family," Kyungok said. After parting ways, she crossed the border and eventually married an older Chinese man of Korean ethnicity (*Joseonjok*). Together, they had a son and a daughter. In between the births, she was deported to North Korea, but she returned to China through the aid of a broker. Her Chinese husband came to pick her up at the border and paid the broker fees. Though Kyungok eventually resettled in South Korea with her five-year-old son, she remains married to her Chinese husband, who resides in China with their daughter. Splitting the family and moving to South Korea was not an easy decision. Although she has been exploring options to bring her husband and teenage daughter to South Korea, her daughter's inability to speak Korean and the cultural gap have prevented Kyungok from permanently reuniting the family in South Korea.

Of course, not all North Korean women willingly become brides. Youngok was twenty-nine years old; she had left North Korea nine years prior to our meeting. An older woman from her hometown in North Hamgyong Province told her she would help Youngok cross the border and find a job. Unaware that she was being sold into marriage, Youngok followed the woman into China with the hope of earning money for her struggling family. She left a note for her mother before she departed, saying she would return in a few months.

"I did not realize I had been sold even when they brought the man that would become my husband," she told me. When the two women crossed the border, a mysterious man picked them up in a car and took them to Liaoning. "Telling me the Chinese authorities were nearby, they briefly hid me in a storehouse. But now that I think about it, that is when they exchanged the money." Youngok's new husband was abusive and an alcoholic. "He loved to drink alcohol, and Chinese alcohol is very strong," she explained. He beat her every time he became intoxicated, but she endured the violence and learned Chinese. Her ultimate goal was to resettle in South Korea, but she first needed to be able to pass as Chinese in case she was stopped by authorities. After living with him for several years, she fled from her husband and worked in an adult entertainment establishment in Yanji until she had saved enough money for the broker fees to reach South Korea.

Scholars studying sex workers and mail-order brides have critiqued and challenged the notion of women as non-agentive victims who are sold into marriage or trafficked into the sex industry. As postcolonial scholars have argued, representations of "third-world women" as victims are highly problematic, orientalist, and ridden with unequal power and positional superiority.[16] Nicole Constable notes that attention to agency "does not imply that they will live happily ever after, or that they are not subject to wider forms of gender discipline and inequality."[17] Despite the varying experiences of North Korean women's mobility across the border, however, human rights narratives present a singular representation of women as victimized subjects. Recognizing the agency of the women allows us go beyond their victim-subject image and see how they assert their strength, negotiate their roles, and pursue opportunities in imperfect situations.

In contrast to the discourse of human trafficking so dominantly featured in NGO narratives, most North Koreans during my fieldwork responded with silence as a kind of resistance to women's overexposure and persistent objectification. North Koreans resettled in South Korea know full well that marriages between North Korean women and Chinese men are prevalent and that many North Korean women have suffered from these experiences. For example, one North Korean man told me, "When we ask each other: 'when did you leave North Korea?' or 'how long were you in China?' Those who were in China for a long time will avoid the questions. Or they might say, 'we came directly to South Korea,' to avoid the topic. But we know that's not true."

When I met with Sun following Dahae's first attendance at church, he said, "We know it happens and that it probably happened to our peers. But we never discuss it. We cover it up for them." Our close group knew that Dahae had suffered some of the same experiences as many other North Korean women. At the age of sixteen, she was sold into marriage and she lived with her Chinese husband until she found a way to escape and seek resettlement in South Korea in 2006. Unlike a few of her high school classmates who have resettled in South Korea with their mothers, Dahae lived alone in South Korea without any family members. However, there has been a glimmer of hope, as she has been able to establish communication with her parents in North Korea through brokers (see chapter 4).

This kind of silence and accommodation shares similarities to the types of strategies used by families in the wake of the 1947 partition of India. Massive collective violence took place as Hindu men abducted Muslim women into the newly formed India, and Muslim men abducted Hindu women into newly formed Pakistan. During this time as many as 100,000 women were abducted and raped.[18] Both states eventually developed policies to exchange and recover the abducted women and children born from sexual violence—figures they saw as polluting the "purity" of the Indian and Pakistani nations. Notions of purity and honor became tied to nationalism and territoriality, and women's bodies became the "semiotic objects on which actions of the state are to be inscribed," as Veena Das writes.[19] However, families in both the Indian and Pakistani communities were flexible and had already developed ways to absorb abducted women of a different nationality. Many women also refused to return to their home country.

In similar ways, resettled North Koreans in South Korea have adopted strategies and practices to purposefully refrain from talking about the past. The stories of trafficking are not told, offering a contrast to their telling and retelling by human rights organizations through defector testimonies, documentaries, White Papers, and fundraising campaigns. The possibility that North Korean women in South Korea were at some point sold into marriage, experienced some form of human trafficking, or had a child with a Chinese husband is high. But these are all experienced as humiliating by the North Korean community. These women are, in essence, tacit subjects.[20] In response, North Koreans protect each other with silence and do what they can to help conceal their past pain. It is a burial of the unspeakable, unspoken words contributing to their own erasure.[21] Despite this preference for silence within the North Korean community in South Korea, the humanitarian impulse by NGOs working with resettled North Koreans is to "give voice" and "hear their testimony." The

gendered migration of North Koreans and their experiences in China further complicate their resettlement experiences in South Korea, as we will
see in the following section.

GENDERED STIGMAS

Even while many North Koreans in South Korea remain silent about
women's experiences of marrying Chinese men or having had children
with them, some held degrading, sexualized perceptions of North Korean
women. One North Korean man told me during an interview,

> As you know, there are a lot of North Korean women in South Korea. These
> women . . . they are okay if they marry, but the women who are not married
> . . . they have no talents, no abilities, and they are not well educated. They
> must eat and make money, right? So, they are in a very difficult situation. A
> lot of girls end up working in karaoke bars and other women sell their
> bodies.

When I asked why he thinks it is these jobs in particular they turn to, he
explained that North Korean women resort to their past experience as
"brides" and "sex workers" in China, echoing the dominant discourse from
human rights organizations. Moreover, he viewed North Korean women's
marriage to Chinese men as a form of sex work even if they had married
the men on their own terms. He saw these marriages as ungenuine, claiming that they were simply temporary solutions for the women's precarious
situation in China.

There are no available statistics on how many North Korean women
participate in the sex industry either in China or in South Korea.[22]
However, I discovered this to be a commonly held stereotype regarding
North Korean women. Another North Korean man I spoke with expressed
his frustration over North Korean women's supposed participation in sex
work. He blamed their material hardship in South Korea as a reason for
their participation in the sex industry.

> Just because they came to South Korea does not mean they will live well.
> Their suffering continues in South Korea because of money. We cannot live
> without money. In China and North Korea, we cannot live because there is

no freedom. Actually, in North Korea, it is not really because of the lack of freedom but because of the lack of food. And in China, there is no freedom. When we arrive in South Korea, we are given freedom. The food is fine. But we all live with greed. It is just frustrating.

Interestingly, this man's comments indicate that he did not view his life in North Korea as one of repression. Instead, he claims, there is no freedom in China, as North Koreans live in fear of arrest and deportation.

I was surprised to hear from my close interlocutor Kang (the student who introduced me to Grandmother Ku) that he too viewed his female North Korean peers with the same stereotype held by the others. "The women from home . . . how do I say it . . . " he mumbled. "To be honest, even my girlfriend, about six months into dating her, I found out that she had a child in China. I was shocked!" Though he was well aware of the gendered migration and the struggles facing North Korean women in China, Kang felt betrayed by this secret his girlfriend withheld from him. He expressed his hesitation to marry North Korean women because of their past: "I am reluctant to marry a North Korean woman. I do not want to marry someone from my home." Although he said he would prefer to marry a South Korean woman, he said he was willing to marry foreigners too. Kang often bragged to me about the many international women he met at the clubs in the popular Hongdae neighborhood of Seoul. Dancing was his hobby, and he would go on weeknights to avoid the weekend crowds.

While the North Korean migration is disproportionately gendered and there are comparably few North Korean men resettled in South Korea, North Korean men are also stigmatized, but in different ways from the women.[23] The commonly held stereotype of North Korean men is that they fled North Korea because they had committed crimes in their home country. Furthermore, North Korean men are supposedly alcoholic and patriarchal, contributing to their othering in South Korea.[24]

As friends around him began to get married, Sun too began to consider dating and marriage. "North Korean women often marry South Korean men, but it is rare to see marriages the other way around," he said, explaining to me that North Korean men were undesirable and unappealing candidates for marriage. Not only did they have to overcome the various beliefs attached to them, but they were also viewed as not having the education, credentials, and skills to succeed in the South Korean labor market.

"I cringe every time I hear the South Korean elders [at church] say that they would never allow their daughters to marry a North Korean man," Sun continued. The sentiment held by the elders, he said, hurt him deeply because it was hypocritical for them as Christians involved in the North Korean ministry. Similar to the prejudice held by the elders, a national survey revealed that though 83.4 percent of South Koreans viewed resettled North Koreans as "our citizens" (*uri gukmin*), only 9.4 percent said they would want them as sons or daughters-in-law.[25]

SEXUALIZED BODIES

In addition to the gendered stigmas attached to North Korean men and women, the women in particular are subject to commercial objectification in South Korea. In a context where South Korea has struggled with the postponement of marriage and low birth rates,[26] marriage matchmaking companies have thrived in recent years by marketing North Korean women (and foreign brides from Southeast Asia) to older South Korean bachelors. While in humanitarian discourse North Korean women have been overwhelmingly represented as victims of human trafficking across the Chinese-North Korean border, South Korean matchmaking companies have portrayed resettled North Korean women as brides to be coveted—beautiful, young, sexually promiscuous, and dutiful. Reading these various forms of digital media as ethnographic text[27] thus reveals interesting insights into the layers of overlapping violence that operate transnationally from North Korea and China to South Korea.

One series of advertisements illustrates the sexualization of North Korean women. A matchmaking company based in Busan (the second largest city in South Korea) posted on its Facebook page ten cartoon ads that explained the "advantages" of marrying North Korean women.[28] The first illustration begins with the exoticization of North Korean beauty: "North Korean women are beautiful even though they do not get cosmetic surgery or do facial care." The ad directly contrasts all-natural North Korean beauty to the normalization and frequency of cosmetic surgery among South Koreans. Subsequently, the second ad asserts that North Korean women are used to marrying older men. This, the ad explains, is because North Korean men serve in the army for ten years and typically marry younger women upon discharge. "I am twenty-two years old," says the woman in the illustration. "In North Korea, a ten-year age difference is not a problem!"

In another ad, a North Korean woman is pictured sitting alone in her apartment daydreaming about marriage. In one of the frames she is depicted on top of a man in a sexual position wearing only her undergarments. The woman says to herself, "I want to stop fantasizing about these things and get married." The ad explains that North Korean women have arrived in South Korea by themselves and are lonely in their small apartments. To quickly adapt to society, it claims, these women sign up for matchmaking services with a sincere desire to meet a good partner. North Korean women are depicted with heightened sexuality and promiscuity, and as a commodity to be sold. At the end of the advertisement, the company boasts its history of success: "an average of 2–3 meetings lead to marriage."

Furthermore, North Korean women are portrayed as submissive, in contrast to "cunning and calculating" South Korean women. The advertisement states that North Korean women embody modesty and frugality, are kind and pure, and are not grasping, unlike South Korean women. "Are you not interested in my occupation and wealth?" a man asks the woman sitting across the table from him. The formality of their clothes and the drinks in their hands indicate that they are on a blind date. Sipping on her iced drink she replies, "I have no interest in those! I want to get married because I want to love, not because of money."

Further differentiating North Korean women from South Korean women, another ad says that North Korean women embrace filial duty, respect their elders, and desire to care for their parents-in-law. A woman in this ad is seen giving a massage to her mother-in-law, washing the dishes, and vacuuming the living room. She says to her (South Korean) mother-in-law, "Please rest, I can do this by myself." The ad explains that because so many North Korean women have come to South Korea alone and are lonely, they long to be around people and be "pestered" by the family. The mother-in-law declares with a smile on her face that "my son has been dutiful through his marriage."

The commodification of North Korean women also occurs in the mainstream media. The South Korean reality television show *Namnam Buknyeo* (*Love Unification: Southern Man, Northern Woman*) depicts fictional marriage between resettled North Korean women and South Korean celebrity men. The show echoes the matchmaking company's series of ads claiming the desirability of North Korean women. One of the ways it does this is through the title itself. "Southern man, northern woman" is a trope that has often been used to foster "an exoticization of North Korean women, who are often depicted as retaining a traditional, wholesome beauty lost by their Southern counterparts."[29] By simulating their married lives, the show portrays resettled North Korean women learning to become good wives to South Korean men and good daughters-in-law within the patriarchal family system.[30] The intent of the show, it claims on its webpage, is to "illustrate, through these marriages, a story of reunification," to explore "what meaning reunification will bring," and to discover "the similarities and differences between North and South."[31]

Other entertainment shows have emerged. *Ije mannareo gapnida* (*Now On My Way to Meet You*) is a Sunday evening talk show that has aired since 2011. One of its main stated objectives is to introduce and paint a better picture of North Korea and the North Korean people to the South Korean public. Although the show claims to generate a greater awareness about the northern neighbors, including North Korea's current conditions, the food and culture, and the struggles of those who flee the country, it has been critiqued for its reinforcement of "pre-existing regimes of knowledge" about North Korea.[32] Furthermore, its effort to create a more positive representation is highly sexualized. The show is anchored on a changing panel of North Korean women who are constantly referred to as *talbuk minyeodeul* (beautiful defectors). It features attractive women in dresses, and the women entertain through performances such as singing and dancing. The show then shifts towards more serious and emotional talk about life in North Korea. North Korean men are glaringly absent throughout.

Some resettled North Koreans feel that these shows contribute to their othering through exaggerated representations of North Korea, the narratives of suffering, and the objectification of the women. Appearances on the South Korean shows can be problematic for other reasons too. For example, for the panelists that have family in North Korea, their appearance could put their family members at risk because South Korean entertainment is increasingly available in North Korea via DVDs and USBs smuggled through China. Although these family members may not have defected to South Korea, they become guilty by association. This is one of the reasons why many resettled North Koreans have changed their names. By taking on new names, they hope to protect their remaining family members in North Korea. Appearances on entertainment shows announce to the North Korean regime that they have betrayed their country for South Korea, and that they are not in China for survival (which is considered a lesser evil than defection to South Korea). Thus, appearances on the shows have been a contentious issue among many resettled North Koreans. Some of my North Korean friends have told me they would never step foot on the entertainment programs no matter how much money North Korean women are paid to be on them.

CHINESE ALLIANCE WITH NORTH KOREA

Human rights activists argue that North Korean border-crossers in China are refugees and should be granted asylum by the Chinese government. Even if North Koreans may have initially left for economic reasons of poverty and hunger, and not due to "persecution" as defined by the 1951 UN Refugee Convention, activists claim that North Korea's hostile policies toward the returned border-crossers—the potential for future persecution— warrants refugee status. However, these humanitarian efforts have been unsuccessful in changing China's policy of arresting and forcibly returning North Koreans to their country.

China is a signatory member state to the 1951 UN Refugee Convention, and it follows the guidelines of the Convention when it comes to other groups seeking asylum on its soil. China allows the UNHCR, the UN's refugee agency, to assist vulnerable populations of various nationalities and it further allows those asylum seekers to request protection from the UNHCR office in Beijing.[33] However, it denies the UNHCR access to the border areas with North Korea, and polices the environs of foreign embassies to prevent North Koreans from entering these grounds with diplomatic immunity. Furthermore, China criminalizes human rights activists and missionaries helping North Koreans in China.

In a similar fashion to the other wealthy nations that make politically and economically motivated decisions about who gets in, who gets what label, and who receives protection, China makes exceptions to its obligations under the Refugee Convention. As political theorist Carl Schmitt claims, all laws are situational.[34] The United Nations has remained powerless, and sometimes voiceless, in convincing the Chinese authorities that North Koreans are deserving of refugee status determination. I explore these global contestations over North Korean deservingness in chapter 5.

China cooperates with North Korea because of their historical alliance, extending back to the Korean War, and because of the geopolitical importance of North Korea. In defense of their forced repatriation of North Korean border-crossers, China cites bilateral agreements with North Korea. These agreements include the 1960 DPRK-China Extradition Treaty, the 1964 Protocol for Mutual Cooperation in Safeguarding National Security and Social Order in Border Areas, the 1986 Mutual Cooperation Protocol for the Work of Maintaining National Security and Social Order in the Border Areas, and the Jilin Province Management Act of 1993. Allowing North Koreans to seek refuge within China would be a public admission that North Korea is an oppressive country and a betrayal of their alliance.

Geopolitical factors also shape China's treatment of North Korean border-crossers. Acceptance of these border-crossers as refugees could lead to a larger outflow of migrants to China. There is a fear that an influx of North Koreans into the Chinese Yanbian Korean Autonomous Prefecture could trigger a new form of ethnic consciousness among ethnic Koreans, challenging Chinese national identity. The outflow of refugees could also contribute to North Korea's destabilization and collapse, which would likely result in South Korea's absorption of the territory, aided by the United States. The absorption would lead to the presence of US troops directly on China's border, as there are approximately 24,000 US troops stationed in South Korea. Keeping the current status quo is in China's best interest, as North Korea provides a buffer zone against US influence in Asia. It allows China to focus its military strength elsewhere, for example, towards the South China Sea, Taiwan, or Tibet.

In July 2016, while I was serving in the South Korean Army, South Korea and the United States deployed the THAAD (Terminal High Altitude Area Defense) missile defense system in the South Korean city Seongju, far enough south to be out of reach of North Korean artillery. China declared the move a threat to their national security, citing the radar system's potential to gather intelligence on its weapons. In retaliation, China pulled its popular group tour packages to South Korea, leading to the loss in millions of dollars for South Korean businesses.

As this chapter has shown, the highly gendered nature of the North Korean migration is closely connected to the domestic affairs of China, the one-child policy, and cross-border marriages. Many human rights organizations have pointed out the issues of human trafficking across the border as brokers seek to profit off the desires of rural Chinese men seeking marriage-aged women. However, the overwhelming representation of and widely held assumption about North Korean women as victims of human trafficking, unwilling wives to Chinese men, and participants in the sex industry contribute to their experience of violence in South Korea through the stigma of impurity and their sexualization. Marriage matchmaking companies and television shows have capitalized on this gendered nature of the North Korean migration. Even when presented in a positive light, South Korean talk shows, reality programs, and marriage matchmaking companies exploit their sexualization, for example, through their portrayal as ideal wives for South Korean customers. Nevertheless, North Koreans have been able to assert their agency despite conditions of limited choice by negotiating border-crossings, choosing partners, or using silence as a form of resistance to the circulating narrative of trafficking.

In addition to these various ways in which bodies are sexualized and commodified, resettled North Koreans often see their bodies in opposition to, or not fitting, a privileged notion of postwar South Koreanness, which in part involves the phenotypical normalization of height and idealized notions of beauty that are naturalized as self-evident and universal. We will see in the next chapter how North Koreans resettled in South Korea confront aesthetic ideals of what modern, cosmopolitan Koreans should look like, in contrast to their North Koreanness.

3 The Body and the Violence of Phenotypical Normalization

> What are North Koreans supposed to look like? Lacking elegance and sophistication? Or are our complexions different? Do we only have one eye? No ears?
>
> Kichul, in conversation with author

CEREMONIAL FIRST PITCH

By the time conscripted soldiers rise in ranks from a private to a corporal in the army, they have enough *jjam* that life in the barracks becomes more relaxed. *Jjam,* meaning experience, originates from the word *janban,* or leftover food. The more food one has eaten in the military, one's military experience—*jjam*—has grown with it. Growing experience also means they are closer to the end of their military service. Unlike the early days as newbies (mockingly called *jjam-jji,* the lowest of the *jjam* hierarchy) when every movement of the body was rigid, voices strong, and military discipline embodied to the fullest, the more experienced conscripts start to slack off here and there within the barracks. It is as simple as walking with their hands in their pockets, wearing their boots unshined, or no longer assembling with a sense of immediate urgency. Many also try to grow out their hair. In a striking contrast to the freshly shaved heads of the privates, corporals and sergeants—most conscripts reach the rank of sergeant by the time of their discharge—push the limits of the 3 cm hair regulation, negotiating and pleading with commanding officers to keep every millimeter possible. Growing out one's hair is symbolic of the transition to civilian, and the faster you grow out your hair, the faster you have rid your body of the *jjam-nnae* (foul military smell).

In October 2016, I was escorted from my regiment to the Division headquarters, about an hour drive away, to meet the Division Commander. When I arrived, the first thing one of the colonels ordered was for my head to be shaved at the base salon for officers, which on normal occasions low-ranking conscripted soldiers are not permitted to use. When I was escorted back for his inspection with my hair freshly cut, he sent me back. "Like a trainee. Shorter. Sharper," he said.

"You're back?" the salon manager asked upon seeing me again. "Why so short?" She looked at me with pitying eyes.

One week prior, my battalion leader had received a memo from the Republic of Korea Army Headquarters that said I would be throwing the ceremonial first pitch at Game One of the Korean baseball World Series. "Only presidents and celebrities throw the first pitch at the Korean Series, *gamunui yeonggwangida* (what an honor to your family)!" my command-ing officer said, patting me on the back as he informed me of the news. The Korean Baseball Organization and the Army Headquarters were planning for the first game to honor active soldiers on duty, and when deciding on who would be a good representative of the military, the top military officials decided that I—the US professor serving in the South Korean Army—would be a good story for the nation. I was told the other candidate they considered was the singer, actor, and entertainer Lee Seung-gi, who was also serving in the army at that time.

On the day of the game, singer Park Jung-hyun sang the national anthem while soldiers held a gigantic 70 m × 45 m (230 ft × 148 ft) South Korean flag on the field. I was transported onto the field by a self-driving Kia and a short video with cinematic music introduced me on the big screens. When the autonomous car reached first base, a security officer wearing a dark suit approached to hold open the door.

I recalled my commander's words as I walked toward the mound. "Soldiers do not smile," he had said. "Do not foolishly wave your hand to the crowd. Walk with purpose. And do not throw the ball into the ground! You are representing our Division but also the entire South Korean mili-tary." Throwing the ball into the ground, he believed, was unfit for a sol-dier and an embarrassment. Once on top of the mound, I saluted the

South Korean flag and the umpire handed me the game ball. Broadcasts of baseball games on television gave the illusion of nearness between the pitcher and the catcher at home base. From my perspective on the mound, however, the catcher seemed incredibly far away, and I wished I had gotten a chance to practice throwing this distance in the bullpen—I had arrived early in the morning but was monitored by two military officers and confined to the stadium's VIP room. I chose not to throw a fastball and risk smashing it into the dirt.

In preparation for this first pitch, my comportment had to be molded and my bodily movement inhibited.[1] I had to pass through multiple inspections that regulated my exemplariness in front of the national audience. The first step was cutting my hair "like a trainee." The sides and back of my head below my military beret had a clean, crisp fade. The army officers inspected my fingernails, the fit of my uniform, the shine of my boots, the precision of my salute, my posture, and the confidence in my stride. They deliberated about what I should say to the media and how I should act on television. The commander had ordered the inhibition of my bodily movement and spatiality—waving at the crowd or throwing the baseball into the ground were deemed unfit for a soldier. My body needed to be disciplined, practiced, and perfected to fit the military's idealized image of a masculine soldier. My fully embodied military disposition was then put on display in front of the nation.

THE FAMINE

The previous chapter showed how resettled North Koreans' past experiences in China contribute to the stigma, discrimination, and sexualization that, I argue, amount to layers of overlapping violence that operate and extend across national borders. This chapter resumes the discussion of the violence continuum through the examination of how the embodied experiences of hunger and idealized notions of body aesthetics contribute to the violence of phenotypical normalization in South Korea. Structural violence, famine, and poor nutrition have molded North Korean bodies; there are often physical disparities between North and South Koreans. The body thus becomes a locus of difference upon their resettlement in

South Korea. South Korean physical and aesthetic normativity marks North Korean bodies as smaller, foreign, and strange in a society where short height is viewed as undesirable for men and where idealized, surgical notions of beauty dominate. In an attempt to assimilate to the normative standards, some North Korean women choose to undergo cosmetic surgery to "correct" a variety of unwanted physical traits, and some men subject themselves to hormone intake or invasive limb-lengthening operations in order to increase their stature. In this chapter, I unravel these various experiences to shed light on the violence of everyday life that is naturalized and rendered invisible in South Korean society.

I met Sun while teaching English at an alternative school for resettled North Koreans in Seoul (introduced in chapter 2). When we first met in 2010, Sun was past his mid-twenties but he attended the school to study for the Korean High School Graduation Equivalency Examination. He aspired to attend university (the government and partnering universities cover the tuition for resettled North Koreans). His hair covered his forehead down to the top of his eyebrows, he had no traces of facial hair, and he wore wire-rimmed rectangular spectacles. Despite his age, his appearance gave the impression of a middle school student. His small boyish body—he was 160 cm (5 ft 3 in) tall and weighed 47 kg (104 lbs)—was the result of the years he lived with malnourishment in North Korea. Sun was born in Musan, a border town separated from China by the Tumen River in North Hamgyong Province and known for its steel and mining industries. Although Sun left North Korea in 1998, it was not until 2007 that he had resettled in South Korea.

North Korea achieved some notable economic success during the postwar reconstruction period. Part of this was due to fraternal aid from China, the Soviet Union, and the Eastern Bloc countries. In addition to cancelled debts by China and the Soviet Union, North Korea received support from many other countries such as East Germany, Albania, Czechoslovakia, Poland, and Romania. These countries aided the reconstruction and restoration efforts of the cities and infrastructure that had been destroyed by US bombing during the Korean War. In exchange for natural resources, the socialist countries rebuilt hospitals, restored communication systems, and reestablished transportation infrastructure.[2] Furthermore, the founding leader of the North Korean state, Kim Il-sung, used propaganda and ideology as tools for mass mobilization. For example, he advanced his ideology of *Juche* (self-reliance) to the North Korean people, which combined the principles of national independence (*jaju*), economic self-sustenance (*jarip*), and self-reliant defense for their national security (*jawi*). Through mobilization of its labor force, Socialist reforms, modernization of agricultural production, and rapid industrialization, North Korea boasted a strong economy. In the 1970s, the CIA estimated the North Korean GNP (Gross National Product) to be greater than that of South Korea's, a country under authoritarian rule at the time.

However, by the 1990s, North Korea faced insurmountable political, economic, and ecological turmoil. With the dissolution of the Soviet Union and the Eastern Bloc, North Korea lost its main trading partners while it continued to face international sanctions. In 1994, Kim Il-sung suddenly died and left the helm to his son Kim Jong-il. To compound these political challenges, North Korea experienced unprecedented rainfall and floods in the summer of 1995 that led to severe famine from 1996–1999.[3] The northern regions of the Korean peninsula are known for mountainous terrain and cool climate while the breadbasket of the country pre-division was in the southern Jeolla Province. Since the division, North Korea has had very little arable land for sustainable food production. The flooding damaged North Korea's farmlands, its underground grain reserves, and its infrastructure and power plants. Deforestation, exacerbated by people searching for fuel, worsened the floods. Drought followed and an unusually frigid series of winters destroyed the seedlings of future crops.

The geopolitical and ecological calamities allowed North Korea to conveniently save face in asking the world for aid without acknowledging its own failures. Prior to losing its trading partners, the death of its founding leader, and natural disasters, North Korea was already struggling to feed its population, as illustrated by its 1992 campaign, "Let's Eat Two Meals a Day." As Sandra Fahy has argued, the famine was insidious and processual, and its effects were felt long before the catastrophic floods.[4] North Korea's failed policies and economic mismanagement were equally to blame. These included the practice of dense rice planting which depletes the soil, energy shortages and its dependence on imported oil, and its prioritization of its military and nuclear ambitions.[5] Facing these challenges, the North Korean regime failed to feed its citizens through its Public Distribution System.[6]

As I have mentioned, an estimated two to three million North Koreans died from widespread starvation.[7] Infections and diseases also contributed to these deaths, as bodies were weak from malnourishment. As Fahy writes, "Famines kill principally through making a population nutritionally deficient enough to then become vulnerable to disease, illness, and inclement weather."[8] In North Korea, this period came to be known as the Arduous March (*gonanui haenggun*), and the regime turned again to propaganda to urge its people to sacrifice, to be strong, and to march forward despite the extreme hardship and suffering. The *Rodong* newspaper, a central outlet of state propaganda, urged its citizens to remember and find strength in the heroic actions of Kim Il-sung who fought off the Japanese Imperial Army in the struggle for independence. Meanwhile, resource distribution to Pyongyang was prioritized over the poorer peripheral regions, and government officials, the elites, and local authorities hoarded limited supplies of food, resources, and international humanitarian aid. Farmers hid whatever crops they had. Others foraged for food. School systems broke down and black markets emerged as people desperately tried to find a way to survive.[9]

Sun's father passed away from illness during the famine. To provide for the family, his mother travelled far distances to find work, and she was often unable to be home. Sometimes, she would be gone for weeks at a time, and Sun took care of his young brother. Often, there was nothing to eat at the house and they scavenged for food and tried to eat grass, roots, and anything else that appeared edible in the mountains. If they were lucky, they caught a frog. Sometimes, they would go to the market and see if anyone had dropped any food scraps on the ground. Many children were severely malnourished and experienced stunted growth, including Sun. In 1998, North Korean children under the age of seven were severely malnourished—approximately 62 percent experienced stunted growth and 60 percent were underweight.[10]

Conditions became increasingly dire, and in April of 1998, Sun and his mother and sister decided to go to China to look for temporary work. They intended to return as soon as possible and Sun's younger brother stayed behind with relatives. As the previous chapter illustrated, thousands of

North Koreans crossed the border to China, both temporarily and permanently, as the cultural familiarity with the ethnic Koreans living in the Chinese borderland provided a solution for the desperate conditions in North Korea.[11]

The China-North Korea border includes the Baekdu Mountain and two rivers that serve as territorial boundaries, the 790-kilometer-long Yalu River (*Amnokgang*) and the 521-kilometer-long Tumen River (*Dumangang*). Sun, his mother, and his sister carefully waded through the Tumen in the dark, the water still frigid and the currents strong. Once they reached land, however, his sister went in a different direction when the family ran from the Chinese border guards. Sun and his mother walked through the night further inland until they came upon a farmhouse. The owner, an ethnic Korean, provided them shelter and fresh clothes. In the morning, a North Korean man came to the farmhouse at the request of the owner, and offered to introduce Sun's mother to a man living in Yanji (a city further north in the Yanbian Korean Autonomous Prefecture). Through marriage, the broker insisted, she could reduce her risk of deportation, and live and work with more freedom. According to Sun, the broker said to them, "If you view me negatively, you could call me a trafficker, but I am merely an intermediary who receives a small commission for the introductions." Sun's mother accepted the offer to secure a better future for the family, and they travelled to Yanji to meet his future stepfather.

MALNOURISHED BODIES

When the green town bus arrived, Sun gestured for me to get on first. The bus would connect us to a hub subway station where we would then go our separate ways. I stepped onto the bus and tapped my transportation card on the electronic reader. It beeped to signal a successful transaction and displayed the fare. Sun followed behind me and he too tapped his card, followed by the beep.

"You should get a student card," I heard the bus driver say to Sun, mistaking him for a much younger student. South Korean public transportations have three fare categories: general (age 19 and above), youth (age

13–18), and children (age 6–12). With the youth card for students, as the bus driver advised him, Sun could save 40 percent on each ride.

"Thank you, but I am not a student," Sun chuckled shyly and smiled at the driver. But most people would have also mistaken Sun for a teenage student. When I first met Sun, I was shocked to learn that he was more than ten years older than his physical appearance suggested. "From the age of nine, I used to go into the woods on a daily basis to collect firewood, I farmed, and I walked over mountains carrying things on my back. I ate grass; there was no meat to eat. How could I have grown?" he said to me when I asked him about the encounter with the bus driver.

For the generation of North Koreans who lived through the famine years, their embodied experiences of hunger and malnutrition—expressed through their stunted growth—often contribute to an experience of violent and gendered phenotypical normalization in South Korea. Poor nutrition and the structural violence in North Korea have molded North Korean bodies, and there are physical health disparities between North and South Koreans. For example, research found that the resettled North Korean children in South Korea between the ages of seven and nineteen were significantly shorter and weighed less than their South Korean peers.[12] The average height differences were 10.1 cm (4 in) for boys and 7.2 cm (2.8 in) for girls. The average weight differences were 11.1 kg (24.5 lbs) for boys and 3.8 kg (8.4 lbs) for girls. Though the physical disparities between North and South Koreans were minimal immediately following national division and war, the disparities increased over the subsequent half century.[13] As North Koreans suffered from food insecurity, South Korea's population grew taller with its economic growth and development.

In South Korea, itself once a war-torn country with very little to eat, height is associated with good nutrition, wealth, and prosperity. Height plays a central role in people's daily lives and being short has come to be viewed as a problem. When women go on blind dates, one of the first questions friends ask is, "Is he tall?" or "What's his height?" For men, height has become a matter of pride and it is very common to see street vendors selling shoe insoles (kkalchang) to help men appear taller. These insoles range anywhere from one to ten centimeters and they are ubiquitous in South Korean society. It is also common to see sneakers, dress shoes, and boots with elevated soles molded into the shoe. In 2009, a

Figure 3. Shoe inserts for extra height sold on the streets in Seoul. Photo: Joowon Park.

female participant on the popular South Korean television show *Minyeodeurui Suda (Chat with Beauties)* referred to short men as losers: "I do not like short men. In an age where looks are one's competitiveness, I think short men are losers. Men should at least be 180 cm tall."[14] Her remarks made national headlines and sparked public conversations and debate about the importance of height.

Children are often assigned seats by height in the classrooms and short children are more likely to be subject to bullying (*wangtta*) in South Korea. In an interview with the *New York Times,* a South Korean growth clinic doctor states that "parents would rather add 10 centimeters to their children's stature than bequeath them one billion won"—or nearly $1 million USD.[15] Growth clinics have become a booming business since the 1990s. Growth treatments (*seongjangchiryo*) involve the inspection of one's bone age, epiphyseal plate, and DNA samples, the use of acupuncture, massages, stretching and special exercises, and the intake of vitamins and growth hormones. There is a steadfast belief that a child's future and fate can be altered for the better even with an incremental increase in height. Research found the existence of a "height premium" in the workplace—wages increased 3.8 percent for every inch in height.[16] Height and looks (aided by cosmetics) have become sources of socioeconomic competitiveness.

In a society obsessed with height, some resettled North Koreans who experienced stunted growth have contemplated growth hormone intake or limb-lengthening operations. One North Korean boy "bought an exercise machine and marked his height on the wall to see if it made him grow." He was conscious of his short height and wanted to "try to restimulate [his] stunted growth."[17] Likewise, Sun had similar concerns about his body. He was approximately 14 cm (5.5 in) shorter than the national average, and though he had gained 10 kg since coming to South Korea, he weighed merely 47 kg.[18]

A few days following the bus driver's comments, I visited Sun in his half-basement room that he rented for $300 a month in northern Seoul. When he arrived in South Korea, he discovered that his sister had already resettled in the country. The government grants one apartment per household, which meant that Sun was ineligible for his own. Instead of living with his sister in a rural area, he rented this room in Seoul. He did not own any furniture and his neatly folded blanket, mat, and pillow were in the corner of the room. On another side were his books, stacked from the ground up. The floral-decorated wallpaper was peeling along the edges and there were some visible watermarks on the wall. His bedroom had been flooded three times that summer from the monsoon rains. Noticeably, Sun had a variety of vitamins next to a 2-liter water bottle, and he pointed out the growth hormones he took on a regular basis to increase his small physical frame. He told me, "I want to be 170 cm. No, even 165 cm would be ok. I wish there was technology to help people grow taller."

Others desired to be taller for more practical reasons of meeting an occupation minimum. Soyang, another of the church group, called Sun *oppa* (older "brother") and was among the students I taught at the alternative school for North Koreans. She left North Korea with her mother when she was just five years old, and they lived with her stepfather in China for nearly ten years. When she was fourteen, Soyang and her mother resettled in South Korea, though they maintained communication with her Chinese stepfather. She aspired to be a police officer when she first arrived in South Korea, but she soon discovered that she did not meet the physical requirements to be a female police officer. For women, the minimum height requirement was 157 cm (5 ft 2 in), with a weight of 47 kg (104 lbs).[19] She fell short by three centimeters and experimented with growth hormone injections. She tried even though her doctor informed her that the shots might at most add two centimeters. There was a strong probability that she still would not pass the qualifying minimum but she told me she had to try, "I wanted to try everything possible before I gave up on my dreams." Soyang today works for a gaming company in South Korea, translating Chinese games into the Korean language.

Soyang and Sun were among my many North Korean interlocutors who embodied the structural violence of famine and the violence of phenotypical normalization in South Korea. Many of the male North Korean students at the church regularly wore shoe insoles, visited growth clinics, experimented with growth hormones, and bought vitamins and supplements. They feared that their short stature would hinder their job opportunities and marriage prospects, and make them "losers" in South Korea. However, though many have tried to undo the violence and inequalities mapped onto their bodies, they often offered each other compliments on how young they look. "You have a small face," they frequently said to one another. "You are *dongan*," others would say, which means "baby-faced." Having a small face and being *dongan* are considered polite compliments about one's appearance in South Korea, and the students often used humor to counter the violence of famine and phenotypical normalization.

ETHNIC BOUNDARY-MAKING

In addition to the embodied experiences of hunger, other differences have emerged between the two Koreas during the seven decades since national division. North and South Koreans have lived under two radically different political and economic systems. Not only do resettled North Koreans have to transition from a communist to a capitalist society, they also have to transition from an industrial to a post-industrial society. Many resettled North Koreans have limited education and few of the skills necessary to adjust to the South Korean economic system where work is highly neoliberalized. Newly arrived North Koreans undergo four hundred hours of mandatory orientation at the Hanawon Resettlement Center where they are taught lessons on capitalism, democracy, and South Korean society, culture, and language. Though the two Koreas theoretically share the same language, Korean anthropologist Chung Byung Ho notes that the spoken and written language "has evolved so much in different directions that many newcomers from the North feel like functional illiterates."[20] And because of their limited exposure to North Korea in the postwar era, for ordinary South Koreans the North Korean dialect is distinctive and unfamiliar—a linguistic marker of foreignness.[21]

Cold War ideologies became a central factor in defining what it meant to be North versus South Korean, and state-based nationalism came to the forefront of identities constructed in opposition to one another. The North Korean state distinguished itself from the "American puppets" of South Korea, identifying South Koreans as traitors in a larger struggle for liberation from Western imperialism. Concurrently, South Korea's authoritarian regimes sought to define the country as anything but North Korean, using anti-Communist rhetoric for nationalistic purposes. South Korea constructed its Koreanness against the figure of the internal Other to delegitimize their northern neighbors who had taken a wrong historical turn. In many ways, the Korean context bore many similarities to pre-unification Germany and West Germany's portrayal of the communist East as "backward."[22]

Despite the postwar struggle for state legitimacy, the two states continue to proclaim the ethnic homogeneity of the Korean people. Both countries rely on what Roy Grinker calls a "master narrative of homogeneity," the belief that the Korean people share the same blood, history, culture, and language.[23] Korea's modern and premodern history is complicated, disparate, and messy, but both Koreas continue to use a sweeping linear and singular narrative of a unified Korean race. For example, in the 2018 meeting between South Korean president Moon Jae-in and North Korean leader Kim Jong-un, the first point of their joint declaration was that "South Korea and North Korea will reconnect the *blood* relations of the people."[24] Reunification thus has been central to the idea of reconnecting blood relations and the South Korean Constitution declares national reunification as a key goal in Article IV: "The Republic of Korea shall seek unification and shall formulate and carry out a policy of peaceful unification based on the principles of freedom and democracy."[25]

The belief in ethnic homogeneity and the shared sense of kinship is illustrated in another advertisement by a South Korean matchmaking company. Marketing North Korean women as desirable partners for South Korean men, the ad emphasizes the shared ethnicity of the Korean people. The storyline depicts a South Korean kindergartener returning home from school. She greets her father and asks, "Dad, dad! My new classmate has strange skin color and has trouble speaking our language. Why is he different?" The image depicts a dark-skinned boy with black eyes. Her father lowers himself to her eye level and responds, "It is because his mother is a foreigner," referring to migrant brides. Explaining this interaction between the father and daughter, the advertisement claims, "Because the two Koreas are of the same ethnic group, North and South Korean families are free from the problem of *honhyeol* (mixed-blood) children that multicultural families experience." The ad ends with the father telling his "princess" to keep this conversation a secret from her mother.

For many North Koreans, the notion of ethnic homogeneity is just ideology and their experiences suggest otherwise. A North Korean refugee living in Fairfax, Virginia expressed to me her disappointment in her resettlement experience in South Korea. With limited education and skills, she could only work part-time jobs, but it was the prejudice and marginalization from South Koreans that pushed her to seek secondary resettlement in the United States.[26] She felt she did not belong in South Korea and she could find no commonality with South Koreans. Asked if she would consider returning to Korea upon reunification, she said she would return to "our home" (*woori gohyang*) in the North. For her, the experience of resettlement in South Korea was one of pain, grief, and regret.

Regarding the ideology of belonging to the same ethnic group, Dahae, one of my students, said to me with much frustration, "I hate being treated as an immigrant. They say that we are South Korean, but in reality, everyone still treats us as North Korean. At best, we are immigrants." When she attended university in Seoul, she was surprised to learn that she was listed as "foreigner" on her professors' rosters, adding salt to the wound of feeling like an outsider in South Korea. When calling Dahae into office hours, her professor wondered which country she was from.

Figure 4. A professor lectures to a group of North Korean and South Korean college students at a Unification Workshop. Photo: Joowon Park.

A vignette I briefly provided in the Introduction illustrates this ethnic boundary-making in South Korea. During fieldwork, I attended a Unification Workshop funded by the South Korean government. It was a weekend retreat with a group of college students composed of both South Korean students and resettled North Korean students. As the first day came to an end, the students reflected on their workshop experience. One South Korean student shared her pleasant surprise that the North Korean students did not appear like they came "from North Korea." Many (South Korean) students laughed and nodded in agreement.

Kichul, one of the North Korean students in attendance, was irritated by this statement. As partially quoted in this chapter's epigraph, he expressed to me his frustration over the negative stereotypes South Koreans have of North Koreans: "There are preconceptions about North Koreans in this country. I can't count the number of times people tell me, 'You don't look North Korean.' And again, last night, 'you don't look like you come from North Korea.' What are North Koreans supposed to look like? Lacking elegance and sophistication? Or are our complexions different? Do we only have one eye? No ears? Why do they look at us differently?"

North Korean bodies, in the imagination of the South Korean student, were marked by foreignness and difference. However, the North Korean students attending the workshop displayed middle-class sophistication in the clothes they wore, the latest cell phones they carried, and the Seoul accent in which they spoke. They were intelligent and, the South Korean student also specifically highlighted, humorous. These North Korean students did not fit the stereotypes that symbolically stigmatize North Koreans as Others through language, body aesthetics, class, and taste.

The oppositional processes of inscribing the body with both real and imagined differences share similarities to the Rwandan context. Liisa Malkki's study of Hutu refugees in Tanzania demonstrates how constructions of Hutu and Tutsi identity became imbued with deep meaning, the body inscribed with physical and social differences, both mythical and historically constituted. The conflict between these two ethnic groups developed a "mythico-history" that created an oppositional past and present between them, lionizing one group as distinctly superior to the Other.[27] Central to the creation of this mythico-history was what Malkki calls "body maps," how the bodies of the Other become articulated and attached with "distinctions of supposedly innate character traits such as laziness, [. . .] life-style and work habits."[28]

North Koreans arriving in South Korea are said to be Korean but in actuality they are not treated as full Koreans. North Koreans gain juridical citizenship of status and rights but not full membership, and they are relegated to the margins of South Korean society symbolically and materially. Upon their arrival in South Korea, at the Hanawon Resettlement Center and beyond, North Koreans must obtain belonging through cultural processes of self-making that are often embodied, for example, through middle-class norms and values, fashion and cosmetics, and the consumption of commodities and goods. Knowing that their bodies had been othered through notions of socioeconomic class and aesthetics, many resettled North Koreans strove to rid themselves of their northern "dust" and to mask their origins.

SURGICAL BELONGING

North Korean bodies are marked in opposition to a privileged notion of Koreanness, which as we have seen in part involves phenotypical normalization of height as well as the ethnicized notions of difference. Attempts to gain a sense of belonging in South Korea thus require many North Koreans to undergo processes of self-making—the embodiment of norms and values, body aesthetics, and dispositions—and the performances of those values. In addition, racialized notions of beauty play a role in the North Korean experience of resettlement, illustrating how the body becomes a manifestation of society's ideas about control, power, and self-worth.[29]

Dahae, Sunmi, and I met weekly to practice conversational English (in chapter 1, I was tutoring these two when I received the phone call about Grandmother Ku). By learning English, a necessity for success in the South Korean education system and in the job market, the two women desired to improve their chances of obtaining good jobs and socioeconomic mobility. Besides their age—Dahae was nearly ten years older than Sunmi, who had just turned nineteen—they had vastly different migration experiences. Sunmi left North Korea at a very young age with her mother and remembered very little of her life in North Korea. Though she lived in China for several years with her Chinese stepfather, Sunmi and her mother eventually migrated to South Korea to obtain resettlement benefits. Dahae, on the other hand, had been sold into marriage in China as a teenager and now lived alone in South Korea, and it had been well over a decade since she last saw her parents in North Korea.

Towards the end of our tutoring session, our conversation turned to the topic of cosmetic surgeries. They were both contemplating cosmetic surgery, and Dahae had even gone to Gangnam for a free consultation (the Gangnam district has the highest concentration of cosmetic surgery clinics in Seoul). When I asked Dahae what kind of surgery she desired, she said, "Everything. I want to do it all. First, I'd start with my nose. You see, women and men are different. Women want to become prettier, and when we become pretty, our *mudae* gets bigger." She used the Korean word for "stage"; her economic situation, she believed, was directly tied to her beauty.

"What's wrong with your nose?" I asked. She complained that her nose was too flat, and that she wished it looked more *seoyang* (Western). Doctors could achieve this by raising her nasal bridge, she said. Sunmi nodded in agreement, complaining that her nose was too flat as well. In addition to her nose, however, she did not like the shape of her face. Sunmi believed it to be too rectangular and therefore not feminine enough. She was considering surgery to make her jawline more v-shaped, though it was much more expensive, risky, and invasive than getting a double-eyelid surgery or a nose job. Both women worried their faces did not live up to the pressures and standards of beauty in South Korea and that they looked too "rural" (*chonseureopda*).

South Korea has often been referred to as the mecca of plastic surgery, as it is the country with the highest number of cosmetic and plastic surgeries performed per capita.[30] Some of the most popular procedures include double-eyelid and eye-widening operations, rhinoplasty (nose jobs), hair transplants, skin whitening, calf reduction, and the "V-line" jaw-reshaping surgery. Idealized notions about a v-shaped face, double eyelids, and higher nose bridges are prominent in South Korean society and reinforced by the cosmetic and skincare industries, pop culture (for example, K-pop stars), advertisements, digital media, and the ever-expanding resolutions of high-definition technology.

Photo requirements have been institutionalized at varying levels of society, from job resumes to college applications. Attractive facial appearance and facial impression (*insang*) are critical factors in evaluation processes and important for one's success. In addition to the job market, others obtain cosmetic surgery to improve their desirability for marriage. Though existing research has often highlighted plastic surgery in relation to women's experiences, South Korean men also partake in cosmetic surgery and skincare to achieve an androgynous masculinity and to become *kkonmi-nam*, a Korean word to describe a stylish and handsome man as soft and beautiful as a flower.[31] Once frowned upon by the South Korean public, cosmetic surgery today is extremely popular across gender lines and has become a sign of affluence, social status, and competitiveness.

The normalization and wide acceptance of cosmetic surgeries in South Korea is rooted in beliefs about physiognomy, neoliberal ideals of self-care and body management, and socioeconomic competitiveness in marriage and the job market.³² Though many Koreans undergo beauty transformations for reasons beyond desires to look "Western," the origins of cosmetic surgery in South Korea are embedded in the history of US militarism and the Korean War. In the postwar years on the Korean peninsula, David Ralph Millard, a surgeon for the US Marine Corps, performed reconstructive surgeries on wounded soldiers but also offered free surgery to Koreans as "evidence of American goodwill in Asia."³³ Some of his patients included local children with congenital diseases such as cleft palates, lepers, and burn victims. He also performed double eyelid surgeries and raised the nasal bridges of Koreans. Millard wrote, "The flat nose and the oriental eye were the two features which seemed to lend themselves to the most striking change with the least radical surgery."³⁴

The Asian eye, without a double eyelid, symbolized deviance and mystery in the orientalist imaginations of Americans like Millard. He claimed that the monolids on Korean eyes gave the impression of "an expressionless eye sneaking a peep through a slit, a characteristic which through fact and fiction has become associated with mystery and intrigue."³⁵ Elsewhere he wrote that the absence of the double eyelid "produces a passive expression which seems to epitomize the stoical and unemotional manner of the Oriental."³⁶ His first patient was a Korean interpreter who desired rounder eyes because the small and slanted shape of his eyes made him untrustworthy to Americans. By surgically transforming himself, the interpreter believed, he could succeed as an interpreter working for the US military. Following surgery on his eyes and nose, the interpreter happily reported that he was now perceived as an Italian or Mexican, and he planned to immigrate to the United States.³⁷

The practice of double eyelid surgeries had existed in East Asia prior to Millard's development of his blepharoplasty technique. In 1895, for example, an American doctor performed eyelid surgeries on many Japanese in Tokyo, wanting to remove the "curse" of their slanted eyes and help them "acquire recognition in the civilized world."³⁸ However, though not the first, Millard played a central role in normalizing and popularizing the procedure in Korea. With the premise of whiteness being the norm, Millard performed cosmetic surgeries on numerous Koreans seeking to deracialize their faces, including local sex workers and nurses near US military bases who wanted to increase their desirability to American

soldiers. Furthermore, the 1945 War Brides Act in the United States ena-
bled American soldiers to bring home Asian women as wives, and Millard
claimed that double eyelid surgeries would be increasingly significant
within that context. In his 1955 publication in *Plastic and Reconstructive
Surgery* he writes: "folds that were exotic in Pusan or Kyoto will become
strangely foreign to Main Street of a mid-west town or under the columns
of a southern mansion. [. . .] The plastic surgeon may be called upon to
help them blend with their surroundings."[39] The presence of the Asian
body, he argued, was a disturbance to the American Main Street and
required assimilation through physical deracialization. Once he returned
to the United States, Millard continued to perform the double-eyelid procedure on Asians as many Asian women in the United States sought to
reduce white anxieties and escape racial prejudice and discrimination.

The cosmetic surgery industry in South Korea is built upon a legacy of
US imperialism. The history of US wars and military presence in Asia crys-
talized a racial hierarchy.[40] It created unequal power relations between the
liberator and the liberated, and contributed to the proliferation of cosmetic
surgeries based on standards of beauty that privileged the white body. The
Asian face, on the other hand, was deemed threatening, mysterious, expressionless, passive, and unattractive. In the decades following Millard's tour of
postwar Korea, clinics offering cosmetic procedures flourished in South
Korea, with the first established in 1961; South Korea today offers medical
tourism to foreigners desiring to replicate the body aesthetics of K-pop stars
and celebrities. No longer strictly tied to Western beauty, the cultural pro-
ductions of *Hallyu* (the Korean Wave) via music, films, and dramas have
helped form new standards of beauty that are regionally specific to Asia.[41]

Within this context where the cosmetic surgery and the culture-export
industries create idealized notions of beauty to be consumed and embodied, many of my North Korean interlocutors contemplated and received
cosmetic surgery to "correct" a variety of unwanted physical traits, despite
the financial burden. Sunmi eventually received the double eyelid surgery,
though she considered it a mere "touch-up" procedure and not surgery. On
Sundays at the North Korean church in Seoul, North Korean women often
came to the worship services wearing baseball caps and face masks to
cover up the still-healing cosmetic procedures they had had. While some
procedures, like the double eyelid surgery, require just a few weeks for the

swelling to disappear, others, like the V-jawline surgery, take several months to properly heal. The women continued to come to church while concealing the bandages on their faces.

The youth pastor said to me, "If they don't come, they lose their scholarships. They come even if they've done surgery. It's so obvious, isn't it? But what can we do?" The church provided approximately $300 per month as scholarship. To become recipients, the North Korean attendees had to participate in the Sunday afternoon Bible studies, and be students in good standing and have "wholesome" morals.

In an effort to reduce these attempts at surgical belonging, one Sunday the head pastor—a resettled North Korean himself—gave a sermon titled, "Healing of the Body." Preceding the sermon, a North Korean man stood in front of the congregation and read the scripture from 1 Corinthians 6:19, "Do you not know that your bodies are temples of the Holy Spirit, who is in you, whom you have received from God? You are not your own; you were bought at a price. Therefore, honor God with your bodies." The pastor preached to the predominantly North Korean congregation: "Many of us in this room have stunted stature from the shortage of food [in North Korea], which has become an inferiority complex. A union with God will restore your bodies, a healing we all need."

In their desire to perform and obtain belonging in South Korea, resettled North Koreans exercise symbolic violence and become complicit in their own subjugation.[42] Buying (literally) into normative, surgical ideals of beauty becomes a form of symbolic violence perpetrated upon themselves. In *Black Skin, White Masks*, Frantz Fanon writes about the psychological effects of colonial racism on the way Antillean blacks in the French Caribbean came to view themselves as "impure" and despise their blackness.[43] The black middle class experienced self-contempt and hated their own appearances, an "epidermalization of [their] inferiority."[44] "I am white," Fanon ventriloquized; "in other words, I embody beauty and virtue, which have never been black. I am the color of day."[45] Elsewhere, Toni Morrison writes in her novel *The Bluest Eye*, "A little black girl yearns for the blue eyes of a little white girl, and the horror at the heart of her yearning is exceeded only by the evil of its fulfillment."[46]

This kind of symbolic violence is produced in the "structures, habituses, and *mentalités* of everyday life."[47] Pierre Bourdieu argues that people's external conditions of existence are embodied as habitus that produce and structure dispositions. The habitus structures an individual's perceptions, experiences, and practices, and it is through habitus that one acquires a sense of one's place in the world or a point of view from which one is able to interpret one's own actions and the actions of others. This process of symbolic violence involves what Bourdieu calls misrecognition, "the fact of recognizing a violence which is wielded precisely inasmuch as one does not perceive it as such."[48] South Korea is a surgically normalized society with extremely high levels of cosmetic surgery, and this influences the pathways North Koreans take as they try to achieve what they perceive as the ideal body aesthetics in South Korea. But it is important to note that this violence of phenotypical normalization is not only confined to the North Korean experience—it is every bit a South Korean experience too, one that has become normalized and embedded in the social fabric of the everyday.

VIOLENCE OF EVERYDAY LIFE

Sun's mother and Chinese stepfather passed away due to illness only a few years after their marriage. Alone and without legal status, Sun found help through Korean missionaries who offered him shelter. The missionaries offered support to a handful of North Korean orphans who all lived together. Their daily routine consisted of praying, singing hymns, and memorizing passages from the Bible, and the missionaries encouraged their conversion to Christianity. After two years of living with the missionaries, Sun returned to North Korea with some of his orphan friends. He had hoped to find his younger brother, but the group of boys was immediately arrested upon crossing the border. Their punishment for leaving North Korea was forced labor for several weeks, though Sun considered the punishment "light." Crossing the border due to hunger—not for the purpose of defection—was considered a lesser crime.

Sun was unable to locate his brother, and he crossed into China again and eventually resettled in South Korea in 2007. What shocked him the most upon resettlement was his small stature compared to his South Korean peers. As a remedy, he took growth hormones for some time, but he eventually stopped taking them as they had a minimal effect on his mature body. When we first met, Sun was embarrassed to talk about any topics in relation to the body, even if it had nothing to do with his own. Over the years, however, Sun has become more comfortable with his body. He is now more open about his experience of stunted growth and small stature, joking with me regularly that his body is "economical" and "advantageous" because he has the option to pay the student fares while I must pay the full price of transportation fees and admission costs.

This chapter has explored the various ways the structural violence of hunger in North Korea and Cold War ethnic boundary-making translate into the violence of phenotypical normalization in South Korea. The embodiment of malnutrition—stunted growth as a consequence of ecological and state violence in North Korea—contributes to the specific ways North Koreans experience belonging in South Korea, which have marked their bodies as smaller, foreign, and strange in a society that obsesses over the undesirableness of short stature. In an effort to undo the violence and material deprivations they have experienced under the North Korean regime, many resettled North Koreans who lived through the famine years participated in processes of self-making that ultimately became symbolically violent. Furthermore, the body aesthetics that resettled North Koreans seek through cosmetic surgery, growth hormones, or self-presentation are tied to their desires to improve their economic situations, to not be "losers," to conform to local idealized notions of beauty, and to obtain belonging.

These types of violence are often overlooked because of the dominance of the narrative of human rights violations in North Korea. However, violence does not merely occur in North Korea, nor is it over when North Koreans resettle in South Korea. As we have seen throughout this chapter, experiences of violence and its legacies often extend into the present with its overlapping layers. Violence is embedded in the everyday, but it becomes so routinized that it becomes a part of the daily sociopolitical formation. Therefore, it is necessary to go beyond the human rights rhetoric that simply focuses on the physical violence and brutalities of North Korean prison camps. We must draw connections between the physical and symbolic, between the visible and invisible, and between intentional and unintentional forms of violence.

How might this violence of everyday life, manifesting in ways that are so intimate and interpersonal—the stigmatization of North Korean women as victims of trafficking, their sexualization, or the phenotypical normalization of body aesthetics for both women and men—change? Change might only conceivably take place through efforts more profound, more collective, and more powerful than what a few individuals in positions of power can provide through policy. It will require a type of "decolonising the mind" and desubjectivation that makes visible, and thus weakens, these forms of normalized, routinized, and thus invisible violence.[49]

4 Remittances and Transborder Kinship

I can send that money to my mother.

Kang, in conversation with author

A fellow soldier and I were walking from the command tower back to our barracks when we discovered small leaflets scattered on the ground. These were *ppira*, propaganda leaflets from North Korea. For the past month our base had been littered with these leaflets that had been launched over the DMZ via airborne balloons. The leaflet I picked up was titled *Cheonbeol* (Divine Punishment), and on the top portion were portraits of former South Korean dictator Park Chung-hee and his daughter Park Geun-hye, the president at the time in 2016. Below the portraits was a provocative and gory depiction of Park Geun-hye receiving punishment via a traditional Korean pillory. Blood and tears poured from her eyes and neck. On the wooden pillory were words associated with the failures during her presidency: *mereuseu* (MERS virus), *segeumpoktan* (tax bomb), *jasarwangguk* (kingdom of suicides), *sewolho* (the sunken Sewol ferry that killed 304 passengers, including 250 students), and *jongbuksanyang* (hunting for pro-North sympathizers). As trained, we returned to the command tower to report the *ppira*. We knew better than to hold onto the leaflets and be accused as threats to national security.

These propaganda leaflets have their origins in the Korean War, when approximately 2.8 billion "paper bombs" were dropped by both sides as part of psychological warfare. "Bury the enemy with paper," ordered Frank Pace, the US Secretary of the Army at the time.[1] Written in Korean, Chinese, or English, the leaflets demanded the enemy's surrender or guaranteed their security upon defection. Although the US and South Korea dropped the overwhelming majority of the leaflets, North Korea was responsible for about 300 million leaflets. The North Korean leaflets often targeted black soldiers fighting for the US forces. Pointing to racial discrimination, the leaflets urged black soldiers to return home and not die in vain for a country that continued to exclude them from their citizenship rights.

Following the armistice, these paper bombs continued to fall from the sky. The leaflets slandered the other political system, boasted about the successes of economic development, and encouraged defections with the lure of lavish compensation. Themes of sexuality, material prosperity, religion, and cultural events were frequently utilized to degrade and demoralize the other side. To this day, leaflet campaigns and other forms of psychological warfare such as shortwave radio broadcasts and loud-speakers directed at frontline soldiers and villages have been at the fore-front of negotiations between the two Koreas. Although both sides first agreed to suspend the leaflet campaigns at the Inter-Korean Summit in 2000, they reengaged in cross-border psychological warfare when rela-tions soured. When I discovered the leaflets in 2016, North Korea had recently conducted its fourth nuclear test and the South Korean military had resumed its loudspeaker broadcasts across the DMZ. The blaring broadcasts rotated between trendy K-pop music and condemnations of North Korea's human rights violations. In retaliation, the North dispersed the leaflets disparaging the South Korean president.

The two states, however, have not been the only actors engaged in the dissemination of leaflets. NGOs began to launch balloons to North Korea at the turn of the twenty-first century when the South Korean government was tempering its leaflet campaigns to ease tensions on the peninsula while an influx of North Koreans resettled in South Korea.[2] These NGOs were staffed by human rights activists, many of whom were themselves North Korean defectors. Their balloons included not only leaflets that rebuked the Kim dynasty, but also dried foods, US dollar bills, small

Figure 5. The balloons launched to North Korea by humanitarian groups include repackaged instant ramen noodles. Photo: Joowon Park.

radios, and USBs with South Korean media contents. Some of the members of the North Korean church where I conducted fieldwork also launched balloons to their "northern brethren." The North Korean pastor and his team carefully tracked wind patterns throughout the year and launched their balloons when the currents were most favorable. However, instead of stuffing the balloons with propaganda leaflets that slandered the North Korean regime, the church members packed the balloons with instant noodles that they had de-branded and repackaged with clear plastic wrap. The pastor emphasized to me that their balloon launches were strictly humanitarian, rather than political, in purpose.

These NGO balloon launches, not surprisingly, have enraged the North Korean regime. In June 2020, Kim Yo-jung, the sister of Kim Jong-un, responded with threats of military retaliation, demolished the North-South joint liaison office, and called the balloon-launchers "human scum" and "mongrel dogs." Shortly thereafter, as inter-Korean tensions deteriorated to the point of cutting off communication, the South Korean parliament passed an amendment to the Development of Inter-Korean Relations Act prohibiting the dissemination of leaflets, loudspeaker broadcasting, and the posting of visual materials, citing these activities as threatening to the lives of residents living near the DMZ. This policy drew criticism from conservatives who viewed the ban as an infringement on freedom of speech and as bending the knee to the North's demands.

While diplomatic negotiations and legal policies have focused on leaflets launched with helium balloons, other forms of transborder connections have materialized across the DMZ. As the previous chapters have illustrated, over 33,000 North Koreans have resettled to South Korea via China, a migratory pattern that emerged following the 1990s famine. Frequently arriving in South Korea alone, resettled North Koreans have sought to reestablish contact with their family members in North Korea, exchange communication, and send monetary remittances. This chapter examines these efforts to maintain transborder kinship and the limitations that arise from the geopolitical barriers to mobility in East Asia. As North Koreans resettled in South Korea engage in giving as a way to improve the lives of their family back home and sustain social ties, these exchanges in return complicate their sense of belonging.

SENDING MONEY TO NORTH KOREA

The summer rain brought some relief to the past several days of blazing hot temperatures. Kang and I usually hung out in Hongdae, a hip neighborhood of Seoul that draws artists, musicians, performers, and youth. Like our mutual friend Sun, Kang had been a *kkotjebi*, North Korean teenagers who scavenged for food around the markets and roamed around various provinces by hopping onto trains.[3] Many were orphans whose parents had passed away during the famine. Kang was malnourished during those years and his body shows it today, though he has gained weight since he resettled in South Korea. At the time of my research, Kang was in his late twenties, 163 cm (5 ft 4 in) tall, and weighing 52 kg (115 lbs), just a few centimeters taller and weighing slightly more than Sun. Kang had crossed into China with other *kkotjebi* boys. They wandered around various towns in China until Kang learned of South Korea's policy toward North Koreans. Unlike other North Koreans who resettle in South Korea by journeying to Southeast Asia, Kang headed towards the Mongolian Gobi Desert to seek an alternative route.

At the end of the evening, we walked toward the subway station huddled underneath his umbrella, sheltering ourselves from the rain. Despite the downpour, the streets were still bustling with people, and we took care to prevent the umbrella from hitting others. One step at a time we heaved our way down the subway entrance stairway in sync with the crowd as the escalator next to us brought up an equal amount of people to the street level. We descended deeper to the mezzanine and passed brightly lit advertisements for K-pop groups to reach the fare gates. We descended again to the train platform where we would wait for the next train to arrive.

I asked Kang, "Do *talbukja* (North Korean escapees) generally support the provision of food aid to North Korea?" I was curious about where resettled North Koreans stood on the politics of humanitarian aid. We were seated on a bench, still surrounded by advertisements on the platform screen walls that exist to prevent people from falling onto the rail tracks.

"I completely oppose providing rice to North Korea because it gets diverted to the military," he replied. As Kang noted, there is a chance that foreign aid will not reach ordinary North Korean citizens, the intended recipients who need it the most. This was especially true during the peak of the famine, when North Korean elites hoarded international aid and redirected supplies to the military. However, there are others who disagree with Kang and argue that the provision of humanitarian aid must remain unconditional and separate from politics.

Kang continued, "In South Korea, there are a lot of North Koreans who have family members in North Korea." His mother too lived in North Korea. If people want to help ordinary North Koreans, he said, a better strategy would be to funnel these funds to resettled North Koreans. "Then, I can send that money to my mother." Remitting money to family members in North Korea intrigued me because North Korea is regarded globally as a country disconnected from the rest of the world. Its regime strictly monitors the flow of information, goods, and people through its shielded borders, but also within it. Considered a nuclear pariah with atrocious human rights violations, North Korea is further excluded from the global economy through international sanctions.

The sending of remittances by North Koreans resettled in South Korea began to surface toward the late 2000s. As thousands of North Koreans arrived in South Korea via China each year in the aftermath of the famine, there was a growing desire to reconnect with loved ones back home. Responding to this need, intermediary brokers, some of whom were already involved in the smuggling of North Koreans across international borders to reach South Korea, developed covert strategies and networks to enable remittances to North Korea. In addition, taking advantage of Chinese cellular signals, they made phone calls possible with family members living in the North Korean borderlands. Today, over three-fifths of resettled North Koreans say that they have experience sending remittances to North Korea, a figure that has increased over the past ten years. Those who have never sent remittances usually do not do so because they do not have enough money to send or because they have no family living in North Korea.

The amount of money resettled North Koreans remit varies. The Database Center for North Korean Human Rights (NKDB), where I was an affiliate researcher during my fieldwork, was one of the first organizations to gather data on the remittances North Koreans sent to their home

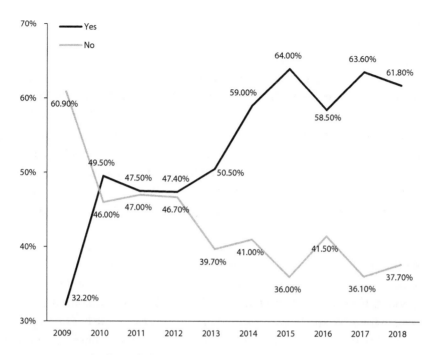

Figure 6. Graph of resettled Koreans sending remittances to North Korea. Source: Database Center for North Korean Human Rights.

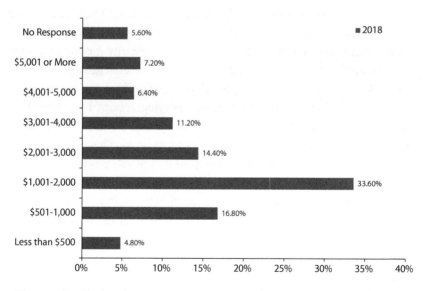

Figure 7. Graph of remittance amounts sent to North Korea. Respondents answered the question, "how much do you remit each time?" Source: Database Center for North Korean Human Rights.

country. The largest number of survey respondents (33.6 percent) sent between $1,000 to $2,000 USD each time, and the average amount sent per transaction was $2,500 USD (₩2.8 million KRW).[4] In South Korea, sending money to North Korea is illegal under the National Security Act. Due to the unresolved war, this law prohibits any unauthorized communications and interactions with North Korea. However, remittances to North Korea and phone calls with family members, though technically criminal, have not been strictly policed. The South Korean government has turned a blind eye for the time being to allow individuals to digitally connect with their families.[5]

Kang sends money to his mother whenever he can, remitting roughly $1,000 USD once or twice a year. To send money, Kang communicates with his broker over the phone and deposits money into the broker's bank account. Brokers, most of whom are Chinese citizens of Korean descent, remain invisible and faceless throughout the process; Kang has never met his broker in person and their interactions occur only through text messages and phone calls. Upon confirming the deposit, the broker contacts a secondary broker inside North Korea to deliver the money, while they take thirty percent as commission. Before I could express my surprise at how high the commission seemed to be, Kang said to me, "There is no other way, at least the money will reach my mother." Kang recognized that the commissions were often used to bribe border security guards and local officials and knew that these illicit activities constituted great risk as broker operations are high crimes in North Korea. The final step in the remittance delivery involves Kang's mother verifying receipt by calling him using the secondary broker's phone. Although some have experienced fraud or improper delivery of remittances, most brokers have held up their end of the bargain to sustain their business and profit-making.

The underground economy of remittances and networks of brokers have been shaped by North Korea's restrictions of freedoms and tight enforcement of its borders, the Chinese policy of repatriating North Korean border-crossers, and the continuing state of war between the two Koreas. Under these geopolitical conditions, my North Korean interlocutors tell me they see the brokers as absolutely necessary. Not only do brokers deliver remittances, mediate communication, and in recent years smuggle family members out of North Korea, brokers play a central role in helping North Koreans navigate the Chinese mainland to reach South Korea. Although the South Korean government has kept its diplomatic doors open to those who seek protection by way of reaching Southeast Asia or Mongolia, it does not actively help North Koreans in China. Therefore, while brokers and smugglers are usually painted as criminal, resettled North Koreans often describe these middlemen as "helpers of North Koreans" (*talbuk doumi*) and their "only hope" (*yuilhan huimang*).

MATERIAL HARDSHIPS AND KINSHIP TIES

Resettled North Koreans send remittances for various reasons. For some, remitting money to family members in North Korea filled a void they felt in South Korea. Most of my North Korean interlocutors sent remittances on major Korean holidays such as *Chuseok* (the Autumn Harvest) and the Lunar New Year, times when many South Koreans return to their home-towns to be with their family. To those separated from their loved ones in North Korea, the family-centered nature of the holidays felt particularly lonely and isolating. Others sent money in order to improve their family's well-being. One North Korean woman said to me during an interview, "I know the miserable living conditions of my family in North Korea. I don't have a prosperous life in this land (South Korea), but I can eat until I am full." She could sympathize with the experiences of hunger and she told me she sent remittances because her heart ached for her family still living in North Korea. There was an emotional dimension to these remittances and many were motivated by feelings of loneliness, regret, and guilt.

When Kang first found his mother in North Korea through a broker, it brought him great joy. The reestablished connection with his mother, whom he had not seen in nearly ten years, provided him a sense of kinship he lacked in South Korea. He told me that while all his South Korean friends had families, he had none. His father died during the famine and his mother still lived in North Korea. The whereabouts of his two siblings were unknown, although he believed they were alive and in China, where he last saw them. Sending remittances to his mother relieved the guilt he felt for having left his mother alone and for living comfortably in South Korea compared to his former life.

However, saving money for remittances while struggling to meet the demands of everyday life was not easy. The initial resettlement money from the government soon ran out and Kang became dependent on welfare. With his education interrupted by the famine and his migration journey, he did not have the necessary credentials or skills for what he considered a good job. Yet, he was unwilling to accept jobs that would relegate him to the lower strata of South Korean society, especially when he had risked his life to come to South Korea with high hopes for a prosperous life. Working full-time also meant he would have to give up his welfare benefits, which he was unwilling to do. In the meantime, he worked part-time jobs and he received a monthly allowance from the church as long as he continued to attend weekly services and Bible study. To achieve upward social mobility, Kang was preparing to attend university in Seoul (his tuition would be covered by the school and the government). Learning English, ironically, was a key requirement for college admission and job prospects in the future, which had initially brought us together.

The renewed connection with his mother through remittances had generated hope that they might physically reunite again someday in South Korea. If he had enough money, the brokers could smuggle his mother out from North Korea to China and ultimately to South Korea. But the cost of the transnational human smuggling was currently out of reach. The price could range anywhere from $5,000 to $10,000 USD, depending on various circumstances such as the region of North Korea where the smuggled person resides, the climate of North Korea's domestic politics and border enforcement, and China's enforcement of repatriation. Since Kang did not have the cash he needed to reunite with his mother, he had contemplated selling his government-subsidized apartment. "I will figure something out," he said, regarding where he would live if he returned his apartment to the government. "Maybe my pastor will let me sleep in the church."

Kang's economic circumstances are not much different from those of other North Koreans resettled in South Korea. Their labor experiences provide a glimpse of the continuing challenges that they face in their transition not only from a communist to a capitalist society, but also from an industrial to postindustrial one. According to a 2019 study, sixty percent of resettled North Koreans were considered "economically active," a category that includes those who are at least fifteen years old and either employed with an income, or unemployed but seeking a job.[6] Their average monthly income was ₩1.95 million KRW (roughly $1,770 USD), at the lower end of the socioeconomic ladder and $1,000 USD less than the average South Korean income.[7] North Koreans who are not economically active cited physical discomfort (39.9 percent), commuting to school (22.2 percent), and child-rearing (22.2 percent) as their biggest reasons.

There are further disparities in the type of occupations that employ resettled North Koreans, raising questions about what it means for them to become "South Korean" within a neoliberal economy. Among the economically active North Koreans, the majority (61.4 percent) were employed in the category of "Crafts, Machines, Operators, and Elementary Occupations," usually performing manual labor as factory workers. This is twice as high a percentage as the South Korean national figure (33.8 percent). Furthermore, while 21.8 percent of South Koreans worked as "Professionals, Technicals, Administrators, and Managers," just 7.4 percent of North Koreans worked in this category. The only occupation category where the disparities are minimal was in the "Service and Sales Worker" sector, where 26.5 percent of North Koreans are employed compared to 23.7 percent of South Koreans. In neoliberal South Korea, where work is highly specialized and stratified, many resettled North Koreans do not have the education, credentials, and skills that allow for successfully achieving a middle-class life. For North Koreans, becoming "South Korean" is often interwoven with socioeconomic inequalities that accumulate into second-class citizenship and marginalization.

On one late afternoon following our after-school English class, some of the students and I walked down the hill from the school to the local bowling alley, situated just a block away from a subway entrance. As usual, we split teams using "rock, paper, scissors," and the losing team would buy a round of ice cream for everyone. When the game was well underway, Kang complained to us that his mother had called him several times recently, but that he purposefully did not answer the calls.

Since they only communicate just a few times a year—his mother has to hike up a hill, away from prying eyes and ears, to place the secretive call using the broker's phone—I presumed Kang would be delighted to speak to his mother. When I asked him why he did not answer his mother's repeated calls, he explained grimly, "It gets stressful. She is calling to ask for more money. I just do not have any at this point."

Perhaps in consolation and in solidarity, a classmate of Kang's jumped in to say, "There's a misconception [in North Korea] that North Koreans live an affluent life in South Korea." Others nodded in agreement, and Dahae, one of the older students in the group, expressed that she too felt a similar sense of burden: "These families [in North Korea] regard remittance-sending as an obligation, but to send money we have to tighten our belts."

As these students revealed, North Koreans in South Korea are not always simply the willing initiators of remittances. Family members in North Korea often call them to request money, demonstrating how the remittance-receiving community can also impact the diaspora in ways that shape diasporic belonging. Comparable to the reality vs the romance of family reunions, the remittances and the phone calls—while reconnecting families and reestablishing intimacy—often become a burdensome obligation, and resettled North Koreans must negotiate kinship and the sense of filial duty, guilt, and the present reality of never having enough money to send back home.

DEMANDS AND BURDENS

Dahae was from Hoeryong, a city in the North Hamgyong Province of North Korea. When she first left her home country, she was just sixteen years old. She had been trafficked into marriage across the border and lived in China for four years before finally resettling alone in South Korea in 2006. Her parents and two younger brothers remained in North Korea—the brothers were unable to serve in the military because of her "disappearance"—and her regular remittances helped sustain their livelihoods.

"If you come [to South Korea] with your family, you can lean on each other. But I was alone," Dahae said when we discussed her experience resettling to South Korea. When she arrived at her apartment, several volunteers from the local social welfare center had just finished cleaning and the space was completely empty besides a cheap rice cooker and a bag of rice gifted from the Hanawon Resettlement Center. Dahae was unable to sleep. On the luxury of her heated apartment floor that winter and in the barren space, she acutely felt the absence of her family.

Dahae worked as a server at a local restaurant for the first four months of her resettlement but she soon quit her job. She wanted to become a hairstylist and registered to attend a *hagwon*, one of the many private institutions in South Korea that offer supplementary education. "I couldn't understand a word. Technical terms. Difficult vocabularies. I realized I needed to learn *hanguk-mal* (South Korean speech) and study before I learned the skills." She came to learn about an alternative school in Seoul for resettled North Koreans. Although the round trip by subway from her apartment in Incheon to Seoul was nearly four hours, this had been her third year attending the school. Dahae had dropped out in North Korea, and she studied hard to make up for her lost education and to pass the South Korean High School Graduation Equivalency Exam.

On a Sunday afternoon following church, Dahae received a phone call while we were eating lunch in the cafeteria. As a new institution—the North Korean pastor was originally from a larger mega-church and had "planted" this North Korean church with their blessing—the church did not have its own building and rented space in a business building in the Guro district of Seoul. The remainder of the building remained dark and empty of everyday employees. The small congregation of resettled North Koreans and a few South Koreans, roughly fifty people in all, ate communally, sitting around folding rectangular tables set up in the cafeteria, a space just across the hallway from the worship room.

On the other end of the phone was Dahae's mother in North Korea. The phone call was not entirely unexpected. As arranged through their broker, her mother had been scheduled to call Dahae a few weeks earlier. However, due to the increased surveillance in her mother's town at the time, the broker had thought it unwise to attempt any illicit activities. To make this call, her mother and the broker had hiked up the mountain to hide from authorities and opportunistic eavesdroppers. Dahae rushed out of the cafeteria to find privacy, and about thirty minutes passed before she returned with a mix of emotions. She was happy to have spoken to her mother but she was also displeased. By the time she returned, the majority of the congregation had finished their meals and had vacated the room.

"You know what? Even if I send money only once a year, I send at least ₩1 million KRW (~$900 USD)," she vented to me and the two *dongsaeng* (younger "siblings") sitting at the table. For North Korean citizens living in the poorer peripheries, that amount had a considerable impact and could help cover a few months of living expenses. In addition to supporting daily livelihoods, many recipients of remittances use the money to repay debt, bribe local officials, or to sell smuggled goods in the black market. "But she always tells me how difficult life is. Always. She only tells me about how hard it is to eat and to live. That's all she tells me, and it's distressing. If she said that my remittance improved her life then I'd think there's at least some worth to it, but she only talks about how hard it is."

The type of discontent on the receiving end that Dahae described is a common theme in ethnographic accounts of remittances, and the recipients are often aware of the emotional burden their discontent puts on the senders.[8] Since life was always going to be difficult in North Korea despite her remittances, Dahae wanted to spend the money on smuggling her parents out of the country instead. Like Dahae, an overwhelming majority (70 percent) of resettled North Koreans say they have hopes and future plans to eventually bring their family members to South Korea.[9] However, her parents refused. It is a common and popular assumption that all North Koreans desire to escape their country, but Dahae's parents were unwilling to leave North Korea. No matter how hard life was, it was home for them, and they did not want to risk their lives to journey across several borders and resettle in a country they did not know.

Dahae continued, "When we talk on the phone, they tell me I need to succeed, that their well-being depends on my success. This is a huge burden to me! My mom told me she wouldn't come here, and so I told her there's no point for me to live here alone. She scolded me, 'if you don't do well there, then we won't do well here.' I told myself that I'd have to succeed to sustain my family.'" Dahae felt it was her duty to provide for her family. However, her mother's constant focus on remittances was deeply frustrating. "Shouldn't a mother be interested in how her daughter is living? *My* well-being?" Dahae asked us. As Marcel Mauss famously theorized, gifts are never free.[10] Without reciprocation, social bonds can weaken, and although Dahae had taken on the economic burden of sending remittances to her family, she felt her family did not return the favor of offering emotional care and intimacy.

I asked Dahae if she had the money to bring her parents to South Korea. "If my parents want to come, maybe I'll get a loan. But the interest is very high and it's risky. If something were to go wrong, I could fall into credit delinquency." Dahae knew that even if her parents wished to come to South Korea, smuggling them out of North Korea involved high risk and many uncertainties. Not only would the brokers have to help her parents secretly cross the border to China undetected or by bribing border security guards, they would have to traverse the Chinese mainland while avoiding arrest. If repatriated to North Korea, her parents would face punishment in North Korea's prison camps for their crime of defection.

LIFE-SAVING REMITTANCE

It was February 2012, and various media outlets were reporting that thirty-one North Korean border-crossers had been arrested in China and were facing deportation to North Korea. The *New York Times* headline read: "China should not repatriate North Korean refugees, Seoul says."[11] The *Washington Post* said, "Spotlight falls on North Korean defectors' treatment in China."[12] For years, human rights activists had been challenging China's official policy of denying asylum to North Korean border-crossers, but what was extraordinary about this circumstance was that North Korean leader Kim Jong-il had just passed away in December of 2011. Kim Jong-un, the son and successor of the deceased leader, decreed that any North Korean citizen caught in the act of defection during the one-hundred-day mourning period would be "exterminated" down three generations—meaning that the punishment would extend from the defector's parents to the defector's children.[13]

This situation was heartbreaking for our friend Youngchul whose younger sister, Hyunmi, was among those detained in China. Youngchul was a university student and one of the student leaders at the North Korean church. He had escaped North Korea in 2004, though his parents and two siblings still lived in North Korea. A few weeks prior to the international headlines, Youngchul had received a call from Hyunmi, who was calling from Yanji, a Chinese city in the Yanbian Korean Autonomous Prefecture bordering North Korea. She had recently crossed into China on her own.

"I don't want to live in North Korea anymore, can you send me to South Korea?" she had asked. Hyunmi had been a frequent border-crosser to China. Her first experience was during the North Korean famine when she temporarily migrated to China for a few years. Though she was eventually arrested and deported back to North Korea, she continued to defy border enforcement over the years. "North Korea was like hell for her," Youngchul told me. Having experienced life outside North Korea, it was difficult for her to readjust to everyday hardships. She decided that she wanted a new life in South Korea.

After receiving this phone call from his sister, Youngchul borrowed money from his friends and paid a migration broker who would guide her to South Korea. Hyunmi met the broker in Yanji and discovered she was in the company of other North Koreans with the same hopes of resettling in South Korea. The group took a nine-hour bus ride to Shenyang. From there, the plan was to continue their journey through Chinese mainland toward Kunming, a Chinese city close to Myanmar, Thailand, Laos, Cambodia, and Vietnam. If they arrived in Thailand, they would likely find a safe passage to South Korea through diplomatic channels and without the risk of forced repatriation. However, when they arrived in Shenyang, the group was immediately arrested by Chinese authorities. With the group was a North Korean agent disguised as a defector, and he had alerted the authorities.

"She had called me just before leaving for Shenyang. When I saw the news about a group of North Koreans arrested in Shenyang, I knew this was my sister," Younchul said. While he hoped to discreetly bribe his sister out of detainment in China, his close friends strongly believed international attention would be the solution. Our friend Jacob had been inspired by the effective use of social media in the Arab Spring and sought to create a movement using the hashtag #SaveMyFriend.

Jacob's hope, he told me, was that the global attention on China would prevent it from forcibly sending those detained back to North Korea. As he expected, the headlines did garner an unprecedented amount of domestic and international attention. Politicians and human rights activists picked up on the slogan and rallied people to demand that the Chinese government abide by its obligations to the 1951 UN Refugee Convention. Protests were held in front of Chinese embassies in Seoul, London, and Washington, DC. Some Korean politicians went on hunger strikes and camped outside the Chinese embassy for days. South Korean celebrities joined the outcry, and soon others joined the chorus publicly expressing their concerns, including US Congressmen and even the UN Secretary-General.

Hundreds of protestors and supporters were gathered outside the Chinese embassy in Seoul, situated a short walk from our school and the bowling alley the North Korean students frequented. Jacob read a letter out loud in front of flashing cameras and journalists. Behind him were human rights activists, NGO workers, and politicians who held up signs that said "Save My Friend," "Stop the forced repatriation of North Korean refugees!," and "North Korean defectors are South Korean citizens." Others held up drawings and illustrations of North Korean border guards brutally inflicting harm on prisoners.

The letter Jacob read was actually written by Youngchul, but Youngchul feared his public exposure might further endanger his family in North Korea. He showed me the letter:

> Our friends and family are currently detained by the Chinese police in Shenyang, China, and are at risk of being sent back to North Korea. We are gathered here to save them. We don't know when they might be deported, but the South Korean press and international human rights organizations have warned that North Koreans caught while fleeing their country during Kim Jong-il's one-hundred-day mourning period will be publicly executed or sent to the prison camps where they will eventually die. Even worse, the North Korean government will also kill all three generations of the family. The detainees do not know when they will be sent back, and they wait with uncertainty and a strand of hope that someone will save them. Those detained need urgent rescue. Your concern and participation will give them strength. Together, our small acts can affect great change. Think of them as your own, and please join our effort to save them. Save them. Please save our friends. Please save them—our parents, our siblings.

However, while these protests were still ongoing, Youngchul received a phone call from his younger brother in North Korea. His brother informed him, to his great surprise, that their sister was already at the North Korean detention facility undergoing investigation. The group had been deported and transferred to North Korea's *Gukgaanjeonbowibu* or State Security Agency (hereafter "SSA").

Despite the international attention, public outcries, and protests held in front of Chinese embassies, the Chinese government had already quietly deported the group to North Korea. The humanitarian outrage, criticism from the international community, South Korean diplomacy, and the appeals from the United Nations, did not—could not—stop the forced repatriation. The Chinese Foreign Ministry spokesman Hong Lei held a press conference and stated, "China has always dealt with the related issues pragmatically based on domestic and international laws and humanitarian principles. This is consistent with all sides involved."[14]

Forcibly returned North Koreans—the North Korean state calls them *bibeobwolgyeongja* or illegal border-crossers—are initially held in detention facilities near the border for interrogation.[15] Many of my North Korean interlocutors with experiences in these SSA detention facilities recall that the cells were often so overcrowded that people slept on the floor, with bodies crisscrossed over one another or in seated positions. Wake-up call is at five in the morning, but the detainees rise only to sit still in a crossed-legged position until eleven in the evening. Any unauthorized movements—stretching, leaning against the wall, or dozing off—can lead to collective punishment for the entire cell. The only rest breaks detainees receive are during meal times. Although meals are provided three times a day, a meal contains less than 100 grams of cooked corn kernels (often mixed together with crushed corn stalk) and a bowl of lightly salted water containing a few cabbage leaves.[16]

During interrogation, one of the first questions the SSA agents ask is the *Juche* year. *Juche* means "self-reliance," and is a North Korean political ideology developed by Kim Il-sung, the grandfather of Kim Jong-un. For example, Kim Il-sung's birth year, 1912, is Year 1 in the *Juche* calendar; "*Juche* 111" is 2022. Forgetting the current *Juche* year signals that the detainee has resided outside North Korea for an extended period of time. The detainees are also bombarded with a series of questions pertaining to why they crossed into China and what they did there. The agents inquire into whether the detainees had any "impure" foreign contact. Did they

come in contact with any anti-state actors such as South Korean missionaries or human rights activists? Did they watch any South Korean television shows or films? Did they attend church or read the Bible? And most
importantly, did they plan to defect to South Korea?

There is a North Korean saying that states, "The slip of the short tongue
severs the long neck" (*jjalpeun hyeo ttaemune gin mogajiga naraganda*).
A casual or miscalculated statement can lead to one's swift death. The
purpose of these interrogations is to separate the "political border-crossers" from the "simple border-crossers." Those considered to have had
impure foreign contact and those who were caught while en route to South
Korea are considered political border-crossers. These prisoners are sent
to North Korea's infamous political prison camps—or "gulags" as human
rights activists call them, alluding to Soviet labor camps.[17] Depending on
the severity of their crime under North Korea's Penal Code, some may be
sentenced to ten years while others are sentenced for life.

However, some North Koreans avoid being categorized as political border-crossers by insisting they were tricked into crossing over to China by
human traffickers and brokers. Others claim that they were hungry and
were merely looking for a way to survive. Although some may have been
genuine defectors, many successfully deny this and manage to become
categorized as simple border-crossers. People who crossed over to China
for "pure" reasons (that is, for economic reasons) are sent to the labor-
training camps (*Nodongdanryeondae*) located near their respective resi-
dences. First-time offenders are sentenced to serve one to six months,
while repeat offenders are sentenced to as many as three years.

Because Youngchul's sister Hyunmi and the other North Koreans were
all caught while en route to South Korea, he knew well the fate that waited
her. North Korean authorities would consider her a political border-
crosser and send her to a prison camp. But his brother in North Korea
reassured him that he did not have to worry: "Just send us money to get
her out [from detention]." Following his brother's instructions, Youngchul
sent him approximately $5,000 USD to bribe the SSA agents. This was
the most urgent and foremost priority because their sister's fate would be
decided in the detention facility. Using a portion of the money, his brother
bribed the SSA agents to cut Hyunmi's interrogation short. She spent less
than two weeks in the border detention facility and the agents classified

her as a simple border-crosser. She was then transferred to a labor-training camp.

The labor-training camps are operated by the *Inminboanbu* or the People's Security Agency (a separate institution from the SSA), and prisoners are forced to work at construction sites, farms, mines, logging, and factories. These camps, in addition to detaining forcibly returned North Koreans, also imprison ordinary citizens who commit minor crimes in North Korea such as the illegal possession and use of mobile phones, theft and embezzlement, smuggling of goods, and unpermitted absence from one's workplace. Hyunmi was repatriated during the winter season, when temperatures in northern parts of North Korea easily drop below −20°C (−4°F). For those arrested during the summer (and wearing light clothes), no special consideration is given and winter coats are not provided. Instead, the authorities allow family visitors to bring prisoners clothes, blankets, and essential toiletries. Prisoners without families are therefore most unfortunate. When the prisoners finish serving their sentences, the authorities send them to a local bathhouse where they bathe and wash their clothes before returning home.

Youngchul's brother bribed the labor-training camp authorities as well, and Hyunmi's time there was brief. With the remaining money, the brother bribed his hometown police, and by mid-April, just a few months after her initial arrest, she returned home. She called Youngchul to thank him when this incident was all over and he rebuked her. "What's wrong with you? You put everyone in danger," he said to her. Youngchul was upset with his sister because her actions had placed his entire family at risk. "I told her not to attempt [leaving North Korea] again. She kept saying, 'I'm sorry. I'm sorry.'" His anger towards his sister was displaced. It was not that he did not desire to reunite with his sister, but rather that there were too many life-threatening risks involved in the attempt to reach South Korea.

Human rights activists had claimed that if Hyunmi and the other North Koreans were deported back to North Korea during the one-hundred-day mourning period, it would certainly lead to their death. However, broker networks, transnational kinship ties, and corrupt North Korean authorities saved Hyunmi's life. Youngchul's only hope resided with the broker system, which had indeed functioned to transform his remittance into a two-month sentence and an eventual safe release for his sister. But once this emergency situation was resolved, Youngchul expressed to me that he would let go of his dream of family reunion for the time being, even if it meant he had to carry the material and emotional burden of sending remittances to his family for the remainder of his life. This experience had brought great emotional toll on Youngchul, Hyunmi, and the family.

PROLONGED SEPARATION AND REUNION

Studies on remittances primarily highlight the impact of the remittance-sending migrants and refugees—culturally, politically, economically—on their country of origin.[18] "Through remitting," Susan Coutin states, "migrants become an absent presence within their countries of origin."[19] However, this chapter has explored some of the circular dimensions of remittances. Although the remittances sent to North Korea have economic and social value, sustaining livelihoods and reestablishing family ties, the receiving family members also directly shape the lives of resettled North Koreans in South Korea through their economic dependence and demands. Within a divided peninsula, these remittances and transborder communication become carriers of intimacy, but also of duty and burden.

A few years later, Kang finally managed to bring his mother out of North Korea, paying his broker $5,000 USD to arrange her border crossing and transnational journey to South Korea. However, her escape from North Korea meant many turbulent weeks of agony, fear, and anxiety. She was arrested by the Chinese border patrol guards when she crossed the Yalu River into Chinese territory. The broker alerted Kang to the situation and requested an additional $3,000 USD to bribe the Chinese police station. Kang had no other options at this point. He feared her repatriation to North Korea would lead to her death, and took out loans from banks and borrowed money from acquaintances to secure the cash. The bribe worked, and his mother continued her journey across the Chinese mainland. Guided by the broker, she travelled with a group of other North Korean defectors towards Thailand where they would claim asylum. From there, she waited her turn to be flown to South Korea for resettlement. But before Kang and his mother could meet face to face, she had to first undergo interrogation (a common procedure to weed out spies) and a mandatory three-month cultural orientation at the Hanawon Resettlement Center.

When she completed her orientation, Kang invited me to his home to greet his mother. He lived in Nowon, a northern neighborhood of Seoul. "My son promised me the trip here would be easy and quick. He said I'd only need to get on a bus once I got to China," she said, describing her journey to South Korea. After the grueling hours and days spent on the bus, she thought that she had arrived in South Korea. "But I saw darker-skinned people. I didn't realize until then that I was in Thailand!"

Kang laughed. "She wouldn't have left [North Korea] if I told her the truth (about the difficult journey)!"

"I thought I was going to die!" his mother exclaimed. "Had I known how challenging the trip would be, I wouldn't have come!" But she was encouraged and mustered strength when she met an older woman within her group of North Koreans seeking resettlement to South Korea: Grandmother Ku, who we met in chapter 1. The two women had crossed paths as they journeyed together across the Chinese mainland and Southeast Asia. Kang's mother said, "There was a grandmother in our group, and I asked her, 'How will you live in South Korea at that age?' The old woman answered that she wanted to die in her birthplace. Seeing a grandmother so determined to reach South Korea gave me strength throughout the journey." Grandmother Ku and Kang's mother arrived in South Korea as part of the same Hanawon cohort, and it was Kang's mother who had asked Kang if he knew anyone from the United States to help search for Grandmother Ku's brother.

Observing Kang and his mother laugh about their past and her exhausting journey to South Korea felt special, especially since I knew Kang had struggled with her demands, the emotional burden, and his own material hardships over the years. They were no longer separated by the DMZ. They talked freely, reminisced, and joked about their past experiences and the time they spent living apart. They were reunited at last. The joy of this moment seemed like a healing closure to Kang's story—except that now he was in overwhelming debt that he would have to pay off for years to come. I also thought of the other North Koreans resettled in South Korea who remain indefinitely separated from their families in North Korea, who may seek and yet never get to reunite with their loved ones.

As Kang celebrated his reunion with his mother, our friend Sun wrote a letter to his younger brother in North Korea. When the church launched their air balloons over the DMZ, Sun included his letter among the leaflets.

One by one I count the stars and I recall my memories of you.
On this evening, it pains me to keep your memories contained.
Congratulations on your twenty-fourth birthday.
It saddens me we cannot share even a bowl of steamy rice.

Thinking of the hardest time,
I remember the days climbing the apartment stairs with you on my back.
Thinking of the happiest time,
I remember the moment I learned you were alive.

When I left, I didn't know that the days without seeing you
Would become longer than the days we spent together.
The tears that you shed have not dried up in my heart.
It has been seventeen years, but my heart is still soaked in tears.

Do you remember your seventh birthday?
It was the last time we saw each other.
Do you remember the noodles we ate?
I ate noodles today thinking of that day, thinking of you.

You live in the furthest place.
A distance greater than heaven to earth.
One day, perhaps, the wall separating us will crumble.
Tonight, your face shines among the stars.

5 Constructing North Korean Deservingness

Humanitarianism [. . .] is several things at once: a structure of feeling, a cluster of moral principles, a basis for ethical claims and political strategies, and a call for action.

Peter Redfield and Erica Bornstein

What, ultimately is gained, and what lost, when we use the
terms of suffering to speak of inequality, when we invoke
trauma rather than recognizing violence, [. . .] when we
mobilize compassion rather than justice?

Didier Fassin

GLOBAL REFUGEE POLICY

When the winter of 2012 came, Sun, Kang, Dahae, Soyang, and Sunmi
accompanied me to the Incheon International Airport with high anticipation for my trip. I was on my way to the University of Oxford to attend
a conference entitled "Understanding Global Refugee Policy." It was to
honor the thirtieth anniversary of the Refugee Studies Centre, and I would
present a paper discussing China's role in the global refugee regime and
China's forced repatriation of North Koreans. Though I reminded my
friends that I was only attending an academic conference and that these
events often took time to yield practical results in policy, they reiterated to
me that I must advocate strongly for the refugee status of North Koreans
in China. We said our goodbyes and I passed through the security gates to
board the British Airways airplane departing Seoul to London.

North Koreans who have left their country are regarded in several ways. To the Chinese government, North Korean border-crossers are "economic migrants," and their official policy is to forcibly return these migrants back to their home country. Human rights activists, on the other hand, argue that those fleeing North Korea are "refugees" in need of international protection. From this perspective, the repression of freedoms in North Korea and the regime's hostile policies give North Koreans the right to refugee status. In international politics and mass media, North Korean escapees are often described as "defectors" from the communist regime. Lastly, whether they are labeled migrants, refugees, or defectors, the South Korean government grants them citizenship based on its constitutional claims to North Korean territory. Article 3 of the South Korean Constitution states that the "territory of the Republic of Korea shall consist of the Korean peninsula and its adjacent islands,"[1] a framing used to claim technical sovereignty over North Korea. South Korea's extension of citizenship to North Koreans, then, is not based on claims to refugee status.

What is the truth of these politics of identification? Is there a truth? Following Walter Benjamin's claim that the "task of a critique of violence may be summarized as that of expounding its relation to law and justice," this chapter explores the global contestations over granting refugee status to North Koreans, and the work of humanitarian actors and various governments to construct North Korean deservingness (and in the case of China, their undeservingness) through a discourse of violence.[2] In these regularized representations, North Korean identities are defined through violence and suffering that are seemingly the only accurate and valid description of their experience. Inscribed with notions of oppression, persecution, and helplessness, North Koreans are reduced to "bare life," figures deprived of political status and rights, and in need of asylum and emancipation to regain qualitative life.[3] North Koreans are thus re-included in politics through their exceptional deservingness, their exceptionality based on an inclusion rather than an exclusion.[4] The humanitarian project becomes a project of delegitimation, intended to symbolize the failure of the North Korean state and citizenship. This chapter illustrates how these constructions of deservingness neglect, and as such reinforce, the structures of power, injustices, and inequalities across multiple national boundaries in which North Koreans are embedded.

POLITICS OF IDENTIFICATION

Following the Second World War and the 1948 Declaration of Human Rights, the Convention Relating to the Status of Refugees was held in Geneva on July 28, 1951 to protect the rights of persons seeking protection from their home countries. Article 1 of this UN Refugee Convention defines a refugee as a person who has a "well-founded fear of being persecuted for reasons of race, religion, nationality, membership of a particular social group or political opinion" and is "outside the country of his nationality and is unable or, owing to such fear, is unwilling to avail himself of the protection of that country."[5] Moreover, the Convention prohibits the contracting States from forcibly returning refugees to their country of origin if their lives would be put in danger. This is the "non-refoulement" principle outlined in Article 33.[6] According to this principle, signatory member-states have an obligation to provide protection to those fleeing persecution and must not forcibly repatriate refugees to the home country they have fled.

China signed the UN Refugee Convention in 1982, but the fundamental pitfall of the Convention is that it leaves significant room for interpretation by its member-states. Although China had leaned toward a policy of tolerance regarding North Korean border-crossers prior to the famine in North Korea, it began to secure its border and enforce deportation due to the mass scale of crossings, the increasing number of crimes committed by border-crossers, and the highly publicized attempts by North Koreans to enter foreign embassies (areas with diplomatic immunity).[7] Framing North Korean border-crossers as illegal economic migrants, Chinese authorities argue that these people are not refugees and have cited the United States' frequent deportation of Central American migrants as an example of other countries taking similar action.

The majority of the North Koreans crossing into China during the 1990s had indeed left for economic reasons as breadwinners and temporary migrants, and in classic understandings of refugee law, many were not fleeing with well-founded fears of persecution. However, while the migrations were driven by economic motives, the root of the problem was political. The migration may have been triggered by famine and the collapse of its main trading partners in the Soviet Bloc, but North Korea's long history of failed policies, economic mismanagement, repression of freedoms, and prioritization of its military and nuclear program had created the conditions for survival migration. Geopolitical and ecological calamities were an opportune excuse for longstanding failure and incompetence.

Furthermore, though the grounds for claiming refugee status commonly depend on one's past persecution (that is, the persecution from which one has fled), it can also be determined based on the potential for future persecution. Given North Korea's policies toward its citizens who leave the country without authorization and its treatment of those forcibly repatriated, most North Korean border-crossers living in China could have a case for refugee status. North Korea's Criminal Law in Article 233 stipulates against unauthorized border-crossings: "A person who illegally crosses a border of the Republic shall be punished by short-term labor for less than two years. In cases where the person commits a grave offence, he or she shall be punished by reform through labor for less than five years."[8] Additionally, Article 62 of the Criminal Law outlines "treason" against the North Korean state:

> A citizen of the Republic who commits treason against the Fatherland by defection, surrender, betrayal; or disclosure of secrets shall be punished by reform through labor for more than five years. In cases where the person commits a grave offence, he or she shall be punished by reform through labor for more than five years and less than ten years.[9]

Contact with missionaries or human rights activists in China, attempting to enter a foreign embassy in Beijing, or being caught while attempting to resettle in South Korea are all regarded as treason and high crimes against the State.

North Koreans who have experienced forced repatriation have cited human rights violations in the North Korean penal system. As I illustrated in the previous chapter, they are subject to various forms of violence including unsanitary conditions, inhumane treatment and forced labor, and starvation. North Korean women suspected of carrying the babies of Chinese men have testified that they experienced forced abortions in the detention facilities.[10] Activists argue that these well-documented violations of basic human rights ultimately amount to persecution (even if projected to be in the future upon return). These testimonies have led humanitarian organizations such as Amnesty International, Human Rights Watch, and other NGOs to produce narratives of suffering as part of a larger project of constructing North Koreans as deserving of refugee status.[11]

Despite this pressure from the international community, the Chinese government has remained unwavering. China polices the surroundings of foreign embassies in Beijing to prevent North Koreans from entering the grounds, blocks UNHCR's access to the borderlands, and criminalizes religious and humanitarian actors that help North Koreans. As I explained in chapter 2, bilateral agreements with North Korea, concerns with ethnic minorities, and a desire to prevent North Korea's collapse and thus maintain a buffer against the US military stationed in South Korea all play a role in China's repatriation policy. Yet, when it comes to other non-North Korean asylum seekers on Chinese soil, China abides by the UN Refugee Convention and allows the UNHCR to do its job.[12] Interpreting the Convention to its own benefit and advantage, China treats North Koreans as a political exception to its refugee policy.

Given China's incessant and steadfast policy to treat North Koreans as economic migrants, human rights activists have alternatively argued that North Koreans could be refugees *sur place*. The UNHCR defines a *sur place* refugee as a "person who was not a refugee when he left his country, but who become a refugee *at a later date*."[13] Using this second principle, it has again been argued that even if North Koreans were economic migrants (and not refugees) when leaving North Korea, the potential for future persecution toward those forcibly repatriated make them refugees *sur place*. However, as the UNHCR Head of Policy Development stressed to me over lunch at the Oxford conference, North Koreans may not fit the *sur place* category since its definition primarily has to do with a *change* in the country of origin, and as he reiterated to me, nothing has fundamentally changed in North Korea since their departure.

The UNHCR has little influence over China's position on the issue of North Korean border-crossers, and I asked the UN policymaker why it was that the UN Refugee Agency was unable to pressure China into granting North Koreans asylum as a signatory member of the Refugee Convention. Explaining his organization's lack of influence, he underlined two points: (1) China is a permanent member of the UN Security Council and wields considerable power within the UN system; (2) if the UN presses too hard on this particular issue, China might prevent the UNHCR from accessing other vulnerable refugee populations on Chinese soil. The UNHCR needs China to open its doors for the organization to do its work there. Because the North Korean refugee issue is numerically not as significant, they were less of a priority compared to the larger scale of other forced migrants and displaced persons. Instead, the official stance of the UNHCR has been that North Koreans are "persons of concern."[14] Viewing the availability of protection from South Korea, which the UNHCR views as "a ready durable solution," it has adopted the position that "refugee status determination is not necessary for North Koreans."[15]

China is no doubt a dominant state within the refugee regime. It wields great power and influence within the UN body as one of the permanent members of the UN Security Council. Although the UNHCR considers North Koreans in China as "populations of concern," China has refused UNHCR access to its border areas with North Korea since 1999.[16] In the early 2000s, when many North Koreans attempted to force their way into foreign embassies in Beijing, thereby garnering attention from the international community, the Chinese government responded by "rounding up and sending hundreds of North Koreans who had previously lived illegally but relatively securely in China, some for several years."[17] But we need not look that far back. Many people participating in the "Save My Friend" campaign (chapter 4) hoped that the unprecedented pressure from the global media coverage and the humanitarian calls to action would force China to change its policy. But despite the loud outcry, the Chinese government forcibly repatriated the group of North Koreans that included Youngchul's sister Hyunmi.

China's repatriation of North Koreans illustrates the limitations of the UN Refugee Convention. Despite UNHCR's judgements on which populations require protection as refugees, the signatory member-states cannot be forced into compliance. Member-states have the power to decide which populations are deserving and undeserving of refugee status, and can contest and resist the UN Refugee Agency's own interpretations. In this regard, the Chinese government continues to argue that North Koreans' motivation is economic in nature, and has urged the international community to take the responsibility of providing food and resources to North Korea to address the root problems that lead to the outflow.

CONSTRUCTING DESERVINGNESS THROUGH VIOLENCE

Due to these debates over granting asylum to North Koreans, various humanitarian actors construct North Korean deservingness using a discourse of violence. In an attempt to give value to North Korean lives, the rhetoric frames them with scripts of oppression and establishes a state of unparalleled suffering by weaving together multiple temporalities, geographies, and contexts to produce a spectacle of the refugee body. Imaginations of North Korea exist in the realm of violence where time and space are collapsed into a single narrative of extraordinary evil. In this discursive formulation, there is only persecution, mass suffering, prison camps, and death, and for the fortunate few, sensational escape stories to "freedom." The perceived misery is of such great magnitude that it can only justify a compassionate response.

Take, for example, the following narrative by Francis Chan, an influential Korean American pastor in the United States. His harrowing depiction of a child's life in North Korea is intended to invoke compassion from the audience:

> Try to imagine what it would be like to be a kid where you're in a place where there's so little food that you and your family are just trying to find clumps of grass to throw in boiling water so that you just have something to fill your stomach. And then imagine as a kid [. . .] watching your parents starve to death or die of tuberculosis, and then you have no family system or any government help to keep you alive and you are on your own, just trying to scrounge, just trying to live, and so you try to escape.[18]

Although his description could be an accurate account of life in North Korea in the late 1990s when the country suffered through years of a destructive famine, he is two decades removed from that period. In Chan's narrative, time in North Korea is suspended and the country exists as an ahistorical place stuck in the peak of the famine.

Chan's depiction becomes even more intense and frightening as he paints a Hollywood-esque, action-packed portrayal of the children's escape from North Korea: "And these kids, man, they're climbing over mountains on their bare feet. They are crawling through jungles just to get out to some place where they can find food. Some of them are swimming across a freezing river—freezing cold river—while soldiers are shooting at them." His representation is like a violent nightmare. Unaccompanied children are being shot at as they run away from soldiers by "climbing over mountains" and "crawling through jungles." However, he does not make clear where these geographical terrains are—there are no jungles in North Korea—and whether it is the North Korean or Chinese soldiers firing their guns.

He continues, "And then once they finally make it to safety in Mongolia, or Vietnam or Cambodia, yet end up in a place where the people there don't want you. And you're there, you don't speak their language, you're not welcome there, and then many of these kids are sold into slavery or just thrown into the sex trade."[19] Chan's description of these paradigmatic children's fates is a distortion of reality and out of chronological sequence. While human trafficking for marriage (not sex) has been an issue many North Korean women have encountered while crossing the border from North Korea to China, this is rarely the case for children. Additionally, the majority of North Koreans who reach Mongolia, Vietnam, or Cambodia are not sold into slavery, as he claims. Instead, unlike China, not all of these countries forcibly repatriate them, and North Koreans usually turn themselves in as illegal border-crossers to seek asylum and eventual resettlement in South Korea. Chan collapses various geographies and contexts to produce a singular discourse of violence that reinforces the now well-established rendering of North Korea as an "axis of evil."

Similar to Chan, others construct North Korea as a place of inhumanity. In a talk at Google, the co-founder of Liberty in North Korea (LINK), an influential and savvy NGO based in the United States, refers to North Korea as a surreal world with brainwashed people, and likens the country to a film setting: "In North Korea [. . .] you have people that are born and raised in the system, and that know nothing else. [. . .] You're dealing with 23 million people that don't know what the real world is like, it's literally like unplugging from *The Matrix*."[20] He further states that "North Korea represents the worst of humanity" and that the country is a "staggering system entirely built and mastered for the express purpose of propagating human suffering and ensuring the continued exploitation of the people."[21] Delineating the leaders as sadistic and the country as populated by a wasteland of bodies, he describes North Korea as a place that is only capable of producing suffering. Human life is stripped of all qualities under necropolitical power and made expendable unto death.[22] This exceptional, omnipresent violence is seemingly the only valid description of the North Korean experience.

These narratives of violence define the North Korean experience in the imagination of non-North Koreans, their lives valued inasmuch as they suffer. Ever since I first embarked on this research, upon explaining the topic, one of the first things resettled North Koreans would say to me was: "let me tell you about my suffering" or "let me tell you about my experiences with human rights violations." They presumed that their stories of violence and suffering were what a researcher interested in North Korea would want to know. Rarely did they initially include in our conversations and interviews the positive memories of their lives—how they had fun as children or as adults, the kinds of food they enjoyed, their friendships, kinship relations, and so on—even though they had no trouble remembering and sharing these experiences with me when I inquired about them. In the words of a North Korean friend, "What value does *naengmyeon* (a popular North Korean noodle dish) have to research?"

This impulse is the result of the structural conditions that make North Koreans repeatedly recount their stories of violence and suffering.[23] When North Koreans arrive in South Korea, they undergo interrogation by the National Intelligence Service and must disavow the communist North before resettling. In addition, North Koreans become subjects of repeated surveys by government agencies and NGOs about their experiences of persecution. As a researcher affiliated with NKDB, I myself participated in some of these processes, visiting the Hanawon Resettlement Center to interview North Koreans about human rights violations. Once resettled, the telling and re-telling of suffering becomes a significant aspect of their lives in resettlement, and often reduces them to notions of oppression and victimhood. In addition to being constant subjects of research, they are asked to provide their testimonies in churches, at international conferences, and on television shows. At other times, they must be willing to provide answers in response to general South Korean curiosity about their lives in North Korea.

When resettled North Koreans are given voice, it is often through their engagement and identification with the discourse of violence.[24] Many

North Koreans in South Korea—some of whom have reached fame—have written memoirs and bestselling books, spoken at global forums such as the TED Conference, and testified in front of the US Congress. The narrative arc has idealized statements which indicate a structured sense of the "right way" to tell their testimonies. Lee Hyeonseo, the first North Korean to appear on the TED stage, unsurprisingly began her story of escape from North Korea with the theme of death:

> When I was seven years old, I saw my first public execution, but I thought my life in North Korea was normal. When I was walking past a train station, I saw something terrible that I can't erase from my memory. A lifeless woman was lying on the ground, while an emaciated child in her arms just stared helplessly at his mother's face. But nobody helped them, because they were so focused on taking care of themselves and their families.

Lee Hyeonseo's TED talk has over twenty million views on YouTube. Lee now frequently appears on television and goes on speaking tours. In the *Wall Street Journal,* she writes that North Korean "lives are spent inside a virtual prison, without knowing whether they will be subject to oppression, and without even knowing what human rights are."[25] What surprised me the most about Lee Hyeonseo was that her story became more sensational each time she gave a presentation about her experiences, culminating in her TED talk.

Another North Korean woman, Park Yeonmi, wore a traditional *hanbok* to speak at the One Young World Summit in Dublin in 2014. She held back tears in front of the hundreds in attendance while describing her country. "North Koreans are being terrorized today," she said, and North Korea is a place without love stories: "no books, no songs, no press, no movies about love stories—there is no Romeo and Juliet." She shared the horrors of everything she had witnessed, from the public execution of a neighbor as punishment for watching an American movie to watching her mother being raped, claiming, "my mother allowed herself to be raped to protect me." Furthermore, she tells her audience, North Korean teenage girls are "victimized and sometimes sold for as little as $200" in China. She provided voyeuristic details when she described her path to liberty in South Korea, walking across "the Gobi Desert following the compass, and when it stopped working, following the stars to freedom."[26]

Both Lee Hyeonseo and Park Yeonmi have published their accounts in books co-written with Western journalists. As Jay Song has shown, these Western co-writers have "played a significant part in shaping North Korean [. . .] narratives."[27] Respectively titled *Girl With Seven Names: Escape from North Korea*, and *In Order to Live: A North Korean Girl's Journey to Freedom*, these memoirs, and many others by resettled North Koreans, draw on the tropes of escape (from a violent North Korea) and freedom (in South Korea and the West).

There have been many concerns raised about the inconsistencies and exaggerations in some of the suffering narratives.[28] North Korean human rights activist movements experienced great embarrassment when Shin Dong-hyuk, known as "the poster boy for human rights atrocities in North Korea," recanted parts of his story of life in a North Korean prison camp.[29] Shin's memoir, *Escape from Camp 14: One Man's Remarkable Odyssey from North Korea to Freedom in the West*, was also co-written with an American journalist. Widely successful and translated into twenty-seven languages, the book had been prominently displayed in the bookstore of the Holocaust Museum in Washington, DC. The English-language version of his memoir recycled his previously published book in Korean, *Sesang bakkeuro naoda* (*Coming Out into the World*, published by NKDB). But the English version had many inconsistencies when compared to his earlier account.

I once shared my concerns about the tendency of many memoirs and testimonies to exaggerate the experiences of violence or to collapse multiple narratives into a singular story with a Korean political scientist. He did not share my concerns. He instead countered by posing a question to me: "Let's say we have a delicious Korean dish. Should we try to pick apart the ingredients that went in to make it tasty, or should we enjoy the final product?" As we will see in the following section, the "savory" discourse of violence also directly shapes US policy.

MANUFACTURED ORPHANS

"There is a bill in Congress right now that will allow North Korean refugee children to be adopted by Americans. Now we all know how dire and hopeless a situation it is in North Korea right now." These were the words of Sandra Oh, the award-winning Korean American actress with starring roles on *Grey's Anatomy,* the spy thriller *Killing Eve,* and *The Chair,* in a 2011 YouTube PSA (Public Service Announcement). She continued her bleak message while pictures of malnourished children accompany the footage. "And these children—these orphans—have escaped and are living in foreign lands alone and without family. And they need us. This bill will allow us to adopt them."[30]

The bill Oh was speaking of was backed by many in the Korean American community, human rights activists, the Han-Schneider International Children's Foundation, and Liberty in North Korea (LINK), which helped draft and campaign for the bill.[31] Congresswoman Illeana Ros-Lehtinen of Florida, Chair of the House Committee on Foreign Affairs, introduced HR 1464, The North Korean Refugee Adoption Act of 2011 to the US House of Representatives, with these words:

> We are all too keenly aware of the extreme repression, malnutrition, and the poverty suffered by so many inside North Korea today. Those threats often take the greatest toll on children. Imagine what happens when a child's natural protectors—parents—are no longer in the picture, and imagine what happens when that child is born or orphaned inside China where the child lacks legal status or dependable access to social services. Malnutrition, abuse, exploitation, lack of education: these are the horrors that are faced by orphans of North Korean origin who are effectively stateless and without protection.[32]

The bill claimed that "thousands of North Korean children do not have families and are threatened with starvation and disease if they remain in North Korea or as stateless refugees in surrounding countries."[33] As a solution, the bill tasked the US Secretary of State to "develop a comprehensive strategy for facilitating the adoption of North Korean children by United States citizens," and claimed that US citizens "would welcome the opportunity to adopt North Korean orphans living outside of North Korea as de jure or de facto stateless refugees."[34] The bill echoed the troubling history of transnational adoptions in relation to American hegemony and postcoloniality in Korea.[35]

Furthermore, the bill only provided vague geographic suggestions about where these orphans resided. If they were "in North Korea," "in surrounding countries," and/or "outside of North Korea," where would the orphanages be established to facilitate the transnational adoptions? How would such children be identified and how would the adoptions be implemented without becoming child trafficking? Moreover, the bill included in the category of orphan "children with Chinese fathers and North Korean mothers who are living in China."[36] By including children of mixed nationalities and using the mother's North Korean nationality to override the father's, the bill tried to legalize the adoption of children who were not "stateless," but Chinese citizens.[37] Ultimately, the figure of the North Korean refugee orphan became, as Christine Hong writes, "a placeholder for children who are, by and large, *not North Korean, not refugees,* and *not orphans.*"[38] The bill misused the label of orphan to describe primarily children who had living parents or were under the care of extended family members in China, and were by birth Chinese citizens.

South Korea categorizes children born in China to North Korean mothers and Chinese fathers as Chinese. Though these children can obtain South Korean citizenship via their mothers' nationality, they are excluded from South Korea's resettlement policy for North Koreans and do not receive the same benefits as others considered to be North Korean under South Korean law.[39] In contrast to the South Korean policy toward the children of North Korean women and Chinese men, however, human rights activists place emphasis on the mother's nationality to categorize the children as "stateless North Koreans."

To construct North Korean children's deservingness of US adoption, the proponents of the 2011 bill relied on the circulation of images of starving North Korean children from the 1990s. During this period of extreme famine and hunger, there were real North Korean orphans—like my friend Sun—who became parentless and began to wander around in search for food and resources. Many scavenged on farms and ate scraps of food on the grounds of black markets and train stations. Their wandering characteristic gained them the nickname *kkotjebi* in Korean, possibly calqued from Russian words—КОЧЕВЬЕ, КОЧЕВНИК, and КОЧЕВОЙ—to describe wanderers, nomads, and vagabonds. However, the orphans from that period were now adults. Most had resettled in South Korea or assimilated into Chinese society. While there may certainly be a number of North Korean children in China, the on-the-ground conditions in

North Korea and China have changed since the era of the famine. The children the bill tried to frame as deserving of adoption were no longer the young, skeletal children portrayed in the images circulated by humanitarian campaigns.

Despite some of the outdated premises upon which the bill was based and the legal complexities of the situation, it gained momentum and public support from sponsored messages by celebrities, backing from prominent Korean American churches, and campaigns by NGOs using a discourse of violence and images of suffering children that invoked compassion. Steven Yeun, a Korean American actor most famous for his role in the show *Walking Dead* and the film *Minari*, appealed for support by referencing "hundreds of thousands" of North Korean refugee orphans who are "displaced everywhere," and are "living and forging and scrounging around for themselves."[40] What is more absurd, Yeun said, is that "we aren't allowed to help them. We can't adopt North Korean refugee orphans."[41]

A particular narrative arc was used in mobilizing public support for the bill. The human rights campaigns collapsed and strung together themes of hunger, trafficking, slavery, and sex work into a single narrative to make it more compelling and appealing for humanitarian compassion. A petition was sent to representatives of each US state, claiming:

> Most North Korean children are not given the chance to be healthy and grow up in a stable home. They are often sent to prison camps and lack the nutrition needed to grow and develop at their age. [. . .] Many flee to China and neighboring countries, where they are still not safe, as most are sold into sex slavery and forced onto the streets as beggars. [. . .] These children do not receive the love, care, safety, and protection they need, and adoption by American families would provide that to them.[42]

Furthermore, in a promotional video by the Han-Schneider International Children's Foundation, a major supporter of this bill, the narrator explains that stateless North Korean children are "left to beg on the streets where these children's fates involve imprisonment, neglect, or human trafficking."[43] In silence, against a pitch-black background, words appear on the screen: "What if they were your children?" Horror hits us at home. These words soon fade away, and another question follows: "What if they could be your children?" These narratives helped raise support for the bill, ultimately leading to US President Barack Obama signing the revised version, The North Korean Child Welfare Act of 2012, into law. This final version tasked the US Secretary of State to "advocate for the best interest of these children, including, when possible, facilitating immediate protection for those living outside North Korea through family reunification or, if appropriate and eligible in individual cases, domestic or international adoption."[44]

COMPASSION CIRCUITS

These widespread humanitarian constructions of North Korean deservingness through the discourse of violence dichotomize those external to North Korea as the standard for human goodness, truth, and freedom, and those internal to North Korea as living without humanity, without truth, and without freedom. Famously declared an "axis of evil" by US President George W. Bush in his 2002 State of the Union Address, North Korea is defined in the negative.[45] "If illegible or impenetrable," Christine Hong writes, "it invites the imposition of phantastic meanings: carceral (prison, gulag, concentration camp), apocalyptic (hell on earth, place of darkness), [. . .] historical (antebellum slavery, the Third Reich), and quasi-scientific (black hole)."[46] Casting North Korea through imageries of darkness and cruelty, the humanitarian discourse of violence constructs a binary opposition, a type of positional superiority that evokes Orientalist imaginaries of "the East" defined in a series of negative oppositions to "the West" and also colonial representations of the African continent as the "Heart of Darkness."[47]

Representations of the inhumanity of North Korea are meant to provoke emotional responses, mobilize empathy, and elicit compassion. If the audience for these kinds of messages does not feel empathy, Robert Meister argues, it risks becoming a complicit bystander instead of a compassionate witness.[48] Addressing the two roles—bystander or witness—in which we observe and perceive the victims of violence, Meister warns of the power of compassion to turn bystanders and even potential beneficiaries of violence into falsely moralized witnesses. Thus, humanitarian campaigns for North Korean human rights become sites for what I call

Figure 8. The majority of North Korean territory is dark at night, illustrating the vast development differences with South Korea. Photo courtesy of Earth Science and Remote Sensing Unit, NASA Johnson Space Center.

compassion circuits, the construction and circulation of narratives and images of violence and suffering to tap into people's moral principles and thereby draw compassion.

The purpose of these representations of North Korean suffering is not only shock value, then, but also to powerfully invoke our emotions, sense of morality, and ethical responsibilities as human beings. The harrowing representations of violence and suffering via photographs, video footage, testimonies, and carefully constructed narratives powerfully elicit compassion, empathy, and pity, making people want to take action to remedy the misfortunes of precarious lives (often situated in faraway places).[49] Though human suffering is a constant and various forms of charity have a long history, the construction of narratives of violence and suffering to invoke compassion in the public sphere is relatively recent.[50] The central tenet of humanitarianism is that all human lives hold equal value, but Didier Fassin argues that it is inherently a "politics of life" because humanitarian actors cannot save all human lives; they must distinguish between the lives that most urgently need saving and the lives worth being risked.[51] These distinctions then reveal the inequality of human lives in reality, and these politics of life open space for politics of death involving the workings of sovereign power over biopolitical bodies.[52]

Although humanitarian action is compelled by the sacredness of human life, it is equally compelled by the voicing of human suffering. Humanitarianism is a politics of suffering as much as it is a politics of life. But what becomes of the lives in question—the lives that are framed through violence and suffering and thus produced into a public spectacle? Constructing North Korean deservingness creates a form of what Alain Badiou has termed "animal humanism," wherein people "only exist as worthy of pity."[53] Molding their North Korean subjects into a state of exception wherein they become included in politics only through their exceptional deservingness, humanitarian actors characterize them as bare, deprived of their political status and rights, and in need of restoration of their humanity. Stripped to this naked form where only their suffering accords their life with meaning and made into mere objects of pity and compassion, humanitarians can only grasp them as life reduced to the breathing of the physical body.[54] At the heart of these compassion circuits is human rights activists' steadfast refusal to let North Korean lives be subjugated to death and their goal to emancipate these lives from the cruelty of violence in North Korea.

These compassion circuits produce a spectacle of violence that render North Korean refugees as a strictly humanitarian, rather than political, issue. For all the focus on the harrowing images of suffering, the North Korean Refugee Adoption Act and its advocates failed to address the structural determinants of North Koreans' survival migration including the state of war, international sanctions, ecological degradations, and food insecurity. Economic sanctions, for instance, wage war by choking a regime's ability to feed its citizens, but in North Korea, they have had an unintended effect of increasing rural-to-urban inequality due to North Korea's redistribution of resources from the peripheries to the core.[55] While poverty and hunger were the main catalysts for the migratory flows into China, supporters of the adoption bill ironically opposed humanitarian aid to North Korea. For example, the Korean American Coalition (KAC), which was one of the main sponsors of the bill, opposed sending humanitarian aid to North Korea. It states prominently on its website that

"KAC will NOT be sending money/food/clothing or any other aid to North Korea. KAC wants to be very clear: KAC's mission is not to provide any support or assistance to North Korea, but rather to bring about greater awareness of the issues surrounding the North Korean people's continued struggles with famine."[56] There is absolutely no promise of assistance or aid. KAC's mission, then, is premised entirely on fostering an emotional and moral response from Americans. Through their depictions of tragedy and misery, humanitarian constructions of North Korean deservingness neglect the ongoing Korean War, and the structural and social inequalities in which North Koreans are embedded.

It is through these narratives of violence and suffering and in the name of humanitarianism that many NGOs deem their clandestine activities to be necessary. Breaking the rule of law and engaging in what China considers human trafficking, religious and humanitarian actors regularly attempt to rescue (that is, smuggle) North Koreans across international borders.[57] For example, calling the cross-border passage "the modern underground railroad"—comparing the situation to that of African American slaves—LINK advertises on its homepage that it has "garnered information about the escape routes through China and Southeast Asia and have established relationships with individuals who work in the 'modern underground railroad' who can help us move refugees safely across borders."[58] Focusing on human rights violations and repression, the US-based organization fundraises for its rescue operations to bring North Koreans to "freedom."

BEYOND NARRATIVES OF SUFFERING

Contentions around categorizing North Koreans who flee their country as migrants, defectors, or refugees is intimately connected to the politics of life and the politics of suffering in constructing North Korean deservingness. Various humanitarian actors construct deservingness through a discourse centered on violence and suffering, relegating North Korea to a place of inhumanity and defining North Koreans exclusively through a lens of misery. Hence, through the production, representation, and circulation of narratives and images, NGOs and human rights activists produce a spectacle of North Korean suffering because the visions of the miserable, wretched, and misfortunate North Koreans elicit emotions, evoke moral responsibilities and obligations, and summon compassion. This spectacle baits us with images of starving children, victims of sex trafficking, and brutally beaten bodies, painting a totalizing portrait of the North Korean experience. But North Koreans' complicity in the compassion circuits is in part an effort to create spaces of belonging in South Korea. With an increasing number of NGOs engaged in these compassion circuits, more North Koreans continue to immerse themselves in these discourses and activities. Their suffering, testimonies, and representations of life in North Korea become a source of income, cultural capital, and fame.

Discourses of violence and suffering influence both state and non-state interventions, for example, in the efforts to mobilize support for the North Korean Refugee Adoption Act. Collapsing together history and temporality with the themes of suffering, hunger, disease, and statelessness that distort and obscure the on-the-ground realities of North Korean children in China, the advocates of this bill proposed adoption by American families as a solution to the human rights crisis in North Korea. Despite legal and ethical complications (such as the strategic deployment of North Korean over Chinese nationality), humanitarian actors engaged in drawing upon moral sentiments and compassion in order to mobilize public support.[59]

Constructing North Korean deservingness through violence depoliticizes North Korea and North Koreans and instead frames the situation as a strictly humanitarian issue. Instead of mobilizing for justice, humanitarian actors mobilize compassion, and fail to address the root causes of the migration and the structural inequalities. Invoking moral sentiments has little impact on North Korea. North Korean hunger remains in place and humanitarian aid is not delivered. Meanwhile, international sanctions continue to strangle the country's economy. The discourse of violence that humanitarian actors produce strengthens the structural violence and the manifestations of inequalities across East Asia by obscuring the root causes of suffering. China's one-child policy and its long historical legacy of son-preference have led to an increase in its sex-ratio disparity, thereby influencing the migratory pattern of North Korean women. Obtaining *hukou* (Chinese household registration) remains an obstacle for many North Korean border-crossers and their children in China. However, the

US adoption of North Korean children was touted as a solution even though it treaded into murky waters by targeting the children of "one North Korean parent" who were Chinese citizens with actual families.

Beyond the invocation of affective dimensions of sympathy and compassion, what is the material impact of framing North Koreans through violence and suffering, those represented as victimized bodies? What is at stake when misery is aestheticized in this way? Whose interest do compassion politics really serve? Violence narratives produce the North Korean experience as a monolithic and a public spectacle in the hope of making them into objects of compassion. But North Koreans do not exist only in the form of dehumanized, pitiable life; they are also political and agentive lives, even in states of misfortune.

Conclusion

A CONTINUUM OF VIOLENCE IN A HOUSE DIVIDED

A house? A house? Let's see if we can put it down sharply. They're families. You can say that. They're families for a lot of children who don't have families.

Dorian Corey in *Paris Is Burning*

[The house is] the site from which to remember the constitutive violence of the home.

Chandan Reddy

GOHYANG—A PLACE OF ONE'S PAST

In October 2012, Sun moved from his tiny half-basement room to a one-bedroom apartment on the ninth floor. His sister had gotten married, and because she was now considered a separate household, Sun became eligible for his own government-subsidized apartment. He held a house-warming party to celebrate. I was the first to arrive. It was a warm autumn day and I was sweating from the fifteen-minute walk from the Junggye subway station. His apartment was tiny. The entryway led directly into a hallway kitchen, and further inside, two light-brown bookshelves on the back wall overwhelmed the small living room space. The twenty-four cubical shelves were stacked with books, neatly organized for the most part and filled to maximum capacity. On the opposite wall was a small desk with a laptop surrounded by more books, notebooks, and writing utensils. Though the building was over two decades old, his space had been refurbished with new white wallpaper and ivory-colored floor mats.

When Sun showed me the bedroom, his roommate was sitting at a desk, playing a video game on his laptop computer. This man, a hometown friend now resettled in South Korea, wanted to find a job in Seoul and needed a place to stay. A closet cabinet ran along the side of the room, making the room feel rather like a walk-in closet. There was no space for beds and I asked where they slept. The roommate replied, "Sometimes in here. Sometimes out there. He sleeps in the living room." But Sun could not stop smiling. "Isn't the apartment spacious?" he asked me. I was unsure if he was serious or if he was being optimistic. Sun was eager for his guests to arrive. When they finally began to trickle in, he greeted each guest by saying, "Look how spacious the place is!" One of his guests bluntly disagreed and teased him that he should earn more money for a larger apartment. "Oh, but it's a perfect fit for a small man like myself," Sun replied cheerfully.

Guests filled the apartment. Sun had told me that he was expecting seven or eight guests in total. By five in the afternoon there were nearly twenty people crammed into the living room and sitting on the floor. A delivery man arrived with Korean-style Chinese food and, from his metal container, he handed us black-bean noodles, spicy *jjamppong*, egg fried rice, dumplings, yellow-pickled radish, and sweet and sour pork. Not everyone in the room knew each other so we did a round of introductions. Sun began, "My name is Sun. I am from Musan, North Hamgyong Province."

In this book, I have used the metaphor of the "house" to comment on the North Korean experience in South Korea, inspired by Jennie Livingston's chronicle of the several Houses of the ball circuits in the documentary *Paris Is Burning*. For the subjects in the film who had been marginalized from their homes due to their gendered and sexual identities, Houses provided them alternative forms of inclusion and belonging, as the quote by Dorian Corey in the epigraph suggests. Additionally, Pepper Labeija, one of the central characters in the film, states, "They come from such sad backgrounds, you know. Broken homes or no home at all. And then the few that do have families and the family finds that they're gay, they ex them completely."[1] The ball circuit Houses came to serve a dialectical purpose in contrast to the violence experienced in the home—the expulsion from kinship circles and their physical dwellings. The house, as Chandan Reddy writes in the epigraph to this conclusion, becomes "the site from which to remember

Figure 9. Food at Sun's housewarming party. Photo: Joowon Park.

the constitutive violence of the home."[2] Similarly, in the Korean context, there is a yearning for a whole home that is no longer divided in two. The division of the Korean peninsula—believed to be in a temporary and liminal condition awaiting reunification—is a place from which we can reflect on the violence of citizenship and belonging.

In Korean, the English word "home" is translated as *gohyang*—a place of one's past. *Gohyang* can be one's birthplace, hometown, or ancestral village, but the significance of the word is its rootedness in a past place (*go*, meaning "past," and *hyang*, which literally means "village"). Home is not merely a geographic location, but one that includes a temporal dimension. The word carries the sentiments of affection (*jeong*) and longing (*geurium*), and though *gohyang* may be a place of positive memories, it can also be one of pain and loss.[3] Thus, *gohyang* is an existential place that combines the elements of space, time, and heart.[4] The Korean language has several words related to home, revealing the significance of the word to the Korean people: *ihyang* (departure from native place); *chulhyang* (departure from hometown); *silhyang* (displaced from home); *tahyang* (foreign land); *gwihyang* (homecoming); *nakhyang* (reluctant return to the countryside); *hyangsu* (nostalgia for home).

Gohyang is a place of the past, but it is also a place to which one is expected to return. This departure/return dichotomy is clearly illustrated in the Korean folk song *Arirang*, sung in both North and South Korea and registered on the UNESCO Intangible Cultural Heritage list.

Arirang, Arirang, Arariyo . . .
Arirang gogaero neomeoganda.
Nareul beorigo gasineun nimeun
Siprido mosgaseo balbyeongnanda.

Arirang, Arirang, Arariyo . . .
Crossing over the Arirang Pass.
The one who abandoned me
Shall not walk even 4 km before their feet hurt.

The national ballad is about a traveler departing one's home, and we can sense the sorrow and harsh resentment felt by the person left behind. While *gohyang* is a place of ancestral origin and social familiarity, the traveler leaves behind these known constants and departs for a place of unfamiliarity. The parting depicted is one of sharp bitterness, and it is suggested that this bitterness can be healed by returning home. Interestingly, when a person dies from old age, Koreans express this as *doragasinda*, which means not only departing from life but literally "to return." In other words, according to Korean scholar Choi Rae-ok, life on earth is metaphorically a traveler's road and the afterlife is the home to which one returns.[5]

North Koreans living in South Korea continue to long for their birthplace, their families, and the place of their childhoods. They may have established new lives in South Korea, but they continue to think of their *gohyang* as North Korea. If reunification was to occur, most resettled North Koreans consistently state that they would desire to return to North Korea. Even if North Korea was a place of suffering, it is also a place of longing and a place of affection. Though they lived under a violent regime, the North is their *gohyang*. Thus, it will require more time and generations for resettled North Koreans to be able to consider South Korea as their home.

When I asked a North Korean man who desires to return to North Korea upon reunification what he expects from South Koreans in the meantime, he responded by saying, "All that we ask is that people do not discriminate against us until we have fully adapted (to South Korea)." Upon resettlement, North Koreans must negotiate their dual identities as North and South Koreans. As one North Korean woman said to me when I inquired into the issue of identity, "I hate those surveys asking me whether I identify as North Korean or South Korean." Laughing at herself, she continued, "People ask me questions about North Korea. I don't know the answers. When people ask me about South Korea, I still don't know the answers. I get confused as to who I am!" Another North Korean woman likened her resettlement experience to belonging to two parents. "If North Korea and South Korea were like a mother and a father, then we are children born between them. They are both our parents. We belong to both Koreas."

Yet, for North and South Koreans, the hope for an eventual reunion of the Korean peninsula is based on a longing for a past that once was, but can never be the same again. It is a romanticized and deceptive yearning for a home that may never be complete or whole. In a study of the *yang-gongju* (literally "Western princesses"), Grace Cho examines the lives of South Korean women who worked as sex workers near American military bases following the Korean War. More than 100,000 Korean women married American GIs and moved to the United States. But, as Cho argues, these women and their families are haunted by their past (what she calls transgenerational haunting), the memories and the silence these women carry with them. For them, she writes, "home and homeland are endlessly fractured."[6] Similarly, resettled North Koreans dwell in a state of displacement, and their notion of *gohyang* is fractured. Their search for *gohyang* is an aching for a distant place one cannot travel to, the nostalgic memory of the past, and a yearning for belonging in a house divided.

VIOLENCE AND ITS INCOMMUNICABILITY

Belonging in a House Divided has been an ethnographic study of the ongoing violence in the lives of North Koreans resettled in South Korea, and its impact on their experiences of citizenship and belonging, drawing attention to not only overt forms of violence but also those that are less visible. A monolithic discourse of violence in North Korea hinders a more nuanced understanding of the experiences of North Koreans' resettlement in South Korea. North Korea is depicted with the thick brush of all-encompassing violence, while South Korea is characterized as a land of freedom. North Korea is represented as evil and South Korea is applauded as a place of human goodness. In these narratives, those external to North Korea are the saviors while those internal are the saved. Unable to comprehend why there is no revolution in North Korea, people often think of North Koreans as living with a false consciousness, indoctrinated and duped into living in their repressive country.

However, citizenship for resettled North Koreans—becoming South Korean through self-making—entails violent processes. The legacies of national division and the unresolved war continue to affect individuals in the form of separated families, espionage activities, and spy discourses. The gendered migration and its relationship to China's one-child policy has produced networks of human trafficking but also the extension of that violence into new forms of sexualization and stigmatization in South Korea. Furthermore, postwar Koreanness ethnicizes North Korean bodies, and symbolic violence operates through socioeconomic competitiveness attached to body aesthetics. For example, as I have shown, the structural violence of hunger and malnutrition in North Korea translates into the violence of phenotypical normalization in South Korea. And while transnational connections established through remittances reconnect families, they also generate material hardships that lead to economic and emotional burdens, familial obligations, and guilt.

Violence on the Korean peninsula transcends time and space, and the rhetoric of healing, recovery, and reconciliation is problematic, for violence is often productive and reproductive, non-linear and transformative. Violence transcends the boundaries of brute force. To fully grasp how violence operates in the lives of North Koreans, it is necessary to go beyond the human rights rhetoric that solely focuses on the physical violence of prison camps, torture, and death. Instead, we must draw connections between the physical and symbolic, between the visible and invisible, intentional and unintentional, and legitimate and illegitimate forms of violence. We must recognize that violence spills over into and overlaps with other categories of violence. It is often in the routinized sociopolitical space of the everyday where these forms of violence exist for resettled North Koreans.

The Korean language operates to enforce the continuum of violence by the word's incommunicability, its failure to communicate the weight of violence. The Korean word for violence focuses on the power of brute force. *Pokryeok* is often used to describe the use of visible force to dominate or repress, resulting in wild unruliness, wreckage, and rampage. Though the character *pok* translates as fierceness or roughness, it also holds another meaning: "to reveal or show" (*deureonada*). Not only is *pokryeok* fierce power, but it is the *visibility* of that power. The meaning of visibility in the root character *pok* is clearly illustrated in the Korean word *pokro* (to expose). With Koreans linguistically unable to grasp and communicate invisible and nonphysical forms of violence, the continuum of violence is enforced and reproduced outside of what is considered to be legitimate or normative.

On July 31, 2019, a forty-two-year-old North Korean woman named Han Sungok was found dead with her six-year-old son Dongjin in a one-bedroom apartment in the Bongcheon neighborhood of Seoul. The neighbors reported a fetid smell like compost coming from Han's apartment. The police arrived to discover that the mother and son had already been dead for two months. No one had noticed that they were missing. Their bodies had decomposed, and had it not been for the foul smell, their deaths might have gone undiscovered for even longer.

Han had resettled in South Korea alone in 2009, arriving via China and Thailand. She had been a cross-border merchant in the Chinese-North Korean borderlands prior to marrying her Chinese husband, an ethnic Korean. She initially seemed to adjust well to her new life in South Korea. She completed various incentivized trainings (including getting a driver's license and obtaining cooking class certifications) and got off welfare within just nine months. Her Chinese husband joined her in 2012 and found work in a South Korean shipyard. Their son Dongjin was born in 2013, and they soon discovered he had epilepsy. When her husband lost his job in 2017, they moved back to China, but within a year, they divorced and she returned to South Korea with her son.

Han Sungok lived with poverty and stigma (as a single mom and as a North Korean), and faced ostracism and indifference in Seoul. It is likely she felt hopeless about their future in South Korea. She had no income except for the $100 per month she received for child support from the government. She had failed to pay rent for over a year. And in May, just before their deaths, Han withdrew the remaining ₩3,858 KRW, or approximately $3 USD, from her bank account. When the police investigated her apartment, there was no food in the refrigerator except a bit of red pepper powder. An empty bottle of soy sauce lay on the ground. Toys were scattered around the apartment and the walls were decorated by Dongjin's doodling. There was no evidence of murder or suicide. Although the investigators could not determine the exact cause of their death due to the severity of their bodily decomposition, they said Han Sungok and her son had most likely starved to death. This was an irony, since she had left North Korea to escape famine and poverty.

Although my North Korean friends did not personally know Han Sungok or her son, they grieved their deaths. They told me they could relate to the woman's hardships in South Korea. They wondered, how could Han and her son have struggled for so long without anyone noticing that something was wrong? Why did she not reach out to the local district office? Why did she not report her son's epilepsy for disability support? The woman and her son were invisible to their neighbors and the welfare system that supports resettled North Koreans, and she was unable to communicate or express the accumulative and overlapping experiences of violence in her everyday life.

ENDLESSNESS OF WAR

Fifteen minutes before my last scheduled night watch from 02:00–04:00, a private whispered in my ear to wake me up; the unspoken rule in our battalion was that one could not touch the body of a higher-ranked soldier, even to wake them. I got up immediately, unlike the other mundane times in the past two years when interrupted sleep was met with groans and sighs. I swiftly changed into my uniform and laced my boots in the pitch dark while the nine other infantrymen slept through the sound of my squeaking locker door and the rustling of my uniform. At 02:00, my partner and I reported for duty and relieved the previous shift. But instead of passing time in silence for the next two hours of night watch, us soldiers on duty reminisced about our experiences of military conscription in anticipation of my discharge.

At 06:30, military war songs blared from the barracks' central speakers and soon the entire battalion assembled on the grassless field for roll call in perfect formation. Breathing in the humid air on this June morning, we sang the national anthem. This was followed by the routine military gymnastic exercises, a five-second battle cry directed toward the war's frontline, and a 3-km jog around our base. After chores and breakfast, at 08:30 my peers and I gathered in our commander's office to report for discharge. As was the traditional ritual at our battalion, soldiers lined up on the sidewalks to congratulate us, the discharged soldiers. We passed down the line to say our goodbyes with handshakes and embraces, and we offered words of encouragement to the junior soldiers: "*Jogeumman deo chama*" ("hold on a little longer"). Though the military clock felt sluggish, time does pass and conscription did indeed end. As the famous Korean saying goes, "*Gukbangbu sigyeneun geokkuro maedarado doraganda*" ("the military clock moves, even upside down"). Yet, as a group of us finished our mandatory military service—at our base but also concurrently at other military bases across the country— newly conscripted soldiers would replace us and the cycle would continue. Each month, eligible South Korean men line up for their physicals, shave their heads, and go through the rituals of becoming a soldier.

The "hot" phase of the Korean War concluded in a cease-fire, with the Armistice Agreement signed between the representatives of the UN Command, China, and North Korea in 1953. However, the war itself has assumed an endlessness through the continued militarization of the DMZ (arguably the world's most militarized border), the ongoing stationing of US troops in South Korea, and North Korea's relentless drive towards nuclearization.[7] Christine Hong likens this unfinished war to a "protean structure, at once generative and destructive."[8] Though the Korean War is often referred to as the "forgotten war" in the United States, it is a part of the Korean habitus, cognitively embedded in schooling, commemoration, military conscription, and the division system that maintains the "peace."[9] The boundary between wartime and peacetime is thus blurred on the Korean peninsula.

If the nature of the North Korean state system is to blame for the migration of North Koreans and their experiences with violence, we must also consider the larger historical context of this unresolved war. North Korea's criminalization of unauthorized exits from its country is itself a form of historical and structural violence rooted in a constant and prolonged state of emergency. For the North Korean regime, repressive policies and nuclear proliferation are necessary under the current state of war. The North Korean laws against what they call "counterrevolutionary activities" should be seen in light of the Korean War's endlessness. In historical context, North Korea is not unique in this regard. Its policies share similarities to the socialist regimes' practice of *Republikflucht*, "frequently used during the Cold War vis-à-vis persons who fled communist regimes, [who] as a result could be severely penalized, if returned, by the internal laws of their country."[10]

And while North Korea punishes those who leave its territory without government approval, South Korea also criminalizes its citizens who visit North Korea without authorization. South Korea's National Security Act Article 6 states,

> Any person who has [. . .] escaped to an area under the control of an anti-government organization [that is, North Korea], with the knowledge of the fact that it may endanger the existence and security of the State or democratic fundamental order, shall be punished by imprisonment for not more than ten years.[11]

The travel prohibition and punishment are necessary, the South Korean government claims, because the two Koreas are still at war. Hence, North Korea's hostile policies should be seen in context as part of the state of emergency that has been established on both sides of the DMZ amid the unending Korean War.

A few years after my discharge from the military, I revisited the DMZ in 2019. There are visible and vivid reminders of ongoing war on the short trip from Seoul to the Joint Security Area, where the Armistice Agreement was signed and the only point within the DMZ where soldiers from North and South Korea directly face one another. On the way, there are barbed-wire fences and guard posts lining the Han River. Anti-tank structures are erected over transportation corridors of roadways and railways. In some areas, rows of "dragon teeth" run through waterways, concrete barricade pillars intended to obstruct the passage of North Korean tanks. Other anti-tank structures resemble highway overpasses, though there are no roads connected on either end. The advertisements on their facades give the impression of an ordinary billboard. These structures are designed to be exploded in the event of a North Korean invasion, with the concrete rubble intended to block the roads to slow down the enemy. During the Korean War, South Korea was defenseless against North Korean tanks, and these defensive structures were built in anticipation of an active re-engagement in war.

We approached the Civilian Control Line (CCL) and South Korean soldiers boarded our bus and checked our identifications. As the name suggests, the CCL restricts the entrance of civilians into the militarized area of the DMZ without authorization. A small number of residents do live in areas north of the CCL, and they are exempt from taxes and mandatory military service as compensation for living in this danger zone. Further into the frontier we frequently came across signs warning about land-mines and our bus travelled through several passageways that had large camouflaged cement blocks lining the side-walls. Similar to the overpass structures on highways, these concrete blocks were designed as "speed bumps." We finally arrived at Camp Bonifas (the UN military base within the DMZ) where we met the American soldiers who would escort us to the Joint Security Area. The UN base and the US soldiers are a bizarre reminder that the endlessness of the war extends far beyond inter-Korean relations, involving and encompassing foreign powers.

The militarization of the Korean landscape, however, goes beyond the restricted space of the DMZ. Military readiness—or the idea of "defensive space"—is embedded in the city planning and architectural structures of South Korea. Ilsan, a city neighboring Seoul to the north and just 25 km from the DMZ, was explicitly designed to be used as a military fortress in case of a North Korean invasion. As revealed in the 1990 memorandum of agreement between the Army Chief of Staff and the Korea Land Development Corporation, at least 60 percent of the apartment buildings

Figure 10. A landmine sign in the DMZ. Photo: Joowon Park.

Figure 11. In the Joint Security Area of the DMZ, a South Korean soldier guards the Military Demarcation Line (MDL) while an American soldier escorts the author. The MDL dividing the two Koreas splits through the buildings and is marked by visible terrestrial difference behind the Korean soldier. Photo: Joowon Park.

were arranged horizontally.[12] The north-to-south roads were made narrow while the east-to-west roads were widened. Public parks, athletic fields, and even children's playgrounds were designed to be used as military strong-holds. Similarly, many of Seoul's northern neighborhoods were designed with these tactics as the city expanded and built much-needed living spaces in the form of high-rise apartments during the 1980s.[13] Satellite photos of the region show a complex grid of horizontally positioned apartment com-plexes that essentially become fortifying structures within the valley leading to Seoul. In South Korea, these apartment complexes have often been called *apateu-geuradeu* (apartment+grad), referencing the Battle of Stalingrad and stressing the defensive function of the cities' designs.[14]

The use of apartment buildings as defensive space has its origins in the years following the Korean War. High-rise structures provided strategic defense mechanisms for a country traumatized and ravaged by an unre-solved war. The South Korean slogan at the time, introduced by the authoritarian leader Park Chung-hee in 1968, was to "construct while fighting" (*ssaumyeo geonseolhaja*). That year, North Korea had sent a commando unit to assassinate Park, and though they successfully infil-trated South Korea and got within 800 meters of the presidential Blue House, they ultimately failed. However, this event and other North-South hostilities left South Koreans apprehensive over the continued threat from North Korea. Following the assassination attempt Park gave a speech to the nation:

> The task before us now is to immediately modernize the country and to accumulate power to fight communism. [. . .] This means to construct while fighting and to fight while constructing. We must fully prepare to defeat the invaders anytime and anywhere while not delaying the work of construction in the slightest. This is the path to success.[15]

To "construct while fighting" meant that the development of Seoul would be inextricably tied to the concept of defensive space.

For example, the Bugak Skyway on top of the Bugak Mountain was built as a tourist attraction, but also for the purpose of increasing the secu-rity of the presidential Blue House located directly below it. The thou-sands of rectangular-shaped flowerpots positioned in Gwanghwamun Square and throughout the city served aesthetic purposes, but were also placed to be used as defensive barricades for soldiers. The Namsan Tunnel, while providing an important thruway under the mountain in central Seoul, could shelter 400,000 people during an emergency. The ubiquitous half-basements, central to the plot in the multiple award-winning South Korean film *Parasite,* have their origins in government plans to use basements as military entrenchments.[16] The apartment buildings in the wealthy neighborhood of Gangnam's Apgujeong, built in the 1970s and 80s, not only strategically faced the Han River in horizontal rows, but were built with rectangular crenels for assault rifles and machine guns, still visible today.

There are other examples of structures that relied on the designs of defensive space. If you take Subway Line 3 to Hongje Station on the northwestern outskirts of Seoul, there is a 200-meter-wide apartment building called *Yujin Maensyeon.* This civilian residence was built with ground-floor piers featuring spaces between the pillars for tanks. Similarly, on the opposite side of Seoul, in the northeast, buildings stretching horizontally in Dobong-gu use the same piloti design, again with the ground floor for tanks. It has now been transformed into the *Pyeonghwamunhwajinji* (Peace-Culture Bunker), a tourist attraction. Both the *Yujin Maensyeon* and *Pyeonghwamunhwajinji* were originally built in the 1970s as Seoul's first line of defense. Because the Bukhan Mountain protects Seoul directly to the north, the northwest and the northeast were considered the areas through which the North Koreans would invade.

Because of the Protection of Military Bases and Installations Act, city planning and construction occurring in areas categorized as "protection zones" must be cleared by the Ministry of National Defense. Roads are built to withstand heavy military vehicles and tanks, and sections of highways are designed to turn into auxiliary airstrips. Civil-defense drills are held each year as emergency preparedness for an imminent attack by North Korea. Furthermore, unknown to even the majority of South Koreans, the tops of high-rise buildings throughout Seoul are purposely left empty for military purposes. Soldiers are secretly stationed on the roofs and top floors of apartment buildings and commercial high-rises, and equipped with Vulcan rotary cannons to protect the air space. Though the exact locations of the bases are a top military secret, the South Korean Army revealed that the 1st Air Defense Brigade had used the top of famous

Figure 12. Colorful ribbons attached to a fence in the DMZ carry messages of hope, peace, and reunification. Photo: Joowon Park.

skyscrapers, the 63 Building and the IFC Tower, as military fortresses. As these examples illustrate, Seoul continues to be a militarized city in the present.

"How's your habitus?" my mentor asked me when I returned to Washington, DC upon my discharge from the army. Though she said this with a smile on her face, it was a serious question and one for which I struggled to formulate a response. The several years I spent in the South Korean military was another layer of the accumulative experiences that I internalized and embodied, ingraining within me certain militarized dispositions that continue to structure the way I think, perceive, and act. Likewise, post-Korean War notions of North Koreanness and South Koreanness are products of the endlessness of war and militarization on the Korean peninsula. North and South Koreans today embody a continuum of violence left unresolved, one that is both enduring and reproductive. It is with this recognition that we should move forward with vigilance, not for the sole aim of reconciliation, healing or closure, but to create spaces of belonging in a house divided.

Acknowledgments

I would like to express my gratitude to all the people whose stories are told in these pages. They allowed me in their homes and shared their lives and experiences with me. I regret I cannot thank everyone by name, as I have used pseudonyms to protect their privacy.

I first embarked on this project as a doctoral student at American University. I owe thanks to my advisor Adrienne Pine for her invaluable mentorship, instruction, and guidance from the very beginning of graduate school. David Vine and Eleana Kim offered critical feedback as committee members and I am appreciative of their advice. I am also fortunate to have received tremendous intellectual solidarity and support from numerous colleagues over the years: Hope Bastian, Jennifer Grubbs, Nell Haynes, Dolores Koenig, Nikki Lane, William Leap, Siobhán McGuirk, Erin Moriarty Harrelson, Sabiyha Prince, Ashanté Reese, Joeva Rock, Ted Samuel, Daniel Sayers, Ayako Takamori, Matthew Thomann, Rachel Watkins, and Brett Williams, among many others.

Many institutions generously provided research support for my work on this project: The National Science Foundation (Award #1324090), the Wenner-Gren Foundation for Anthropological Research, the Explorers Club Washington Group, the Association for Asian Studies Northeast Asia Council Research Travel Grant, the Robyn Rafferty Mathias Grant for International Research, the American University Vice-Provost Doctoral Dissertation Research Award, and the Skidmore College Faculty Development Grant. I also want to thank the Database for North Korean Human Rights for offering an institutional base in South Korea during the early stages of this research, and especially to thank its Chief Director, Dr. Yoon Yeo Sang, and Senior Director of Operations, Lim Soon Hee.

I am fortunate to work with wonderful colleagues in the Department of Anthropology at Skidmore College. Thank you to everyone in the Department—faculty, staff, and students—for the vibrant community and making Skidmore a new home to me. I am also grateful to several former students who provided research assistance on this project: Sean Boehme, Xiyu Erik Cai, Christian Saralegui, and Sophia Rubien.

At the University of California Press, I would like to thank Kate Marshall, Enrique Ochoa-Kaup, and Emily Park for their editorial guidance. Kate, thank you for your enthusiastic support for this book from its very inception. I would also like to thank Catherine Osborne and Victoria Baker. Furthermore, my appreciation goes to Grace Cho, who graciously identified herself as one of the reviewers of the manuscript, as well as to the other two anonymous reviewers whose thoughtful critiques and suggestions have been constructive.

Parts of this book were presented at conferences, invited talks, and workshops at various institutions, and I benefited from the feedback offered by these audiences. I am especially grateful for the invitations from the Truman Research Institute at the Hebrew University of Jerusalem, the Hong Kong Institute for the Humanities and Social Sciences at the University of Hong Kong, Stanford University's Walter H. Shorenstein Asia-Pacific Research Center, and the Social Science Research Council Korean Studies Dissertation Workshop to present earlier iterations of the various chapters from this book project.

An earlier version of chapter 1 was previously published in 2020 as "Voices of War's Legacies: Reconciliation and Violence in Inter-Korean Family Reunions" (*Anthropology and Humanism* 45, no. 1: 25–42). Some of the exploration of issues in chapters 2 and 3 was previously published in 2016 as "The Gendered Contours of North Korean Migration: Sexualized Bodies and the Violence of Phenotypical Normalization in South Korea" (*Asian Ethnicities* 17, no. 2: 214–27). However, these two chapters have been fully rewritten and revised from this original publication. I am grateful to Taylor & Francis Ltd (http://www.tandfonline.com) and John Wiley and Sons for permission to use these materials.

My family is a constant source of love, energy, and support, and I am always enormously grateful to them: my wife Eunmi Grace, my children Davitt and Roey, my brother Jooyoung, and my parents. This book is dedicated to my parents, who have nurtured and supported me for many years.

Notes

INTRODUCTION

The epigraph is often attributed to Abraham Lincoln, but it originates in the Bible: "If a house is divided against itself, that house cannot stand" (Mark 3:25, NIV).

1. See Cumings 2005, 187, and Oberdorfer 2001, 6. The two officers' names were Lieutenant Colonels Dean Rusk and Charles Bonesteel. Rusk would later become the US secretary of state and Bonesteel a US military commander in South Korea.

2. The length of compulsory military service in South Korea ranges from eighteen months to three years depending on the branch of the military (Army, Navy, Air Force, or Marines). Over the last few decades, the South Korean government has generally reduced the length of mandatory service. In North Korea, military service is ten years and is required of all men, and in some cases, women too.

3. Sociologist Seungsook Moon (2005) writes that South Korea took a path toward a "militarized modernity" beginning in the early 1960s, mobilizing various forms of gendered citizenship.

4. My military conscription was not related to the purpose of conducting research for this book. As I stated earlier, I have lived outside of South Korea since the age of eight. For those holding onto South Korean citizenship, South Korea allows for the postponement of military service for varying circumstances such as living, studying, or working overseas. If a draft notice is issued, however,

155

evading conscription can have severe consequences, such as imprisonment or barred entry to the country. Steve Yoo (Yoo Seung-jun), once a famous pop star in South Korea in the 1990s, obtained US citizenship and evaded military service despite having received his physical examination and draft notice. The South Korean government, in response, banned him indefinitely from entering the country, and has repeatedly denied his visa requests to visit the country.

5. Woo-Cumings 2002; Yoo 2020.

6. The North Korean regime acknowledged that roughly 200,000 North Koreans crossed over to China at the peak of the famine (Crossette 1999). Other sources cite estimations up to 300,000 North Koreans in China during that time (Choo 2006; Chung 2009; Crossette 1999; Tanaka 2008).

7. Kwon and Chung 2012, 168.

8. For a discussion on the materiality of landmines in the DMZ, see Eleana Kim 2016. In highlighting the nonhuman agencies of the explosives, she brings attention to the shared ecology and cohabitation between the mines and borderland residents.

9. In the processes of decolonization and nation-building, North Korea created a hereditary class system called *seongbun* that divided its citizens into three groups—the core, wavering, and hostile classes. Those in the hostile class (such as descendants of landlords, Japanese collaborators, and Christians) were relocated to the peripheral regions, where they worked as miners and farmers. This class system today continues to determine one's status, opportunities, and responsibilities.

10. Sung Kyung Kim 2016; NKIDP 2012; H. Park 2015. Sung Kyung Kim writes that the Chinese-North Korean borderland had "frequent linkages denoting a regional and cultural sense of kinship specific to the borderland than cultural ties with the state to which it belongs" (2016, 118).

11. Bell and Fattig 2014; Charny 2005.

12. Constitution of the Republic of Korea 1987, 2, emphasis added.

13. Han 2013; J. Jung 2011; Jiyoung Song 2015.

14. Chung 2014; Joowon Park 2012.

15. The amount of resettlement money North Koreans receive usually depends on the size of the household and other conditions. In 2019, North Koreans received ₩16–23 million KRW ($15,000-$20,000 USD) for housing support as well as ₩8–39 million KRW ($7,000-$35,500 USD) as resettlement money. The amount offered has significantly decreased over the years. This is both a humanitarian and political gesture, a legacy of the Cold War conflict between the two Koreas (see Chung 2014, 337). North Korean defectors were a validation of the "superiority" of South Korea, capitalism, and liberal democracy.

16. See Bell 2013; E. Cho 2018; Choo 2006; Chung 2009; J. Jung 2016; Lankov 2006; Joowon Park 2016; Sands 2019.

17. The fear of difference in South Korea, or the desire for homogeneity, has a deep political history. In particular, the belief in ethnic homogeneity led to normative expressions of (South) Koreanness, suppression of deviance, strict enforcement over people's bodies and fashion, and even the discrimination and marginalization of "impure" *hyonhol* (mixed-blood) Koreans who were offspring of American soldiers stationed in South Korea. John Lie writes that "deviance and marginality became matters of private and public opprobrium" (2014, 11).

18. Chung 2014, 338.

19. Jin-Heon Jung (2011, 2015, 2016) has vividly captured the active role of Protestant churches helping North Koreans resettle to South Korea as part of their evangelical mission.

20. An et al. 2018; Jin Kang Kim 2019. For a discussion on the impact of social networks on suicidality of North Korean women living in South Korea, see Um et al. (2020, 2021).

21. South Korea's rate is 24.6 suicides per 100,000 persons, the highest suicide rate among OECD countries. For comparison, the United States falls in 9th place with 13.9 suicides per 100,000 persons (OECD 2018).

22. Yonhap 2018.

23. Bauböck 1994; Brubaker 1992; Hammar 1990; Kymlicka 1998; Rosaldo 1994; Soysal 1994; Young 1989.

24. Kymlicka 1998. This emphasis on cultural diversity and social pluralism in what constitutes citizenship was rooted in Thomas Marshall's thesis that the concept of citizenship must include not only civil and political rights, but also *social* rights. For Marshall (1950), the focus on these dimensions of citizen rights was a crucial process of democratization. Kymlicka argues for the addition of a fourth, *cultural* dimension to Marshall's framework of citizenship based on civil, political, and social rights.

25. Rosaldo 1994, 402.

26. Anzaldúa 1987; Blanc, Basch, and Schiller 1995; Brettell 2007; Glick Schiller, Basch, and Blanc 1995; Kanna 2010; Pandolfo 2007; Tambiah 2000.

27. Gordon and Stack 2007; Sassen 1996.

28. Soysal 1994.

29. Ong 1999, 2005, 2006.

30. Baghdasaryan 2011; Das 2011; Parla 2011; Rosaldo 2003; Shindo 2009.

31. See respectively, Baghdasaryan 2011; Shindo 2009; Das 2011.

32. For example, Deborah Thomas argues that citizenship is more than a set of rights, but rather is a "set of performances and practices directed at various state and non-state institutions or extraterritorial or extralegal networks" (2011, 6)

33. See, for example, Agamben 1998; Arendt 1958; Betts and Loescher 2011; Fassin 2011.

34. I draw from Aihwa Ong's suggestion that citizenship involves a dual process of "self-making and being-made in relation to nation-states and transnational processes" (1996, 737). Ong utilizes the Foucauldian notion of biopolitics to focus on the processes of subjectification through both the state and civil institutions. Ong's definition of cultural citizenship, focusing on biopolitical statecraft and subjectification, diverges from Renato Rosaldo's (1994) usage of the concept as a right to cultural difference.

35. "National order": Malkki 1995b. For refugees symbolizing a failure of citizenship see Agamben 1995; Arendt 1958; Betts and Loescher 2011; Haddad 2008; Nyers 1999.

36. Malkki 1992, 33.

37. Nyers 1999; Malkki 1992, 1995b.

38. Brysk and Shafir 2004; Malkki 1995b; Nyers 2006.

39. See Ahn 2005; Haggard and Nolan 2011.

40. Amnesty International 2011; Human Rights Watch 2012.

41. Charny 2005; Eunyoung Kim et al. 2009; Kurlantzick and Mason 2006.

42. Scheper-Hughes and Bourgois 2004.

43. Farmer 1997; Galtung 1969.

44. Farmer 1997, 263.

45. Bourdieu 2001; Bourdieu and Wacquant 1992.

46. Pine 2008, 23.

47. Scheper-Hughes 1993.

48. Scholars studying refugee resettlement in the United States have shown that experiences of violence and displacement persist throughout resettlement and are even a continuance of unresolved pasts. See Besteman 2016; Fadlalla 2019; Ong 2003; Tang 2015.

49. Scheper-Hughes and Bourgois 2004, 27.

50. Chan and Schloenhardt 2007; Charny 2005; Fahy 2011; Haggard and Nolan 2007, 2011; E. Lee 2000, 2004; Lee and Kim 2011; Sung 2019.

51. The framework of trauma is highly developed in South Korean public culture and politics. See Choi et al. 2011; Chung and Seo 2007; W. Jeon et al. 2008; B. Jeon et al. 2009; Hyo Hyun Kim et al. 2011; Min 2008; B. Song et al. 2011. In Korean diaspora studies, see Grace Cho's work on "haunting" in the Korean American diaspora (2008).

52. Some have offered critiques of this focus on securitization, as these analyses often portray North Koreans as "incompetent citizens" needing to learn to become a modern subject (Ryang 2009; Sung 2010). Becoming "modern" is deemed important because resettled North Koreans are often viewed in South Korea as a testcase for the future reunification of the two Korean states. See Bleiker 2004; Chung, Jeon, and Chung 2006; Chung 2009; W. Jeon 2007; I. Yoon 2009.

53. See Chung 2009; Lankov 2006; Son 2016. Lankov argues that the government started to quietly discourage defection, for example, through reducing

resettlement benefits. Sarah Son expands on Lankov's argument, and explains these policy changes to competing, collective identity frames used in South Korea to regard North Koreans.

54. Rogers Brubaker and Frederick Cooper suggest the use of "identification," a term that gives agency to the persons doing the identifying and to focus on the processes rather than the condition. They write, "As a processual, active term, derived from a verb, 'identification' lacks the reifying connotations of 'identity.' It invites us to specify the agents that do the identifying. [. . .] 'Identification' calls attention to complex (and often ambivalent) *processes*, while the term 'identity,' designating a *condition* rather than a *process*, implies too easy a fit between the individual and the social" (2000, 14–17).

55. David Rosenhan's classic research on the effects of psychodiagnostic labels, "On Being Sane in Insane Places" (1973) provides insight into the dangers of labeling. In this study, eight pseudopatients were admitted to psychiatric hospitals and diagnosed with schizophrenia. Once categorized and labeled, the pseudopatients were stuck with it and could not get unlabeled. They could not free themselves from that tag. Even worse, the schizophrenic label began to influence other people's perceptions of the patients and their associated behaviors. The label continued to follow the pseudopatients upon their discharge from the hospital.

56. Feldman 2007; Valentine 2004. David Valentine argues that we should use categories as "tools" to understand the multitude of our experiences (217).

57. Reddy 1998, 357.

58. Turner 1969, 95.

59. Sociologist Gi-Wook Shin claims, "Korea is the only place in which the ethnic homogeneity (real or perceived) remains broken into two political entities" (2006, 19). In recent years scholars have challenged the notion of ethnic homogeneity and the oneness of North and South Koreans, and have called for an analysis of a multicultural Korea (Nora Hui-Jung Kim 2012; Lie 2014; Y. Park 2020). North Koreans have been entering South Korea for two decades, coinciding with the South Korean state projects of globalization and multiculturalism. However, the multicultural turn has had its challenges, with South Korean citizens often expressing their *ban damunhwa*, or anti-immigration, anti-multicultural sentiments (E. Jung 2019). What is certain is that South Korea can no longer be considered ethnically homogenous. This rise in multiculturalism has led some to ask if North Koreans should be regarded as foreign migrants or if they should be considered "co-ethnics" (Choo 2006; Nora Hui-Jung Kim 2016).

60. As one anonymous reviewer pointed out, being a citizen of any nation (whether in a totalitarian North Korea or in South Korea) is to ultimately subject oneself to the sovereign and violent power of the state.

61. My appreciation goes to Eleana Kim for pointing this out.

62. South Korea is also one of the largest senders of Christian missionaries throughout the world, only second behind the United States.

63. Jin-Heon Jung's work (2011, 2015, 2016) on the religious encounters of North Koreans and South Korean evangelicals has been an important contribution to the study of the North Korean migration. He argues that the activities of these religious organizations shed light on the processes of acculturation, anticommunism and nationalism, and the ideologies of human rights and freedom.

64. Bell 2013; E. Cho 2018; Choo 2006; Chung 2009; J. Jung 2015; Y. Kim 2016; Soo-Jung Lee 2011; S. Park 2016; Sands 2019. Various ethnographic studies have provided vivid accounts of North Korean experiences in South Korea. Yoon Young Kim (2009, 2016) approaches North Korean subjectivity from their interactions with South Korean counterparts in educational institutions. Jin-Heon Jung (2015) looks at the religious conversion of North Koreans as they migrate to China, and later in their resettlement to South Korea. Seo Yeon Park (2016) has analyzed the role of Hana Centers in the depoliticization of North Korean identity. Hae Yeon Choo (2006), though not focused on any one specific institution, provides an ethnographic account of the gendered and ethnicized nature of South Korean citizenship through the experiences of North Koreans and how they negotiate their identities.

CHAPTER 1

Epigraphs: Butler 2003, 10; Behar 1996, 63.

1. The funeral song's origin is said to derive from a king who once sought refuge in this region from the tumult in Hangyang (present day Seoul). Curious about the ongoing affairs at Hanyang, he sent a person to seek information. "When will he return once he leaves?" the king asked. Repeatedly, his informants did not return and he said in distress, "I can't live because of the pain."

2. MacArthur 1964, 350.

3. Addressing people—particularly people older than you—by the first name is considered rude. Instead, people often refer to one another by the relationship they have with that person. I addressed this woman as *halmeoni,* which means grandmother in Korean.

4. Nan Kim 2017, 2.

5. See C. Kim 1988; Nan Kim 2017; Soo-Jung Lee 2006.

6. *Korea Times* 2018.

7. Das 1996; G. Cho 2008.

8. R. Liem 2003.

9. The ethnic Koreans in Japan who have become Japanese citizens or permanent residents following their immigration to Japan prior to 1945 are often referred to as *Zainichi* Koreans. This reference distinguishes them from the later

wave of Korean migrants who arrived in Japan towards the end of the twentieth century. *Zainichi* is a Japanese word that means "foreigner living in Japan." For an extensive study of this population, see Ryang 2000. For letters from the diaspora, see Liem and Liem 2013.

10. Sung Kyung Kim (2014, 556) offers a detailed analysis of the many legal ways North Koreans travel to China. She describes three main ways: obtaining a travel permit from the North Korean government to visit Chinese relatives, visas issued from China, or travel pass available for borderland residents under the agreement of both China and North Korea.

11. Korean artist Ahn Seok-ju composed this song prior to the Korean division during the Japanese occupation of the Korean peninsula (1910–45). Ahn's original lyric was "Our wish is independence," to reflect the desire of the Korean people to be liberated from Japanese imperialism. However, he substituted "reunification" for "independence" when Korea was divided into two parts.

12. Nan Kim 2017, 23.

13. *The Guardian* 2014.

14. *Chosun Ilbo* 2010.

15. Funabashi 2007.

16. Sang Yong Lee 2013.

17. Bell and Chee 2013; *JoongAng* 2014a, 2014b.

18. Levi 1988.

19. Tae Hong Kim 2011.

20. *Chosun Ilbo* 2011.

21. Collier, Rosaldo, and Yanagisako 1997, 78.

22. Behar 1996, 177.

CHAPTER 2

1. This account of the Chinese "human wave" has likely been embellished over time. Brigadier General Edwin H. Simmons writes, "U.S. Marines' and soldiers' imaginations sometimes magnified what they saw and heard while under attack. The Western press was soon filled with fantasies of 'human sea attacks' by 'hordes' of Chinese. Chinese propaganda photographs and films showing wave after wave of Chinese advancing in line across the snow with bravely flying red banners reinforced these exaggerations" (2002, 48).

2. According to MacArthur's own reflections on the possibility of China's intervention in the Korean War: "my own military estimate was that with our largely unopposed air forces, with their potential capable of destroying, at will, bases of attack and lines of supply north as well as south of the Yalu, no Chinese military commander would hazard the commitment of large forces upon the devastated Korean peninsula" (MacArthur 1964, 362).

3. Stueck 1995, 37–38, 65. In regards to China's decision to enter the Korean War, Bruce Cumings emphasizes Chinese reciprocity to North Korea's assistance in the Chinese Civil War (2005, 238).

4. The second branch was located in various cities until December 2012 when the more permanent facility was established.

5. Shinui Kim 2013.

6. Thanks to Xiyu Erik Kai who informed me of these Chinese slogans.

7. Fan 2013.

8. Denyer and Gowen 2018.

9. Sung Kyung Kim 2014.

10. Writing about migrant farmworkers in the United States, Seth Holmes critiques the tendency of migration studies to categorize migrants' motivations based on a push/pull dichotomy (2013, 17).

11. Sung Kyung Kim 2016; NKIDP 2012. Hazel Smith (2012) argues that cross-border activities and migrations did not suddenly emerge in the 1990s, but that the famine solidified the migration flows in one direction, from North Korea to China.

12. The 1961 report by the Chinese 4th Bureau of the Ministry of Public Security states, "Last November [1960] a low food [provisions] standard was implemented, and since that time the [Yanbian Korean Autonomous] Prefecture has witnessed a clear increase in the outflow of border residents" (NKIDP 2012, 10). In that same year, the Chinese Ministry of Foreign Affairs sent a telegram to its embassy in North Korea expressing its concerns about increased border crossings by Chinese people into North Korea: "There are many reasons causing the increase in border crossings, though mainly it is because these people do not understand the temporary difficulties [facing] our country." The Chinese Ministry of Foreign Affairs and the Ministry of Public Safety estimated that, in 1961 alone, over 28,000 Chinese citizens crossed over to North Korea (NKIDP 2012, 18). These migrations were viewed as a worthwhile option given that the majority of the Korean-Chinese spoke the Korean language and had extended family in North Korea.

13. NKIDP 2012, 7.

14. This was reported in the *New York Times* (Crossette 1999).

15. Sung Kyung Kim (2014) notes that there are informal networks of brokers that facilitate cross-border marriages in addition to the less common criminal networks that traffic women into the sex industry.

16. Abu-Lughod 2002; Burton 1992; Mohanty 2003; Said 1979; Teng 1996.

17. Constable 2003, 90.

18. Veena Das writes that the "woman's body became a sign through which men communicated with each other. The lives of women were framed by the notion that they were to bear permanent witness to the violence of Partition. Thus, the political programme of creating the two nations of India and Pakistan was inscribed upon the bodies of women" (1995, 56).

19. Das 1995, 71.

20. Carlos Decena has theorized on the "tacit subject" in his research on Dominican immigrant gay men in New York City. He writes, "what is tacit is neither secret nor silent" (2008, 340).

21. See Grace Cho's work on "haunting" (2008).

22. The sex industry in South Korea is not small. There are between five hundred thousand to one million women who work in the sex industry, according to the South Korean Ministry for Gender Equality and the Korean Feminist Association (Ghosh 2013).

23. Recent research found that South Korean public perception of resettled North Koreans and resettlement policies vary by the presentation of the gender of North Koreans. Public support for resettlement policy decreased significantly when focused on North Korean men (Rich et al. 2020).

24. See Choo 2006 for a discussion on how gender and state-based identities intersect to marginalize resettled North Koreans as "backward."

25. Gim 2019.

26. Young Koreans refer to the current generation as *Sampo Sedae,* a generation that must give up three things: dating, marriage, and children. As socioeconomic life has become more and more difficult, people have expanded the term to *N-po Sedae:* a generation that must give up "N" number of things in life (including careers, homeownership, dreams and aspirations, human relationships, health, and appearance).

27. Ginsburg, Abu-Lughod, and Larkin 2002; Pink et al. 2016.

28. *Hankyoreh* 2014.

29. Green and Epstein 2013, 4.

30. E. Cho 2018.

31. *TV Chosun* 2015.

32. Green and Epstein 2013.

33. According to Kurlantzick and Mason, "China permits non-North Korean asylum seekers of all nationalities to openly approach the UNHCR offices in China and to receive UNHCR refugee status determination and remain in China pending resettlement" (2006, 37).

34. Schmitt 2005.

CHAPTER 3

1. I am thinking here of Iris Marion Young's classic essay, "Throwing Like a Girl: A Phenomenology of Female Body Comportment Motility and Spatiality" (1980).

2. Yoo 2020, 44–45. South Korea also received significant aid from its allied countries like the United States and Japan.

3. Meredith Woo-Cumings (2002) argues that the unprecendented rainfall and massive flooding were directly associated with changing global climatic conditions.

4. Fahy 2015.

5. Christine Ahn (2005) argues that this practice of dense rice planting is a direct legacy of Japanese colonial policy.

6. The PDS was not an "equal" distributive system, as it gave out provisions in varying amounts depending on one's political rank, region, and class. Furthermore, the PDS, by establishing assigned distribution centers, structurally restricted human mobility between regions (Fahy 2015).

7. Woo-Cumings 2002, 3; Yoo 2020, xviii.

8. Fahy 2015, 111.

9. Chung 2003; Woo-Cumings 2002.

10. Central Bureau of Statistics, DPRK 1998.

11. NKIDP 2012.

12. Pak 2010.

13. Pak 2004, 2010.

14. M. Park 2010.

15. S. Choe 2009.

16. K. Park and Lee 2010, 138.

17. Chung 2009, 18.

18. The national average here refers to the men who received physical examinations for the military draft (Korean Statistical Information Service 2021).

19. For men, the requirement used to be 167 cm (5 ft 6 in) and 57 kg (125.7 lbs). The South Korean government eventually got rid of these qualifications in 2008 due to public concerns that they were human rights violations. But this was too late for Soyang, who gave up her aspirations to be a police officer.

20. Chung 2009, 16.

21. Hough 2021.

22. Berdahl 1999.

23. Grinker 1998, 4.

24. *Korea Times* 2018, emphasis added.

25. Constitution of the Republic of Korea 1987.

26. Some North Korean refugees have sought asylum directly with Western countries while in Southeast Asia. However, there have been a number of resettled North Koreans seeking secondary asylum *despite* having already received South Korean citizenship. A few have sought asylum by disguising details of their resettlement in South Korea. For an extensive analysis of North Koreans' secondary asylum, see Jay Jiyoung Song and Bell 2019.

27. Malkki 1995a, 55.

28. Malkki 1995a, 80.

29. Bordo 1993.

30. S. Choe 2011; *Daily Mail* 2012.

31. For women: Balsamo 1996; Blum 2003; Brush 1998; Davis 1995; Frost 2005; Kaw 1993; Morgan 1991; Negrin 2002. For men: Holliday and Elfving-Hwang 2012; Yoo 2020, 244.

32. Holliday and Elfving-Hwang 2012; Sharon Heijin Lee 2016; Leem 2017.

33. Millard 1955, 319.

34. Millard 1955, 331.

35. Millard 1955, 333.

36. Millard 1964, 647.

37. Millard 1955, 334.

38. *Los Angeles Times* 1895.

39. Millard 1955, 336.

40. Nadia Kim 2008; Palumbo-Liu 1999.

41. Sharon Heijin Lee 2016, 18.

42. Bourdieu and Wacquant 1992; Bourgois 2009.

43. Fanon 2008.

44. Fanon 2008, xv.

45. Fanon 2008, 27.

46. Morrison 2007, 204.

47. Scheper-Hughes and Bourgois 2004, 19.

48. Bourdieu and Wacquant 1992.

49. "Decolonising the mind": Thiong'o 1986. By "desubjectivation," I am referring to the Foucauldian notion of "subjectivation" which involves the process of becoming a subject in relation to power, structural forces, and inequalities. Desubjectivation, then, requires the recognition of and active resistance to this subjugation. For further discussion, see Pine 2008.

CHAPTER 4

1. Sonya Lee 2017.

2. J. Jung 2014.

3. Chung 2003, 199.

4. Although it is impossible to know the total amount of remittances sent to North Korea, it is estimated that at minimum $2 million USD have been sent to North Korea via family remittances (NKDB 2019). Though these remittances are valuable for the ordinary North Korean citizens living under extreme material hardships, this figure is likely not a significant amount that would drastically alter the North Korean economy or politics for the time being.

5. CGNTV 2012.

6. NKDB 2019, 10.

7. NKDB 2019, 13. The average income of South Koreans is approximately ₩2,870,000 KRW ($2,600 USD).

8. Glick Schiller and Fouron 2001; Lindley 2010; Mazzucato, Kabki, and Smith 2006; Riak Akuei 2005; Tacoli 1999. For recipient awareness see Åkesson 2011.

9. NKDB 2014.

10. Mauss 1990.

11. S. Choe 2012.

12. Harlan 2012.

13. Ju 2012.

14. *CNN* 2012.

15. NKDB 2012b.

16. NKDB 2012b.

17. See Hawk 2012.

18. Ahmed 2000; Goldring 2003; Fagen and Bump 2006; Horst 2008; Levitt 1998. In the context of North Korea, anthropologist Byung Ho Chung describes North Koreans' migration and transnational activities as "penetrant" (2014).

19. Coutin 2007, 123.

CHAPTER 5

Epigraphs: Redfield and Bornstein 2011, 17; Fassin 2012, 8.

1. Constitution of the Republic of Korea 1987.

2. Benjamin 1978, 277.

3. Agamben 1998.

4. Critiquing the theory of the state of exception as advanced by Carl Schmitt and Giorgio Agamben, Aihwa Ong argues that exceptionality "can be deployed to include as well as to exclude" (2005, 5).

5. UNHCR 2007, 16.

6. UNHCR 2007, 32.

7. Crimes: Charny 2005, 15.

8. DPRK 2009, 39.

9. DPRK 2009, 11.

10. Amnesty 2011; NKDB 2012a.

11. Cohen 2010; Kurlantzick and Mason 2006; E. Lee 2000, 2004; Haggard and Noland 2006; Milanova 2005.

12. Kurlantzick and Mason 2006, 37.

13. UNHCR 2011, 19, emphasis added.

14. Janice Marshall, the former representative of the UNHCR office in Seoul, writes, "North Koreans, even if not, in the strictest sense of the international def-

inition, refugees, are clearly *persons of concern* to the Agency if they are at risk of being returned to North Korea to face disproportionate punishment for having left [. . .] Therefore, just like other refugees, they need assistance to access a long-term solution to their plight" (2007, emphasis added).

15. J. Marshall 2007.

16. Mahr 2002, ii.

17. Smith 2012, 3.

18. Chan 2012.

19. Chan 2012.

20. A. Hong 2007.

21. A. Hong 2011.

22. Mbembe 2003.

23. Hough and Bell 2020.

24. See Jay Song 2021 for an analysis of the "savage-victim-saviour" narratives of three prominent North Korean human rights activists. Green and Epstein (2013) argue that these discourses hinder our nuanced understandings of North Korea.

25. H. Lee 2011.

26. One Young World 2014.

27. Jay Song 2021, 55.

28. Jolley 2014; Joo Park 2014.

29. S. Choe 2015.

30. S. Oh 2011.

31. Campbell 2010.

32. Ros-Lehtinen 2012.

33. HR 1464 – 112th Congress 2011, 1–2. The final, enacted version states: "(1) hundreds of thousands of North Korean children suffer from malnutrition in North Korea, and North Korean children or children of one North Korean parent who are living outside of North Korea may face statelessness in neighboring countries" and "(2) the Secretary of State should advocate for the best interest of these children, including, when possible, facilitating immediate protection for those living outside North Korea through family reunification or, if appropriate and eligible in individual cases, domestic or international adoption" (HR 1464 – 112th Congress 2012, 1).

34. HR 1464 – 112th Congress 2011, 2–3.

35. Eleana Kim 2010; Hosu Kim 2016; Jodi Kim 2009, 2015; Klein 2003; A. Oh 2015; Pate 2014; Stryker 2010.

36. HR 1464 – 112th Congress 2011, 5.

37. Article 4 of the Nationality Law of the People's Republic of China reads: "Any person born in China whose parents are both Chinese nationals or one of whose parents is a Chinese national shall have Chinese nationality."

Furthermore, Article 6 states: "Any person born in China whose parents are stateless or of uncertain nationality and have settled in China shall have Chinese nationality" (Nationality Law of the People's Republic of China 1980).

38. C. Hong 2012.

39. G. Lee 2012; National Human Rights Commission of Korea 2012. When a North Korean mother enters South Korea alone but has had a child with a Chinese man, she must initially inform the government agents that her child is still in China. Otherwise, it will be difficult for her child to obtain South Korean citizenship at a later time. And if a child of a North Korean mother and Chinese father seeks resettlement in South Korea but the whereabouts of his or her mother is unknown (for example, if the mother was deported to North Korea while in China), then the child must prove to the South Korean government that his or her mother is indeed a North Korean national in order to claim and obtain South Korean citizenship.

40. Yeun 2012.

41. Yeun 2012.

42. Han-Schneider Petition Letter 2010.

43. Han-Schneider 2010.

44. HR 1464 – 112th Congress 2012.

45. US President George W. Bush, in his 2002 State of the Union Address, grouped together North Korea, Iran, and Iraq as "axis of evil" countries seeking weapons of mass destruction and sponsoring acts of terrorism.

46. C. Hong 2013, 519.

47. Said 1978. See also Massad 2002. Regarding Africa, I am referencing here Joseph Conrad's novel, *Heart of Darkness*, but also Achille Mbembe's *On the Postcolony:* "Africa as an idea, a concept, has historically served, and continues to serve, as a polemical argument for the West's desperate desire to assert its difference from the rest of the world" (2001, 2).

48. "In Human Rights Discourse we, as compassionate witnesses, resist seeing the sufferer as a vicarious surrogate for ourselves, a human sacrifice from which we benefit. Instead, we project ourselves back into the image of starved, mutilated, genocided bodies whose suffering is fantasmatically our own. The *compassionate* bystander is no longer a beneficiary who *has* a victim; rather, he is the witness that his imaginary victim wants" (Meister 2012, 226).

49. Kleinman and Kleinman 1996.

50. Redfield and Bornstein 2011, 3.

51. Fassin 2007. Didier Fassin's use of the phrase "politics of life" differs from the Foucauldian "biopolitics" in that it does not concern the ways in which technologies of power regulate human populations. The establishment of refugee camps and detention centers are examples of humanitarian biopolitics.

52. Agamben 1998; Hansen and Stepputat 2006; Jennings 2011; Mbembe 2003.

53. Badiou 2007, 175.

54. See Redfield 2005 for his critique of Doctors Without Borders, a nongovernmental organization that provides medical relief in humanitarian disasters.

55. Y. Lee 2014.

56. THINK 2013.

57. Jiyoung Song 2013.

58. LINK 2015.

59. See Bass 2008, Berlant 2004, and Fassin 2012 for a further discussion on the politics of compassion.

CONCLUSION

Epigraphs: Livingston 1991; Reddy 1998, 357.

1. Livingston 1991.

2. Reddy 1998, 357.

3. Sharon Yoon notes that for diasporic Koreans forcibly displaced by colonialism, division, and war, *gohyang* has often been intertwined with the sentiments of loss and longing for the homeland (2021, 31).

4. R. Choi 1995.

5. R. Choi 1995.

6. G. Cho 2008, 91.

7. C. Hong 2015; Suzy Kim 2015.

8. C. Hong 2015, 598. See the special journal issue entitled "The Unending Korean War" in *positions: asia critique*.

9. Paik 2011.

10. Mahr 2002, 18.

11. National Security Act 1997.

12. *Yonhap News* 1994.

13. *Chosun Ilbo* 1994.

14. The web of concrete apartment buildings will essentially become military pillboxes in the event of an invasion. Tanks can easily be targeted and destroyed, and it becomes difficult for the enemy to discern where the snipers are shooting from.

15. *Chosun Ilbo* 1968. Additionally, to read Park Chung-hee's new year speech where he urges the nation to "construct while fighting," see JoongAng 1969.

16. The revised Building Act in 1970 mandated the construction of basements in apartment buildings for military purposes in the event of war. However, with increased urbanization, the basements became gradually used as residential space. In response, the government mandated in 1984 that basements be raised to allow ventilation and natural light, leading to the proliferation of half-basement apartments in South Korea.

References

Abu-Lughod, Lila. 2002. "Do Muslim Women Really Need Saving? Anthropological Reflections on Cultural Relativism and Its Others." *American Anthropologist* 104, no. 3: 783–90.

Agamben, Giorgio. 1995. "We Refugees." *Symposium* 49, no. 2: 114–19.

———. 1998. *Homo Sacer: Sovereign Power and Bare Life.* Translated by Daniel Heller-Roazen. Stanford: Stanford University Press.

Ahmed, Ishmail. 2000. "Remittances and Their Economic Impact in Post-war Somaliland." *Disasters* 24, no. 4: 380–89.

Ahn, Christine. 2005. "Famine and the Future of Food Security in North Korea." *Institute for Food and Development Policy/Food First Policy Brief No. 11.* http://www.kpolicy.org/documents/policy/050531christineahnnkfoodsecurity.pdf.

Åkesson, Lisa. 2011. "Cape Verdean Notions of Migrant Remittances." *Cadernos de Estudos Africanos* 20: 139–59.

Amnesty International. 2011. "Annual Report 2011: North Korea." http://www.amnesty.org/en/region/north-korea/report-2011.

An, Ji Hyun, et al. 2018. "Prevalence and Correlates of Suicidal Thoughts and Behaviors among North Korean Defectors." *Psychiatry Investig* 15, no. 5: 445–51.

Anzaldúa, Gloria. 1987. *Borderlands: The New Mestiza.* San Francisco: Aunt Lute Books.

Arendt, Hannah. 1958. *The Origins of Totalitarianism*. New York: Meridian Books.

Badiou, Alain. 2007. *The Century*. Translated by Alberto Toscano. Malden, MA: Polity Press.

Baghdasaryan, Milena. 2011. "Contesting Belonging and Social Citizenship: The Case of Refugee Housing in Armenia." *Citizenship Studies* 15, no. 3–4: 529–42.

Balsamo, Anne. 1996. *Technologies of the Gendered Body: Reading Cyborg Women*. Durham, NC: Duke University Press.

Bass, Gary J. 2008. *Freedom's Battle: The Origins of Humanitarian Intervention*. New York: Alfred A. Knopf.

Bauböck, Rainer. 1994. *Transnational Citizenship: Membership and Rights in International Migration*. Gloucestershire, UK: Edward Elgar Publishing.

Behar, Ruth. 1996. *The Vulnerable Observer: Anthropology That Breaks Your Heart*. Boston: Beacon Press.

Bell, Markus. 2013. "Manufacturing Kinship in a Nation Divided: An Ethnographic Study of North Korean Refugees in South Korea." *The Asia Pacific Journal of Anthropology* 14, no. 3: 240–55. https://doi.org/10.1080/144422 13.2013.789070.

Bell, Markus, and Sarah Chee. 2013. "Southern Inhospitality." *Foreign Policy in Focus,* September 18. https://fpif.org/southern-inhospitality.

Bell, Markus, and Geoffrey Fattig. 2014. "International Cooperation on the North Korean Refugee Crisis." *Forced Migration Review* 45: 59–60.

Benjamin, Walter. 1978. *Reflections*. Edited by Peter Demetz. Translated by Edmund Jephcott. New York: Schocken Books.

Berdahl, Daphne. 1999. *Where the World Ended: Re-Unification and Identity in the German Borderland*. Berkeley: University of California Press.

Berlant, Lauren, ed. 2004. *Compassion: The Culture and Politics of an Emotion*. New York: Routledge.

Besteman, Catherine. 2016. *Making Refuge: Somali Bantu Refugees and Lewiston, Maine*. Durham, NC: Duke University Press.

Betts, Alexander, and Gil Loescher. 2011. "Refugees in International Relations." In *Refugees in International Relations*, edited by Alexander Betts and Gil Loescher, 1–27. Oxford: Oxford University Press.

Blanc, Cristina Szanton, Linda Basch, and Nina Glick Schiller. 1995. "Transnationalism, Nation-States, and Culture." *Current Anthropology* 36, no. 4: 683–86.

Bleiker, Roland. 2004. "Identity, Difference, and the Dilemmas of Inter-Korean Relations: Insights from Northern Defectors and the German Precedent." *Asian Perspective* 28, no. 2: 35–63.

Blum, Virginia. 2003. *Flesh Wounds: The Culture of Cosmetic Surgery*. Berkeley: University of California Press.

Bordo, Susan. 1993. "Reading the Slender Body." In *Unbearable Weight: Feminism, Western Culture, and the Body*, 185–212. Berkeley: University of California Press.

Bourdieu, Pierre. 2001. "Gender and Symbolic Violence." In *Masculine Domination*, translated by Richard Nice, 34–42. Stanford: Stanford University Press.

Bourdieu, Pierre, and Loïc Wacquant. 1992. "Symbolic Violence." In *An Invitation to Reflective Sociology*, 167–73. Chicago: University of Chicago Press.

Bourgois, Philippe. 2009. "Recognizing Invisible Violence: A Thirty-Year Ethnographic Retrospective." In *Global Health in Times of Violence*, edited by Barbara Rylko-Bauer, Linda Whiteford, and Paul Farmer, 17–40. Santa Fe, NM: School of Advanced Research Press.

Brettell, Caroline. 2007. "Theorizing Migration in Anthropology: The Social Construction of Networks, Identities, Communities, and Globalscapes." In *Migration Theory: Talking Across Disciplines*, edited by Caroline Brettell and James Frank Hollifield, 113–59. London: Routledge.

Brubaker, Rogers. 1992. *Citizenship and Nationhood in France and Germany*. Cambridge, MA: Harvard University Press.

Brubaker, Rogers, and Frederick Cooper. 2000. "Beyond 'Identity.'" *Theory and Society* 29: 1–47.

Brush, Pippa. 1998. "Metaphors of Inscriptions: Discipline, Plasticity and the Rhetoric of Choice." *Feminist Review* 58, no. 1: 22–43.

Brysk, Alison, and Gershon Shafir, eds. 2004. *People Out of Place: Globalization, Human Rights, and the Citizenship Gap*. New York: Routledge.

Butler, Judith. 2003. "Violence, Mourning, Politics." *Studies in Gender and Sexuality* 4, no. 1: 9–37.

Burton, Antoinette. 1992. "The White Woman's Burden: British Feminists and 'The Indian Woman,' 1865–1915." In *Western Women and Imperialism: Complicity and Resistance*, edited by Nupur Chaudhuri and Margaret Strobel, 137–57. Bloomington: Indiana University Press.

Campbell, Kimberly Hyo-Jung. 2010. "De Facto Statelessness Places Adoption on the Table for Children of N. Korean Women in China." *Hankyoreh*, June 18.

Central Bureau of Statistics, DPRK. 1998. "Nutritional Survey of the Democratic People's Republic of Korea." https://reliefweb.int/report/democratic-peoples-republic-korea/nutrition-survey-democratic-peoples-republic-korea.

CGNTV. 2012. "Talbukjaui daebuk songgeum." *CGNTV*, September 21. Season 1 Episode 67.

Chan, Francis. 2012. "Francis Chan on N. Korean Refugee Orphan Adoption Bill." *YouTube*, March 15. https://www.youtube.com/watch?v=Qh81-ToZfnY.

Chan, Elim, and Andreas Schloenhardt. 2007. "North Korean Refugees and International Refugee Law." *International Journal of Refugee Law* 19, no. 2: 215–45.

Charny, Joel R. 2005. *Acts of Betrayal: The Challenge of Protecting North Koreans in China.* Washington, DC: Refugees International.

Cho, Eun Ah. 2018. "'Becoming' North Koreans: Negotiating Gender and Class in Representations of North Korean Migrants on South Korean Television." *Cross-Currents: East Asian History and Culture Review* 27 (June): 26–50.

Cho, Grace M. 2008. *Haunting the Korean Diaspora: Shame, Secrecy, and the Forgotten War.* Minneapolis: University of Minnesota Press.

Choe, Sang-Hun. 2009. "South Korea Stretches Standards for Success." *New York Times,* December 23.

———. 2011. "In South Korea, Plastic Surgery Comes Out of the Closet." *New York Times,* November 3.

———. 2012. "China Should Not Repatriate North Korean Refugees, Seoul Says." *New York Times,* February 22.

———. 2015. "Prominent North Korean Defector Recants Parts of His Story of Captivity." *New York Times,* January 18.

Choi, Rae-ok. 1995. "Gohyang." *Encyclopedia of Korean Culture.* http://encykorea.aks.ac.kr/Contents/Item/E0004040.

Choi, Seul Ki, et al. 2011. "Anxiety and Depression among North Korean Young Defectors in South Korea and Their Association with Health-Related Quality of Life." *Yonsei Medical Journal* 52(3): 502–509.

Choo, Hae Yeon. 2006. "Gendered Modernity and Ethnicized Citizenship: North Korean Settlers in Contemporary South Korea." *Gender and Society* 20, no. 5: 576–604.

Chosun Ilbo. 1968. "Buganghan jajugukgaro je2ui gwangbogeul." August 16. https://newslibrary.chosun.com/view/article_view.html?id=1456419680816m1012&set_date=19680816&page_no=1.

———. 1994. "Jeongukjuyosiseol jeonryakseolgye dangyeon." September 28. https://newslibrary.chosun.com/view/article_view.html?id=2281419940928m1031&set_date=19940928&page_no=3.

———. 2010. "N. Korean Leader Gives 160 Luxury Cars to Top Officials." August 10. http://english.chosun.com/site/data/html_dir/2010/08/02/2010080200980.html.

———. 2011. "N. Korea Purges Deputy Spy Chief." May 20. http://english.chosun.com/site/data/html_dir/2011/05/20/2011052000884.html.

Chung, Byung-Ho. 2003. "Living Dangerously in Two Worlds: The Risks and Tactics of North Korean Refugee Children in China." *Korea Journal* 43, no. 3: 191–211.

———. 2009. "Between Defector and Migrant: Identities and Strategies of North Koreans in South Korea." *Korean Studies* 32: 1–27.

———. 2014 "North Korean Refugees as Penetrant Transnational Migrants." *Urban Anthropology and Studies of Cultural Systems and World Economic Development* 43, no. 4: 329–61.

Chung, Byung-Ho, Wook Taek Jeon, and Jean-Kyung Chung, eds. 2006. *Welcome to Korea: Bukjoseon saramdul ui namhan sari*. Seoul: Hanyang University Press.

Chung, Soondool, and Ju-Yun Seo. 2007. "A Study on Posttraumatic Stress Disorder among North Korean Defectors and their Social Adjustment in South Korea." *Journal of Loss and Trauma* 12, no. 4: 365–82.

CNN. 2012. "China has Repatriated North Korean Defectors, South Korean Official Says." March 9.

Cohen, Roberta. 2010. "Legal Grounds for Protection of North Korean Refugees." *Brookings Institution*. http://www.brookings.edu/research/opinions/2010/09/north-korea-human-rights-cohen.

Collier, Jane, Michelle Z. Rosaldo, and Sylvia Yanagisako. 1997. "Is There a Family? New Anthropological Views." In *The Gender/Sexuality Reader: Culture, History, Political Economy*, edited by Roger Lancaster and Micaela di Leonardo, 71–81. New York: Routledge.

Constable, Nicole. 2003. "Feminism and the Myths of 'Mail-Order' Marriages." In *Romance on a Global Stage: Pen Pals, Virtual Ethnography, and "Mail-Order" Marriages*. Berkeley: University of California Press.

Constitution of the Republic of Korea. 1987. https://korea.assembly.go.kr:447/res/low_01_read.jsp.

Coutin, Susan Bibler. 2007. *Nations of Emigrants: Shifting Boundaries of Citizenship in El Salvador and the United States*. Ithaca, NY: Cornell University Press.

Crossette, Barbara. 1999. "Korean Famine Toll: More Than 2 Million." *New York Times*. August 20.

Cumings, Bruce. 2005. *Korea's Place in the Sun: A Modern History*. New York: W. W. Norton.

Daily Mail. 2012. "South Korean Girls' Obsession with Double Eyelid Surgery as they Strive to Look Like 'Pretty Western Celebrities.'" October 24. http://www.dailymail.co.uk/femail/article-2222481/South-Korean-girls-obsession-double-eyelid-surgery-strive-look-like-pretty-western-celebrities.html.

Das, Veena. 1995. "National Honour and Practical Kinship: Of Unwanted Women and Children." In *Critical Events: An Anthropological Perspective on Contemporary India*, 55–83. Delhi: Oxford University Press.

———. 1996. "Language and Body. Transactions in the Construction of Pain." *Daedalus* 125, no. 1: 67–91.

———. 2011. "State, Citizenship, and the Urban Poor." *Citizenship Studies* 15, no. 3–4: 319–33.

Davis, Kathy. 1995. *Reshaping the Female Body: The Dilemma of Cosmetic Surgery*. New York: Routledge.

Decena, Carlos Ulises. 2008. "Tacit Subjects." *GLQ: A Journal of Lesbian and Gay Studies* 14, no. 2-3: 339–59.

Denyer, Simon, and Annie Gowen. 2018. "Too Many Men." *Washington Post,*
April 18.

DPRK (Democratic People's Republic of Korea). 2009. *The Criminal Law of the
Democratic People's Republic of Korea.* Seoul: Citizens' Alliance for North
Korean Human Rights.

Fadlalla, Amal Hassan. 2019. *Branding Humanity: Competing Narratives of
Rights, Violence, and Global Citizenship.* Stanford, CA: Stanford University
Press.

Fagen, Patricia Weiss, and Micah Bump. 2006. "Remittances in Conflict and
Crises: How Remittances Sustain Livelihoods in War, Crises, and Transi-
tions to Peace." *Security-Development Nexus Program Policy Papers.* New
York: International Peace Academy.

Fahy, Sandra. 2011. "'Like Two Pieces of the Sky': Seeing North Korean through
Accounts of the Famine." *Anthropology Today* 27, no. 5: 18–21.

———. 2015. *Marching Through Suffering: Loss and Survival in North Korea.*
New York: Columbia University Press.

Fan, Jiayang. 2013. "The Children of China." *The New Yorker,* April 24. http://
www.newyorker.com/online/blogs/newsdesk/2013/04/the-one-child-policy
.html.

Fanon, Frantz. 2008. *Black Skin, White Masks.* New York: Grove Press.

Farmer, Paul. 1997. "On Suffering and Structural Violence: A View from Below."
In *Social Suffering,* edited by Arthur Kleinman, Veena Das, and Margaret
Lock, 261–83. Berkeley: University of California Press.

Fassin, Didier. 2007. "Humanitarianism as a Politics of Life." *Public Culture* 19,
no. 3: 499–520.

———. 2011. "Policing Borders, Producing Boundaries: The Governmentality of
Immigration in Dark Times." *Annual Review of Anthropology* 40: 213–26.

———. 2012. *Humanitarian Reason: A Moral History of the Present.* Berkeley:
University of California Press.

Feldman, Ilana. 2007. "Difficult Distinctions: Refugee Law, Humanitarian
Practice, and Political Identification in Gaza." *Cultural Anthropology* 22,
no. 1: 129–69.

Frost, Liz. 2005. "Theorizing the Young Woman in the Body." *Body and Society*
11, no. 1: 63–85.

Funabashi, Yoichi. 2007. *The Peninsula Question: A Chronicle of the Second
Korean Nuclear Crisis.* Washington, DC: Brookings Institution Press.

Galtung, John. 1969. "Violence, Peace, and Peace Research." *Journal of Peace
Research* 6, no. 1: 167–91.

Ghosh, Palash. 2013. "South Korea: A Thriving Sex Industry in a Powerful,
Wealthy Super-State." *International Business Times,* April 29. http://www
.ibtimes.com/south-korea-thriving-sex-industry-powerful-wealthy-super-
state-1222647.

Ginsburg, Faye D., Lila Abu-Lughod, and Brian Larkin. 2002, eds. *Media Worlds: Anthropology on New Terrain.* Berkeley: University of California Press.

Gim, Jeongbeom. 2019. "'Talbukmindo Uri Gukmin' 84% 'Nae Myeoneuriro Gwaenchanha' 9%." *Maeilgyeongjae,* October 21. https://www.mk.co.kr/news /politics/view/2019/10/855711.

Glick Schiller, Nina, Linda Basch, and Christina Szanton Blanc. 1995. "From Immigrant to Transmigrant: Theorizing Transnational Migration." *Anthropological Quarterly* 68, no. 1: 48–63.

Glick Schiller, Nina, and Georges Fouron. 2001. *Georges Wakes Up Laughing: Long-Distance Nationalism and the Search for Home.* Durham, NC: Duke University Press.

Goldring, Luin. 2003. "Re-thinking Remittances: Social and Political Dimensions of Individual and Collective Remittances." *CERLAC Working Paper Series.* New York: Centre for Research on Latin America and the Caribbean.

Gordon, Andrew, and Trevor Stack. 2007. "Citizenship Beyond the State: Thinking with Early Modern Citizenship in the Contemporary World." *Citizenship Studies* 11, no. 2: 117–33.

Green, Christopher K. and Stephen Epstein. 2013. "Now On My Way to Meet Who? South Korean Television, North Korean Refugees, and the Dilemmas of Representation." *The Asia-Pacific Journal: Japan Focus* 11, no. 41: 1–18.

Grinker, Roy Richard. 1998. *Korea and its Futures: Unification and the Unfinished War.* London: Macmillan.

The Guardian. 2014. "Japan and North Korea meet over abductions." October 28. http://www.theguardian.com/world/2014/oct/28/japan-and-north-korea-meet-over-abductions.

Haddad, Emma. 2008. *The Refugee in International Society: Between Sovereigns.* Cambridge, UK: Cambridge University Press.

Haggard, Stephan, and Marcus Noland, eds. 2006. *The North Korean Refugee Crisis: Human Rights and International Response.* Washington, DC: US Committee for Human Rights in North Korea.

———. 2007. *Famine in North Korea: Markets, Aid, and Reform.* New York: Columbia University Press.

———. 2011. *Witness to Transformation: Refugee Insights into North Korea.* Washington, DC: Peter G. Peterson Institute for International Economics.

Hammar, Tomas. 1990. *Democracy and the Nation State: Aliens, Denizens, and Citizens in a World of International Migration.* London: Ashgate Publishing.

Han, Ju Hui Judy. 2013. "Beyond Safe Haven: A Critique of Christian Custody of North Korean Migrants in China." *Critical Asian Studies* 45, no. 4: 533–60.

Han-Schneider. 2010. "S3156 Information—English Version." *YouTube,* June 12. https://www.youtube.com/watch?v=wNrCMkf-5Ys.

Han-Schneider Petition Letter. 2010. "North Korean Refugee Adoption Act." *KoreAm,* July 19. http://iamkoream.com/north-korean-refugee-act.

Hankyoreh. 2014. "Sogot charimeuro 'seobangnim'? Gyeolhonjeongboeopche 'talbuk yeoseong biha' gwanggo murui." August 26. http://media.daum.net /society/others/newsview?newsid=20140826161013112.

Hansen, Thomas Blom, and Finn Stepputat. 2006. "Sovereignty Revisited." *Annual Review of Anthropology* 35: 295–315.

Harlan, Chico. 2012. "Spotlight Falls on North Korean Defectors' Treatment in China." *Washington Post,* March 23. https://www.washingtonpost.com /world/for-north-korean-defectors-a-higher-profile-about-their-treatment-in-china/2012/03/19/gIQA6UHqVS_story.html.

Hawk, David. 2012. *The Hidden Gulag: The Lives and Voices of "Those Who Are Sent to the Mountains."* 2nd edition. Committee for Human Rights in North Korea: Washington, DC.

Holliday, Ruth, and Joanna Elfving-Hwang. 2012. "Gender, Globalization and Aesthetic Surgery in South Korea." *Body & Society* 18, no. 2: 58–81.

Holmes, Seth. 2013. *Fresh Fruit, Broken Bodies: Indigenous Mexican Farmworkers in the United States.* Berkeley: University of California Press.

Hong, Adrian. 2007. "Liberty in North Korea: The North Korean Human Rights Crisis." *Google Tech Talks,* June 29. https://www.youtube.com/watch?v= 3dqTNqhSR5I.

———. 2011. "How to Free North Korea: The Time to Topple the Criminal Government in Pyongyang is Now. Here's How to Do It." *Foreign Policy,* December 19. http://www.foreignpolicy.com/articles/2011/12/19/how_ to_free_north_korea.

Hong, Christine. 2012. "The Fiction of the North Korean Refugee Orphan." *38 North,* September 19. http://38north.org/2012/09/chong091912.

———. 2013. "Reframing North Korean Human Rights." *Critical Asian Studies* 45, no. 4: 511–32.

———. 2015. "The Unending Korean War." *positions: asia critique* 23, no. 23: 597–617.

Horst, Cindy. 2008. "The Transnational Political Engagements of Refugees: Remittance Sending Practices amongst Somalis in Norway." *Conflict, Security and Development* 8, no. 3: 317–40.

Hough, Jennifer. 2021. "The Racialization of North Koreans in South Korea: Diasporic Co-Ethnics in the South Korean Ethnolinguistic Nation." *Ethnic and Racial Studies,* https://doi.org/10.1080/01419870.2021.1921237.

Hough, Jennifer, and Markus Bell. 2020. "North Koreans' Public Narratives and Conditional Inclusion in South Korea." *Critical Asian Studies* 52, no. 2: 161–81.

HR 1464 – 112th Congress. 2011. "An Act to Develop a Strategy for Assisting Stateless Children from North Korea, and for Other Purposes." *GovTrack.us.* https://www.govinfo.gov/content/pkg/BILLS-112hr1464ih/pdf/BILLS-112hr1464ih.pdf.

HR 1464 – 112th Congress. 2012. "North Korean Child Welfare Act of 2012." *GovTrack.us.* http://www.govtrack.us/congress/bills/112/hr1464.

Human Rights Watch. 2012. "World Report 2012: North Korea." http://www.hrw.org/world-report-2012/world-report-2012-north-korea.

Jennings, Ronald C. 2011. "Sovereignty and Political Modernity: A Genealogy of Agamben's Critique of Sovereignty." *Anthropological Theory* 11, no. 1: 23–61.

Jeon, Bong-Hee, et al. 2009. "Prevalence and Correlates of Depressive Symptoms among North Korean Defectors Living in South Korea for More than One Year." *Psychiatry Investigation* 6: 122–30.

Jeon, Woo Taek. 2007. *Saramui Tongil Ttangui Tongil (Unification of People, Unification of Land).* Seoul: Yeonsei University Press.

Jolley, Mary Ann. 2014. "The Strange Tale of Yeonmi Park." *The Diplomat,* December 10. http://thediplomat.com/2014/12/the-strange-tale-of-yeonmi-park.

JoongAng. 1969. "Ssaumyeo geonseolhaja." January 1. https://www.joongang.co.kr/article/1183787#home.

———. 2014a. "Time to Revamp Spy Agency." *Korea JoongAng Daily,* March 12. http://koreajoongangdaily.joins.com/news/article/article.aspx?aid=2986164.

———. 2014b. "Ruling Party Rep Calls for NIS Chief Resignation." *Korea JoongAng Daily,* March 12. http://mengnews.joins.com/amparticle/2986217.

Ju, Seong-ha. 2012. "Hujintao jungguk gukga juseogege bonaeneun pyeonji." *Dong-a Ilbo.* http://blog.donga.com/nambukstory/archives/23738. Accessed 10 November 2012.

Jung, EuyRyung. 2019. "'Voices of Ordinary Citizens': *Ban Damunhwa* and its Neoliberal Affect of Anti-Immigration in South Korea." *Critical Asian Studies* 51, no. 3: 386–402.

Jung, Jin-Heon. 2011. "Underground Railroads of Christian Conversion: North Korean Migrants and Evangelical Missionary Networks in Northeast Asia." *Encounters: An International Journal for the Study of Culture and Society* 4: 163–88.

———. 2014. "Ballooning Evangelism: Psychological Warfare and Christianity in the Divided Korea." *Max-Planck Institute Working Paper* 14–07.

———. 2015. *Migration and Religion in East Asia: North Korean Migrants' Evangelical Encounters.* New York: Palgrave MacMillan.

———. 2016. "The Religious-Political Aspirations of North Korean Migrants and Protestant Churches in Seoul." *Journal of Korean Religions* 7, no. 2: 123–48.

Kanna, Ahmed. 2010. "Flexible Citizenship in Dubai: Neoliberal Subjectivity in the Emerging 'City-Corporation.'" *Cultural Anthropology* 25, no. 1: 100–29.

Kaw, Eugenia. 1993. "Medicalization of Racial Features: Asian American Women and Cosmetic Surgery." *Medical Anthropology Quarterly* 7, no. 1: 74–89.

Kim, Choong Soon. 1988. *Faithful Endurance: An Ethnography of Korean Family Dispersal*. Tucson: University of Arizona Press.

Kim, Eleana. 2010. *Adopted Territory: Transnational Korean Adoptees and the Politics of Belonging*. Durham, NC: Duke University Press.

———. 2016. "Toward an Anthropology of Landmines: Rogue Infrastructure and Military Waste in the Korean DMZ." *Cultural Anthropology* 32, no. 2: 162–87.

Kim, Eunyoung, et al. 2009. "Cross Border North Korean Women Trafficking and Victimization Between North Korea and China: An Ethnographic Case Study." *International Journal of Law, Crime and Justice* 37: 154–69.

Kim, Hosu. 2016. *Birth Mothers and Transnational Adoption Practice in South Korea: Virtual Mothering*. New York: Palgrave Macmillan US.

Kim, Hyo Hyun, et al. 2011. "Prevalence and Correlates of Psychiatric Symptoms in North Korean Defectors." *Psychiatry Investigation* 8: 179–85.

Kim, Jin Kang. 2019. "Ganan·oeroume goripdoen talbukmindeul, jasal seontaek neureoganda." *Skyedaily,* October 9. http://www.skyedaily.com/news/news_view.html?ID=91608.

Kim, Jodi. 2009. "An 'Orphan' with Two Mothers: Transnational and Transracial Adoption, the Cold War, and Contemporary Asian American Cultural Politics." *American Quarterly* 61, no. 4: 855–80.

———. 2015. "'The Ending Is Not an Ending At All': On the Militarized and Gendered Diasporas of Korean Transnational Adoption and the Korean War." *positions: asia critique* 23, no. 4: 807-835.

Kim, Nadia. 2008. *Imperial Citizens: Koreans and Race from Seoul to LA*. Stanford, CA: Stanford University Press.

Kim, Nan. 2017. *Memory, Reconciliation, and Reunions in South Korea: Crossing the Divide*. Lanham, MD: Lexington Books.

Kim, Nora Hui-Jung. 2012. "Multiculturalism and the Politics of Belonging: The Puzzle of Multiculturalism in South Korea." *Citizenship Studies* 16, no. 1: 103–17.

———. 2016. "Naturalizing Korean Ethnicity and Making 'Ethnic' Difference: A Comparison of North Korean Settlement and Foreign Bride Incorporation Policies in South Korea." *Asian Ethnicity* 17, no. 2: 185–98.

Kim, Shinui. 2013. "Why are the majority of North Korean defectors female?" *NK-News.org,* July 31. http://www.nknews.org/2013/07/why-are-the-majority-of-north-korean-defectors-women.

Kim, Sung Kyung. 2014. "'I Am Well-Cooked Food': Survival Strategies of North Korean Female Border-Crossers and Possibilities for Empowerment." *Inter-Asia Cultural Studies* 15, no. 4: 553–71.

———. 2016. "Mobile North Korean Women and their Places in the Sino-North Korea Borderland." *Asian Anthropology* 15, no. 2: 116–31.

Kim, Suzy. 2015. "Introduction to '(De)Memorializing the Korean War: A Critical Intervention.'" *Cross-Currents: East Asian History and Culture Review* 14: 51–62.

Kim, Tae Hong. 2011. "Kim Jong Il Associate Purged from NSA." *Daily NK,* May 20. http://www.dailynk.com/english/read.php?cataId=nk00100&num=7706.

Kim, Yoon Young. 2009. "Making National Subjects: Education and Adaptation Among North Korean Immigrants in South Korea." PhD diss., University of Hawai'i.

———. 2016. "Negotiating Cultures and Identities: Education and Adaptation Among Young North Korean Settlers in South Korea." *Journal of International Migration and Integration* 17, no. 4: 1015–29.

Klein, Christina. 2003. *Cold War Orientalism: Asia in the Middlebrow Imagination, 1945–1961.* Berkeley: University of California Press.

Kleinman, Arthur, and Joan Kleinman. 1996. "The Appeal of Experience; The Dismay of Images: Cultural Appropriations of Suffering in Our Times." *Daedalus* 125, no. 1: 1–23.

Korea Times. 2018. "Panmunjeom Declaration." April 27. http://www .koreatimes.co.kr/www/nation/2018/04/731_248077.html.

Korean Statistical Information Service. 2021. "Byeongyeokpanjeonggeomsa hyeonhwang - sinjang bunpobyeol, cheongbyeol." https://kosis.kr/statHtml /statHtml.do?orgId=144&tblId=TX_14401_A041.

Kurlantzick, Joshua, and Jana Mason. 2006. "North Korean Refugees: The Chinese Dimension." In *The North Korean Refugee Crisis: Human Rights and International Response,* edited by Stephan Haggard and Marcus Noland, 34–52. Washington, DC: US Committee for Human Rights in North Korea.

Kwon, Heonik. 2020. *After the Korean War: An Intimate History.* Cambridge, UK: Cambridge University Press.

Kwon, Heonik, and Byung-Ho Chung. 2012. *North Korea: Beyond Charismatic Politics.* Lanham, MD: Rowman and Littlefield.

Kymlicka, Will. 1998. "Multicultural Citizenship." In *The Citizenship Debates,* edited by Gershon Shafir, 167–88. Minneapolis: University of Minnesota Press.

Lankov, Andrei. 2006. "Bitter Taste of Paradise: North Korean Refugees in South Korea." *Journal of East Asian Studies* 6: 105–37.

Lee, Eric Yong-Joong. 2000. "Protection of North Korean Escapees Under International Law." *Journal of Human Rights and the Law* 2: 111–34.

———. 2004. "Human Rights Protection of North Koreans in a Third Country: A Legal Approach." *Journal of Korean Law* 4, no. 1: 155–77.

Lee, Gyuchang. 2012. "Mugukjeok talbukja bohoreul wihan beopjedojeok daeeung bangan mosaek." *Tongiljeongchaegyeongu* 21(1): 213–38.

Lee, Hyeonseo. 2011. "Life on the Other Side: A North Korean's Account of Life in South Korea." *Wall Street Journal*, July 11. http://blogs.wsj.com /korearealtime/2011/07/11/a-defectors-tale-lee-hyeon-seo.

Lee, Sang Yong. 2013. "49 NK Spies: 21 Disguised as Defectors." *DailyNK*, October 11. Http://www.dailynk.com/english/read.php?cataId= nk00100&num=11069.

Lee, Sharon Heijin. 2016. "Beauty Between Empires: Global Feminism, Plastic Surgery, and the Trouble with Self-Esteem." *Frontiers: A Journal of Women's Studies* 37, no. 1: 1–31.

Lee, Sonya. 2017. "Korean War Propaganda Leaflet Collection at the Library of Congress." September 26. https://blogs.loc.gov/international-collections /2017/09/ korean-war-propaganda-leaflet-collection-at-the-library-of-congress.

Lee, Soo-Jung. 2006. "Making and Unmaking the Korean National Division: Separated Families in the Cold War and Post-Cold War Eras." PhD diss., University of Illinois Urbana-Champaign.

———. 2011. "Education for Young North Korean Migrants: South Koreans' Ambivalent 'Others' and the Challenges of Belonging." *The Review of Korean Studies* 14, no. 1: 89–112.

Lee, Woo-young, and Yuri Kim. 2011. "North Korean Migrants: A Human Security Perspective." *Asian Perspective* 35: 59–87.

Lee, Yong Suk. 2014. "Countering Sanctions: The Unequal Geographic Impact of Economic Sanctions in North Korea." *Stanford University Freeman Spogli Institute for International Studies Working Paper.* http://fsi.stanford.edu /sites/default/files/nksanctions_fsiworkingpaper.pdf.

Leem, So Yeon. 2017. "Gangnam-Style Plastic Surgery: The Science of Westernized Beauty in South Korea." *Medical Anthropology* 36, no. 7: 657–71.

Levi, Primo. 1988. "The Gray Zone." In *The Drowned and Saved*, 37–58. New York: Simon & Schuster.

Levitt, Peggy. 1998. "Social Remittances: Migration Driven Local-Level Forms of Cultural Diffusion." *International Migration Review* 32, no. 4: 926–48.

Lie, John, ed. 2014. *Multiethnic Korea? Multiculturalism, Migration, and Peoplehood Diversity in Contemporary South Korea.* Berkeley: University of California Press.

Liem, Deann, and Ramsay Liem, dirs. 2013. *Memory of Forgotten War.* 37 min. Berkeley: Mu Films and The Channing & Popai Liem Education Foundation.

Liem, Ramsay. 2003. "History, Trauma, and Identity: The Legacy of the Korean War for Korean Americans." *Amerasia Journal* 29, no. 3: 111–29.

LINK (Liberty in North Korea). 2015. "Refugee Rescues." *Liberty in North Korea.* http://www.libertyinnorthkorea.org/rescue-refugees.

Lindley, Anna. 2010. *The Early Morning Phone Call: Somali Refugees' Remittances.* New York: Berghahn Books.

Livingston, Jennie, dir. 1991. *Paris Is Burning.* 76 min. Burbank, CA: Miramax Home Entertainment.

Los Angeles Times. 1895. "How the Japs Get New Eyes." February 3.

MacArthur, Douglas. 1964. *Reminiscences: General of the Army.* New York: McGraw-Hill Book Company.

Malkki, Liisa. 1992. "National Geographic: The Rooting of Peoples and the Territorialization of National Identity Among Scholars and Refugees." *Cultural Anthropology* 7, no. 1: 24–44.

———. 1995a. *Purity and Exile: Violence, Memory, and National Cosmology among Hutu Refugees in Tanzania.* Chicago: University of Chicago Press.

———. 1995b. "Refugees and Exile: From 'Refugee Studies' to the National Order of Things." *Annual Review of Anthropology* 24, no. 1: 495–523.

Mahr, Christian F. 2002. "North Korea: Scenarios from the Perspective of Refugee Displacement." *Rosemarie Rogers Working Paper No. 11.* The Inter-University Committee on International Migration. http://web.mit.edu/cis/www/migration/pubs/rrwp/11_mahr.html.

Marshall, Janice. 2007. "International Attitudes in Acknowledging North Korean Defectors' Refugee Status." *International Symposium on North Korean Human Rights: International Trends Concerning Human Rights for North Korean Defectors.* November 7. Seoul, South Korea.

Marshall, T. H. 1950. *Citizenship and Social Class and other Essays.* Cambridge: University of Cambridge Press.

Massad, Joseph Andoni. 2002. "Re-Orienting Desire: The Gay International and the Arab World." *Public Culture* 14, no. 2: 361–85.

Mauss, Marcel. 1990. *The Gift: The Form and Reason for Exchange in Archaic Societies.* Translated by W. D. Halls. New York: W. W. Norton.

Mazzucato, Valentina, Mirjam Kabki and Lothar Smith. 2006. "Transnational Migration and the Economy of Funerals: Changing Practices in Ghana." *Development and Change* 37, no. 5: 1047–72.

Mbembe, Achille. 2001. *On the Postcolony.* Berkeley: University of California Press.

———. 2003. "Necropolitics." *Public Culture* 15, no. 1: 11–40.

Meister, Robert. 2012. *After Evil: A Politics of Human Rights.* New York: Columbia University Press.

Milanova, Nadia. 2005. "Lack of International Protection of North Korean Refugees." *Human Rights Without Frontiers International.* http://www

.hrwf.net/images/advocacy/2005–2008/international%20protection%20
nk%20refugees.pdf.

Millard, David Ralph, Jr. 1955. "Oriental Peregrinations." *Plastic and Reconstructive Surgery: Journal of the American Society of Plastic Surgeons* 16,
no. 5: 319–36.

———. 1964. "The Oriental Eyelid and Its Surgical Revision." *American
Journal of Ophthalmology* 57, no. 4: 646–49.

Min, Sung Kil. 2008. "Divided Countries, Divided Mind 1: Psycho-Social Issues
in Adaptation Problems of North Korean Defectors." *Psychiatry Investigation* 5: 1–13.

Mohanty, Chandra T. 2003. *Feminist Without Borders*. Durham, NC: Duke
University Press.

Moon, Seungsook. 2005. *Militarized Modernity and Gendered Citizenship in
South Korea*. Durham, NC: Duke University Press.

Morgan, Kathryn Pauly. 1991. "Women and the Knife: Cosmetic Surgery and
the Colonization of Women's Bodies." *Hypatia* 6, no. 3: 25–53.

Morrison, Toni. 2007. *The Bluest Eye*. New York: Vintage International.

National Human Rights Commission of Korea. 2012. *Haeoecheryu bukhanitaljumin adong ingwonsanghwang siltaejosa*. Seoul: National Human
Rights Commission of Korea.

National Security Act. 1997. *The National Security Act of the Republic of Korea*.
Seoul: National Assembly.

Nationality Law of the People's Republic of China. 1980. https://www.mfa.gov
.cn/ce/ceus//eng/ywzn/lsyw/vpna/faq/t710012.htm#:~:text=Article%20
4%20Any%20person%20born,national%20shall%20have%20Chinese%
20nationality.

Negrin, Llewellyn. 2002. "Cosmetic Surgery and the Eclipse of Identity." *Body
and Society* 8, no. 4: 21–42.

NKDB (Database Center for North Korean Human Rights). 2012a. *White Paper
on North Korean Human Rights 2012*. Seoul: Database Center for North
Korean Human Rights.

———. 2012b. *Prisoners in North Korea Today*. Seoul: Database Center for
North Korean Human Rights.

———. 2014. *Trends in Economic Activities of North Korean Defectors in 2013*.
Seoul: Database Center for North Korean Human Rights.

———. 2019. *Trends in Economic Activities of North Korean Defectors in 2018*.
Seoul: Database Center for North Korean Human Rights.

NKIDP (North Korea International Documentation Project). 2012. *E-Dossier
#11*. Washington, DC: Woodrow Wilson International Center for Scholars.

Nyers, Peter. 1999. "Refugees and Humanitarian Ethics: Beyond the Politics of
the Emergency." *YCISS Occasional Paper Number 58*. http://www.yorku.ca
/yciss/publications/OP58-Nyers.pdf.

———. 2006. *Rethinking Refugees: Beyond States of Emergency*. Abingdon, UK: Routledge.

Oberdorfer, Dan. 2001. *The Two Koreas: A Contemporary History*. New York: Basic Books.

OECD. 2018. "Suicide Rates." *OECD.org*. https://data.oecd.org/healthstat /suicide-rates.htm.

Oh, Arissa. 2015. *To Save the Children of Korea: The Cold War Origins of International Adoption*. Stanford, CA: Stanford University Press.

Oh, Sandra. 2011. "Sandra Oh on North Korean Refugee Adoption Act." *YouTube*, December 1. *https://www.youtube.com/watch?v=O-dO1u6H5Ik*.

Ong, Aihwa. 1996. "Cultural Citizenship as Subject-Making." *Current Anthropology* 37, no. 5: 737–51.

———. 1999. *Flexible Citizenship: The Cultural Logics of Transnationality*. Durham, NC: Duke University Press.

———. 2003. *Buddha is Hiding: Refugees, Citizenship, The New America*. Berkeley: University of California Press.

———. 2005. "(Re)Articulations of Citizenship." *Political Science and Politics* 38, no. 4: 697–99.

———. 2006. *Neoliberalism as Exception: Mutations in Citizenship and Sovereignty*. Durham, NC: Duke University Press.

One Young World. 2014. "Yeonmi Park Introduced By James Chau." *YouTube*, October 20. https://www.youtube.com/watch?v=Ei-gGvLWOZI.

Paik, Nak-chung. 2011. *The Division System in Crisis: Essays on Contemporary Korea*. Berkeley: University of California Press.

Pak, Sunyoung. 2004. "The Biological Standard of Living in the Two Koreas." *Economics and Human Biology* 2: 511–21.

———. 2010. "The Growth Status of North Korean Refugee Children and Adolescents from 6 to 19 years of age." *Economics and Human Biology* 8: 385–95.

Palumbo-Liu, David. 1999. *Asian/American: Historical Crossings of a Racial Frontier*. Stanford, CA: Stanford University Press.

Pandolfo, Stefania. 2007. "The Burning: Finitude and the Political-Theological Imagination of Illegal Migration." *Anthropological Theory* 7, no. 3: 329–63.

Park, Hyun Ok. 2015. *Capitalist Unconscious: From Korean Unification to Transnational Korea*. New York: Columbia University Press.

Park, Joo. 2014. "YeonMi Park: The Defector Who Fooled the World." *The Peace Wager*, December 27. http://thepeacewager.org/2014/12/27/yeonmi-park-the-defector-who-fooled-the-world.

Park, Joowon. 2012. "'I Can Send That Money to My Mother': Remittances, Telecommunication and Post-Migration Strategies of North Koreans." *Anthropology News* 53, no. 2: 11.

———. 2016. "The Gendered Contours of North Korean Migration: Sexualized Bodies and the Violence of Phenotypical Normalization in South Korea." *Asian Ethnicity* 17, no. 2: 214–27.

———. 2020. "Voices from War's Legacies: Reconciliation and Violence in Inter-Korean Family Reunions." *Anthropology and Humanism* 45, no. 1: 25–42.

Park, Ki Seong, and In Jae Lee. 2010. "Height Premium in the Korean Labor Market." *Korean Journal of Labour Economics* 33, no. 3: 129–49.

Park, Min-young. 2010. "'Loser' Girl in Hot Water." *The Korea Herald,* March 30. http://www.koreaherald.com/national/Detail.jsp?newsMLId= 20091113000069.

Park, Seo Yeon. 2016. "Street-level Bureaucracy and Depoliticized North Korean Subjectivity in the Service Provision of Hana Center." *Asian Ethnicity* 17, no. 2: 199–213.

Park, Young-a. 2020. "North Korean Migrants in South Korea: 'Multicultural' or 'Global' Citizens?" *Korean Studies* 44: 123–48.

Parla, Ayşe. 2011. "Labor Migration, Ethnic Kinship, and the Conundrum of Citizenship in Turkey." *Citizenship Studies* 15, no. 3-4: 457–70.

Pate, SooJin. 2014. *From Orphan to Adoptee: U.S. Empire and Genealogies of Korean Adoption.* Minneapolis: University of Minnesota Press.

Pine, Adrienne. 2008. *Working Hard Drinking Hard: On Violence and Survival in Honduras.* Berkeley: University of California Press.

Pink, Sarah, et al. 2016. *Digital Ethnography: Principles and Practice.* London: SAGE.

Reddy, Chandan C. 1998. "Home, Houses, Non-Identity: *Paris Is Burning.*" In *Burning Down the House: Recycling Domesticity,* edited by Rosemary Marangoly George, 355–79. Boulder, CO: Westview Press.

Redfield, Peter. 2005. "Doctors, Borders, and Life in Crisis." *Cultural Anthropology* 20, no. 3: 328–61.

Redfield, Peter, and Erica Bornstein. 2011. "An Introduction to the Anthropology of Humanitarianism." In *Forces of Compassion: Humanitarianism Between Ethics and Politics,* edited by Erica Bornstein and Peter Redfield, 3–30. Santa Fe: School of Advanced Research Press.

Riak Akuei, Stephanie. 2005. "Remittances as Unforeseen Burdens: The Livelihoods and Social Obligations of Sudanese Refugees." *Global Migration Perspectives No. 18.* Geneva: Global Commission on International Migration.

Rich, Timothy S., et al. 2020. "South Korean Perceptions of North Korean Immigration: Evidence from an Experimental Survey." *Political Science* 72, no. 2: 77–92.

Ros-Lehtinen, Illeana. 2012. "North Korean Orphans Need Our Help, Ros-Lehtinen Says." *YouTube,* September 11. https://www.youtube.com/watch?v= TuoM9rZV2eo.

Rosaldo, Renato. 1994. "Cultural Citizenship and Educational Democracy." *Cultural Anthropology* 9, no. 3: 402–11.

———, ed. 2003. *Cultural Citizenship in Island and Southeast Asia: Nation and Belonging in the Hinterlands.* Berkeley: University of California Press.

Rosenhan, D. L. 1973. "On Being Sane in Insane Places." *Science* 179: 250–58.

Ryang, Sonia. 2000. *Koreans in Japan: Critical Voices from the Margin.* New York: Routledge.

———, ed. 2009. *North Korea: Toward a Better Understanding.* Lanham, MD: Lexington Books.

Said, Edward. 1978. *Orientalism.* New York: Vintage Books.

Sassen, Saskia. 1996. *Losing Control? Sovereignty in an Age of Globalization.* New York: Columbia University Press.

Sands, Iain. 2019. "Performing in the 'Cultural Borderlands': Gender, Trauma, and Performance Practices of a North Korean Women's Musical Troupe in South Korea." *Cross-Currents: East Asian History and Culture Review* 8, no. 1: 41–67.

Scheper-Hughes, Nancy. 1993. *Death Without Weeping: The Violence of Everyday Life in Brazil.* Berkeley: University of California Press.

Scheper-Hughes, Nancy, and Philippe Bourgois, eds. 2004. *Violence in War and Peace: An Anthology.* Malden, MA: Blackwell Publishing.

Schmitt, Carl. 2005. *Political Theology: Four Chapters on the Concept of Sovereignty.* Translated by George Schwab. Chicago: University of Chicago Press.

Shin, Gi-Wook. 2006. *Ethnic Nationalism in Korea: Genealogy, Politics, and Legacy.* Stanford, CA: Stanford University Press.

Shindo, Reiko. 2009. "Struggle for Citizenship: Interaction between Political Society and Civil Society at a Kurd Refugee Protest in Tokyo." *Citizenship Studies* 13, no. 3: 219–37.

Simmons, Edwin H. 2002. *Frozen Chosin: U.S. Marines at the Changjin Reservoir.* Washington, DC: History and Museums Division, Headquarters, U.S. Marine Corps.

Smith, Hazel. 2012. "Introduction: Explaining North Korean Migration to China." In *North Korea International Documentation Project E-Dossier #11*, 1–4. Washington, DC: Woodrow Wilson International Center for Scholars.

Son, Sarah. 2016. "Identity, Security, and the Nation: Understanding the South Korean Response to North Korean Defectors." *Asian Ethnicity* 17, no. 2: 171–84.

Song, Byoung-A, et al. 2011. "Post-Traumatic Stress Disorder, Depression, and Heart-Rate Variability among North Korean Defectors." *Psychiatry Investigation* 8: 297–304.

Song, Jay. 2021. "The 'Savage-Victim-Saviour' Story Grammar of the North Korean Human Rights Industry." *Asian Studies Review* 45, no. 1: 48–66.

Song, Jay Jiyoung, and Markus Bell. 2019. "North Korean Secondary Asylum in the UK." *Migration Studies* 7, no. 2: 160–79. https://doi.org/10.1093/migration/mnx074.

Song, Jiyoung. 2013. "'Smuggled Refugees': The Social Construction of North Korean Migration." *International Migration* 51, no. 4: 158–73.

———. 2015. "Twenty Years' Evolution of North Korean Migration: 1994–2014: A Human Security Perspective." *Asia and the Pacific Policy Studies* 2, no. 2: 399–415. https://doi.org/10.1002/app5.82.

Soysal, Yasemin Nuhoğlu. 1994. *Limits of Citizenship: Migrants and Postnational Membership in Europe.* Chicago: University of Chicago Press.

Stryker, Rachael. 2010. "The War At Home: Affective Economics and Transnationally Adoptive Families in the United States." *International Migration* 49, no. 6: 25–49.

Stueck, William. 1995. *The Korean War: An International History.* Princeton, NJ: Princeton University Press.

Sung, Minkyu. 2010. "The Psychiatric Power of Neo-liberal Citizenship: The North Korean Human Rights Crisis, North Korean Settlers, and Incompetent Citizens." *Citizenship Studies* 14, no. 2: 127–44.

———. 2019. "Balloon Warriors for North Korean Human Rights Activism: A Critique of North Korean Defector-Activists' Post-Humanitarianism." *Critical Asian Studies* 51, no. 3: 355–67.

Tacoli, Cecilia. 1999. "International Migration and the Restructuring of Gender Assymetries: Continuity and Change Among Filipino Labor Migrants in Rome." *International Migration Review* 33, no. 3: 658–82.

Tambiah, Stanley J. 2000. "Transnational Movements, Diaspora, and Multiple Modernities." *Daedalus* 129, no. 1: 163–94.

Tanaka, Hiroyuki. 2008. "North Korea: Understanding Migration to and from a Closed Country." *Migration Policy Institute.* http://www.migrationinformation.org/feature/display.cfm?ID=668.

Tang, Eric. 2015. *Unsettled: Cambodian Refugees in the NYC Hyperghetto.* Philadelphia: Temple University Press.

Teng, Jinhua E. 1996. "The Construction of the 'Traditional Chinese Woman' in the Western Academy: A Critical Review." *Signs: Journal of Women in Culture and Society* 22: 115–51.

THINK. 2013. "Topple Hunger in North Korea (T.H.I.N.K) Program." *Think Children.* http://thinkchildren.org/about-us.

Thiong'o, Ngugi wa. 1986. *Decolonising the Mind: The Politics of Language in African Literature.* Portsmouth, NH: Heinemann.

Thomas, Deborah. 2011. *Exceptional Violence: Embodied Citizenship in Transnational Jamaica.* Durham, NC: Duke University Press.

Turner, Victor. 1969. *The Ritual Process: Structure and Anti-Structure.* Chicago: Aldine.

TV Chosun. 2015. "Aejeongtongil namnambuknyeo sijeun1." http://broadcast
.tvchosun.com/broadcast/program/2/C201400042/edit/5936.cstv.

Um, Mee Young, Eric Rice, Lawrence A. Palinkas, and Hee Jin Kim. 2020.
"Migration-Related Stressors and Suicidal Ideation in North Korean
Refugee Women: The Moderating Effects of Network Composition." *Journal
of Traumatic Stress* 33: 939–49.

Um, Mee Young, Jungeun Olivia Lee, Hee Jin Kim, Eric Rice, and Lawrence A.
Palinkas. 2021. "Testing the Pathway from Pre-migration Sexual Violence to
Suicide-Related Risk among North Korean Refugee Women Living in South
Korea: Do Social Networks Matter?" *Social Psychiatry and Psychiatric
Epidemiology* 56: 485–95.

UNHCR. 2007. *Convention and Protocol Relating to the Status of Refugees.*
Geneva: UNHCR.

UNHCR. 2011. *Handbook and Guidelines on Procedures and Criteria for
Determining Refugee Status: Under the 1951 Convention and the 1967
Protocol Relating to the Status of Refugees.* Geneva: UNHCR.

Valentine, David. 2004. "The Categories Themselves." *GLQ: A Journal of
Lesbian and Gay Studies* 10, no. 2: 215–20.

Woo-Cumings, Meredith. 2002. "The Political Ecology of Famine: The North
Korean Catastrophe and Its Lessons." *ADB Institute Research Paper 31.*
Tokyo: Asian Development Bank Institute Publishing.

Yeun, Steven. 2012. "Steven Yeun on North Korean Refugee Adoption Act."
YouTube, April 12. https://www.youtube.com/watch?v=dzLN3VuisQw.

Yonhap. 2018. "Young Defectors from N. Korea Struggle to Adapt to S. Korean
Schools." *The Korea Herald,* April 28. http://www.koreaherald.com/view
.php?ud=20180428000065.

Yonhap News. 1994. "Isansindosi yusasi jinjihwaryong seolgye." September 26.
https://n.news.naver.com/mnews/article/001/0003804938?sid=100.

Yoo, Theodore Jun. 2020. *The Koreas: The Birth of Two Nations Divided.*
Oakland, CA: University of California Press.

Yoon, In-Jin. 2009. *Bukhanijumin: Saenghwalgwa Uisik, Geurigo Jeongchakji-
wonjeongchaek (North Korean Migrants: Life and Consciousness, and
Settlement Support Policy).* Seoul: Jipmundang.

Yoon, Sharon. 2020. *The Cost of Belonging: An Ethnography of Solidarity and
Mobility in Beijing's Koreatown.* New York: Oxford University Press.

Young, Iris Marion. 1980. "Throwing Like a Girl: A Phenomenology of Female
Body Comportment Motility and Spatiality." *Human Studies* 3, no. 2:
137–56.

———. 1989. "Polity and Group Difference: A Critique of the Ideal of Universal
Citizenship." *Ethics* 99, no. 2: 250–74.

Index

191

claim of, as a trick to get categorized as "simple border-crosser," 113; marriage as most common goal of, 59, 125; nonconsensual marriage, 61–63, 87, 106; postcolonial scholarship challenging victim narrative of, 62; sex industry trafficking, 59, 125, 162n15; silence within the NK community as resistance to the narrative of, 53–54, 62–63, 71; slavery, humanitarian construction of North Korean asylum seekers and, 125; stereotypes and stigmas of impurity against women resettled in SK, 23–24, 64–65, 71, 94, 143; and women as tacit subjects, 63, 163n20. *See also* cross-border marriage; human rights narrative of North Korean women as victimized subjects

Cumings, Bruce, 162n3

Czechoslovakia, 75

Dandong, China, 35

Das, Veena, 63, 162n18

Database Center for North Korean Human Rights (NKDB): overview, 20–21, 54; Hanawon Resettlement Center survey project of human rights violations, 21, 54–55, 59, 126; publisher of Shin Dong-hyuk's *Sesang bakkeuro naoda*, 128; remittances survey, 100–102; statistics on number of North Koreans who crossed to China, 58; *White Paper on North Korean Human Rights*, 55

Decena, Carlos, 163n20

"decolonising the mind," 94, 165n49

desubjectivation, 94, 165n49

digital culture, cosmetic surgery reinforced by, 88

discrimination against North Koreans. *See* stereotypes, stigmas, and discrimination against North Koreans

discrimination against South Koreans with kinship ties to North Korea, and emigration, 33, 41–42, 48

DMZ (Demilitarized Zone): overview, 1, 53; airborne balloon launches, both NK and SK sending propaganda leaflets (*ppira*), 95–96, 98; airborne balloon launches to NK, by churches (ramen noodles), *97*, 98, 117; airborne balloon launches to NK, by NGOs (leaflets and culturally useful items), 96, 98; as blocking direct entrance to SK, 5–6, 33, 156n8; Camp Bonifas (UN military base), 148; Civilian

Control Line (CCL), 148; fence decorations with hope for reunification, *39, 152*; incursion tunnels, 3; Joint Security Area, 147–48, *149*; landmines and, 148, *149*, 156n8; map of, *x*; Military Demarcation Line, 53, *149*; postwar crossings on foot, 32; psychological warfare (e.g., radio broadcasts, loudspeakers, leaflets), 95–98; psychological warfare, banning of, 98; as world's most militarized border, 146. *See also* Korea, division of; Korean War as endless

dokaebi (creature in Korean folklore), 35

domestic violence, marriage trafficking and, 61–62

Eastern Bloc: dissolution of, and North Korea's loss of trading partners, 5, 34, 55, 56–57, 76, 120–21; fraternal aid given to NK, 75

East Germany, 75; reunification of East and West, 38, 83

ecological degradation. *See* famine of 1996–1999 (North Korea); global warming and ecological degradation

education: alternative school for resettled North Koreans, 20, 107; English language study requirement for resettled North Koreans, 20; English language teaching as form of violence, 20; English proficiency needed for education and employment, 87, 104; habitus formation and, 14; of North Korean refugees in preparation for resettlement, 7, 21, 54, 115–16; private supplementary education institutions (*hagwon*), 107; resettled North Koreans as ill-prepared for post-industrial work, 82–83, 104–5; resettlement benefit of subsidized tuition, 6, 75, 104; South Korean High School Graduation Equivalency Exam, 107; study of South Korean speech by resettled North Koreans, 83, 107. *See also* university education

employment: average monthly income, 105, 166n7; cosmetic surgery and prospects for, 88–89; disparities in occupations held by resettled North Koreans vs. South Koreans, 105; English proficiency as necessity in, 87, 104; "height premium" in, 81, 82; job training as benefit for resettled North Koreans, 6; percent of resettled North Koreans considered "economically active," 104–5; resettled North

Marshall, Thomas, 157n24
masculinity: androgynous (*kkonminam*), 88; military ideal of, 73–74
Mason, Jana, 163n33
Mbembe, Achille, 168
media: getting SK entertainment into NK, 69, 98; and humanitarian pleas for China to change its policy of forced repatriation of NK refugees, 109, 123; and the Korean War, 161n1; and North Korean escapees as "defectors," 119; as romanticizing family reunions and reunification, 39. *See also* television (South Korea)
Meister, Robert, 132
methodology, 17–18, 19–22, 66; literature review, 21, 160n64; pseudonyms used throughout, 22. *See also* positionality of the researcher
militarization of the Korean peninsula: and the endless Korean War, 3, 146–47; as "peaceful" status, 51; separation of families due to, 33; South Korean architecture and development designed as defensive space, 148, 150–52, 169nn14–16. *See also* DMZ (Demilitarized Zone); Korean War as endless; United States military stationed in South Korea
military (North Korea): the famine, and humanitarian aid redirected to, 99–100; resources redistributed to, 12, 14, 77, 99–100, 134, 164n6. *See also* military conscription, mandatory (North Korea); nuclear weapons development
military (South Korea): overview, 3; annual exercise with the US military, 3; body movement and spatiality inhibited to represent ideal masculinity, 73–74; Cheonan naval vessel, NK torpedoing, 3; high alert after nuclear tests by NK, 51–52; orders to report propaganda leaflets from NK, 95; THAAD (Terminal High Altitude Area Defense) deployed with US, 71. *See also* military conscription, mandatory (South Korea)
military conscription, mandatory (North Korea): the gendered migration and mobility limitations of, 55–56; length of mandatory service, 55–56, 155n2; portrayed as preparing NK brides for older SK men, 67. *See also* Korean War as endless
military conscription, mandatory (South Korea): overview, 3; as central to citizen-

ship, 22; discharges, 145–46; and the endless war, preparation for, 22, 26; establishment of the 102nd Battalion, 1; evasion of conscription, banishment for crime of, 3, 155–56n4; experience (*jjam*) gained, and difference in attitudes, 72–73; folk song mourning, 27, 160n1; hair cuts and hair length during, 72–73; indoctrination of NK as the "enemy," 22; length of mandatory service, 3, 155n2; positionality of the researcher and, 1, 2, 3, 22–23, 152; rising in rank, 72; social isolation of conscripts, 27; training of conscripts, 1, 22–23, 26. *See also* Korean War as endless
Millard, David Ralph, 89–90
Minyeodeurui Suda (Chat with Beauties) (South Korean television), 79–80
modern subject, becoming, 158n52
Mongolia, North Korean asylum claims in, 7, 58–59, 99, 103; humanitarian constructions of NK asylum seekers and distortions of reality, 125
Moon Jae-in: derided as "commie" for overtures to NK, 45; Inter-Korean Summits with NK leader Kim Jong-un, 30, 39, 83, 96; reunification pledge, 30, 39, 83
Moon, Seungsook, 155n3
Morrison, Toni, 91
multicultural turn, 159n59
Musan, North Korea, 75
Myanmar, and North Korean refugees, 36, 110

Namnam Buknyeo (Love Unification: Southern Man, Northern Woman) (South Korean television), 68
Namsan Tunnel (Seoul), 151
nationalism: inscribed on women's bodies, 63, 162n18; and purity, 63
neoliberalism: cosmetic surgery and, 88–89; and the transnational decoupling of citizenship from the state, 10; work and, 82–83, 105
NGOs. *See* human rights activists and organizations
NKDB. *See* Database Center for North Korean Human Rights
North Hamgyong Province, South Korea, 75, 106
North Korea: Agreed Framework between the United States and North Korea (1994), 42; assassination attempts on presidents

of SK, 3, 150; assistance to China in Chinese Civil War, 162n3; "axis of evil" rendering of, 125, 132, 168n45; correspondence allowed from Korean diaspora to family in, and censorship of, 34; developmental differences with South Korea, *133*; economic sanctions on, 3, 76, 100, 134; economy of, postwar, 75–76; entertainment from SK increasingly available in, 69; imports of luxury goods, 42; interrogations by authorities of, 35, 112–14; isolation from the rest of the world, 100; *Juche* (self-reliance), and *Juche* year, 75–76, 112; kidnapping of people from various countries, 42; "Let's Eat Two Meals a Day" (1992 campaign), 76; propaganda used by, 75–76, 77; rebuilding after the Korean War, 75–76; religious organizations considered enemies of the state, 20; and *Republikflucht,* similarities of policies to, 147; retaliation for NGOs launching airborne balloons into NK, 98; *Rodong* newspaper (state propaganda), 77; *seongbun* class system of, 156n9; spying on Korean Americans, 42. *See also* black markets (*Jangmadang*) in North Korea; China, alliance with North Korea; China, illegal crossings of North Koreans into; family reunions; famine of 1996–1999; home; human rights violations in North Korea; Korean War as endless; North Koreans who have left their country, labels used for; North Korea, unauthorized departures as crime; nuclear weapons development (North Korea); Pyongyang, North Korea; reunification; social factors contributing to the vast increase in migration

North Korean Criminal Law: Article 62: defection defined as treason, 121; Article 233: unauthorized border-crossings forbidden, 121

North Korean labor-training camps (*Nodongdanryeondae*): for ordinary minor crimes, 114; for "simple border-crossers," 113, 114

North Korean People's Security Agency (*Inminboanbu*), 114

North Korean political prison camps, 59, 113, 121

North Korean State Security Agency (*Gukgaanjeonbowibu*, SSA), 34, 112–14

North Koreans who have left their country, labels used for: as "defectors" (international politics and mass media), 119; as "economic migrants" (China), 119; and politics of identification, 119; as "refugees" (human rights activists), 119; as survival migrants, 120–21, 134–35. *See also* China, forced repatriation of North Koreans; North Korea, unauthorized departures as crime; resettlement of North Koreans in South Korea; UN Refugee Convention (1951), and refugee status of North Koreans

North Korean Worker's Party, 47

North Korea, unauthorized departures as crime: and assumption of death of remaining family members by North Koreans who have left, 6; bribes lightening the outcomes of, 113–14; decisions not to leave due to, 109; decisions not to return due to, 36; decisions to leave again despite punishment, 59, 110; execution proclaimed as punishment during mourning period for Kim Jong-il, 109, 111, 114; executions, as constant threat, 113; executions, public, 54–55; human rights violations experienced in penal system, 12, 54–55, 112, 114, 121, 128; the Korean War's endlessness as historical context of, 147; labor-training camps (*Nodongdanryeondae*), 113, 114; laws governing, 121; political prison camps, 59, 113, 128; punishment of remaining family members as guilty by association, 36, 41, 69, 109, 111; refugee status based on future persecution due to, 121, 122; SSA detention facilities, 112; SSA interrogation to separate the "political border-crossers" ("impure") from the "simple border-crosses" ("pure"), 112–14; as stain on family background (*todae*), 35, 106; transfer from China to NK State Security Agency (SSA, *Gukgaanjeonbowibu*), 112; as "treason," 121. See also human rights violations in North Korea

Nowon (Seoul neighborhood), 116

nuclear weapons development (North Korea): agreement with the US to halt, 42; economic sanctions due to, 3, 76, 100, 134; and isolation of NK from the rest of the world, 100; the Korean War as endless and, 3, 146; testing, 51, 96

pop culture: phenotypical normalization and, 88, 90. *See also* celebrities; K-pop; television

positionality of the researcher: and China's policy of forced repatriation of North Koreans, 118; and compulsory military service, 1, 2, 3, 22–23, 152; as English teacher/tutor, 20; and espionage suspicions, 44, 45; and family reunion efforts for Grandmother Ku and her brother, 37–39, 40–41, 44, 45–46, 48, 49–50; in the Korean diaspora, 19; the Korean War and, 3–4; and repeated recounting of stories of violence and suffering, 126. *See also* methodology

postcoloniality: transnational adoptions and, 129; victim narrative and cross-border trafficking of NK women, 62

Protestant churches in South Korea: overview, 20, 107, 157n19, 160n63; airborne balloon launches to NK (ramen noodles), *97*, 98, 117; and attempts to cover up still-healing cosmetic surgeries, 90–91; evangelical mission of, 20, 160n62; as limited source of community, 8; monthly allowances for resettled North Koreans as incentive to attend, 20, 53, 91, 104; name changes of converts, 56; SK elders saying they would never allow their daughters to marry NK men, 66; social interactions in, 53–54, 107

Public Distribution System (PDS, North Korea), collapse of, 5, 56–57, 76–77, 164n6. *See also* famine of 1996–1999 (North Korea); social factors contributing to the vast increase in migration (North Korea)

purity: nationalism and territorialism and, 63; and punishment for unauthorized departures from NK, 112–14; stigma of impurity, and trafficking of NK women resettled in SK, 23–24, 64–65, 71, 94, 143

PyeongChang Winter Olympics (2018), 4

Pyeonghwamunhwajinji (Peace-Culture Bunker), 151

Pyongyang, North Korea: fewer resettled North Koreans come from, 6, 29; higher quality of life in, 29; in the Korean War, 28; Pan-National Reunification Concert (*Beomminjok Tongir Eumakhoe*), 33–34; reduced opportunity for escape in regions close to, 6; resource redistribution to the

elite, the military, and area of, 12, 14, 77, 99–100, 134, 164n6; and the *seongbun* class system, 156n9

racism: colonial, and symbolic violence, 91; NK propaganda urging Black US soldiers to refuse to fight due to, 96; and whiteness as norm in origins of SK cosmetic surgery, 89–90

Reddy, Chandan, 18, 138, 139–40

Redfield, Peter, 118

refugees: as defined by loss of citizenship identity, 12; displacement of, as pathological condition of the refugee, 12; and false notion that regaining citizenship is emancipation from violence, 12–13, 158n48; methods of resolution as focusing on restoring order, security, and reinstatement of persons "out of place," 12; as symbolizing the failure of the nation-state basis of citizenship, 12. *See also* humanitarian construction of North Korean deservingness (of refugee status) through the discourse of violence; UN Refugee Convention (1951), and refugee status of North Koreans

religious organizations: assisting the journey from China to South Korea, 7, 135; China criminalizing efforts to help North Koreans, 70, 122, 135; contact with, as treason in NK, 112–13, 121; as limited form of community for resettled North Koreans, 8; North Korea view of, as "enemies of the state," 20; support for resettled North Koreans, 20. *See also* Protestant churches

remittances by resettled North Koreans to family in North Korea: overview, 24, 98, 100; amount of money sent each time, 100, *101*, 102; amount sent to NK in total, 165n4; bribing security guards and local officials for transmittals, 102; broker commissions, 102; broker operations as high crime in NK, 102; brokers for, 24, 100, 102–3, 105, 107; as compensation for the guilt of having left, 15, 103; and desire to bring family members to SK, 104, 108, 109, 115–16; discontent and lack of reciprocity by recipients of, 108–9; economic struggle to pay, 104–6; effect on country of origin, as area of study, 115, 166n18; famine survival due to, 34; and global isolation of NK, 100; Korean holi-

Founded in 1893,
UNIVERSITY OF CALIFORNIA PRESS
publishes bold, progressive books and journals
on topics in the arts, humanities, social sciences,
and natural sciences—with a focus on social
justice issues—that inspire thought and action
among readers worldwide.

The UC PRESS FOUNDATION
raises funds to uphold the press's vital role
as an independent, nonprofit publisher, and
receives philanthropic support from a wide
range of individuals and institutions—and from
committed readers like you. To learn more, visit
ucpress.edu/supportus.